AF469247

LOVE MUSIC LOVE FOOD

THE ROCK STAR COOKBOOK

With Special thanks to Paul King for tireless efforts to keep the project on course and many a late night phone call of support. Ben Cole at Stanley's Post for dedicating his first class retouchers to the cause and Paul, Mark and Sophie who worked so hard amongst others at Stanley's to help produce these images. To Andy and Sylviane at Peartree for all the camera and lighting kit, Lawrie for tech advice whether in Mexico or Shoreditch and Darius/Ben. Heston Blumenthal for making me blush when I read the foreword for the first time and providing a great recipe for Roger. Alec and all the staff at Street Studios who always tried to accommodate us with great shooting spaces and put on a brave face for our food-flinging, cove-endangering finale shoot. To Johnny and Josh and everyone at The Shoreditch.com for use of their amazing studios (I apologise you got all the slightly whiffy seafood shoots) and for some fabulous spaces through JJ Locations.

For our gorgeous brand identity, adapted to work on everything from banners to badges, napkins and books, Jonathan and Dan at Barnbrook. Terri and Gillian at HallorNothing for being easily lured into doing our PR with the promise of chocolate puddings at meetings and Dean Chalkley for my new squid siren look plus tips on the idiosyncrasies of shooting musical folk. To my blisteringly hardworking assistants, Marie for her retouching and commitment, Gidz being in from the start, Pablo, Chris, Dan, Mark, Daria, Eleni and Louis for extra hours on all aspects of the project and stacks of others who never complained if they had to sit in a tub of cold noodles for a pre light or lug tons of compost/kit and the odd stuffed deer up six flights of stairs. My agents, Carolyn and Skye at Trayler & Trayler for sponsoring our exhibition frames and for their patience whilst I veered off into the world of people with food, and to my producers at Bare Films, Helen and Clare, for the same. To my dear friend Claire for support in darker times and to John at PSL. For those who provided exhibition prints to promote the project, Tony at White and Black for beautiful B&W bromides, Stuart and Dave at The Printspace for perfect colour prints and to Art Finish for slaving over hot dry mounting presses for us.

SPECIAL THANKS

To Angie for bringing great artists into studios and coffee bars for us and introducing me to the industry folk who've been so instrumental in helping this go forward. Ronnie Tee, who cajoled artists into our festival pop-up studios and rallied round the project on all fronts with gusto, and to Bev, best booker and biggest Biffy fan, for endless emails to industry contacts night and day. And to Barnaby for turning my illegible concept scribbles into works of beautiful illustration for the artists to sign, often adding unthought-of backgrounds and touches which ended up in the final shot. For Des, Jane and all at *Teenage Cancer Trust* who work so hard to raise funds and got behind the concept. And to Adrian and Myrna Whiteson; you inspire those around you with your devotion to the charity you created, thank you for entrusting the good name of the charity to be associated with *Love Music Love Food* and for your encouragement. To Kedge at Tomato for crafting the book design, loving a gorgeous glass of vino and tweaking typography so elegantly. Steph, not enough space left here to gush as I'd like to, heaps of design reworks, pesky photographers being indecisive and not a cross word – just great design. To Liz, Heidi and Ewan at Selfridges for not being angry when we broke one of your knives and instead ensured this project made it into book form with your love of the idea, and to Jane O' Shea and Clare Lattin at Quadrille for taking that on board and making this book a reality. For my co-authors, Andrew and Sarah, who've added the cherries to the top of the bakewell and Lili for being the first to get excited by the concept and on hand to help find anything from sheep to locations. To Gill for letting me raid the instruments cupboard, be it violins or ukuleles. And to Rupert and Dylan, long-suffering family with only a great collection of gig t-shirts and a generously signed guitar for comfort over the past year, you've been very patient.

To all the above and those listed in the contributors section, without your goodwill, forbearance and support this project would not have been possible.

Peace, love, gigs & pies

Patrice

For my mother Patricia, God bless, and my son Dylan —with love.

DEDICATION

In memory of Heather Burns-Mace

A woman of great spirit, Heather gave her children the following advice '*Try and do something that scares you every day*,' followed by: '*Never, never give up*'. Well, this has scared us from time to time but *we never gave up*. Thank you Heather for your lust for life and your faith in us.

Gibson
CUSTOM

IF MUSIC BE THE FOOD OF LOVE, does that mean that the love of music and the love of food are somehow intertwined? That is certainly what we discovered in putting together ***Love Music Love Food:*** *The Rock Star Cookbook*, an epic undertaking which saw the cream of musical talent agree to be slathered in Marmite, buried in wine gums, transported into the Middle Ages and much more – all in aid of the best cause imaginable, the *Teenage Cancer Trust*, which works to give young people diagnosed with cancer world-class support and state-of-the-art facilities.

Music is an epicurean thing and we wanted to capture that love of life in pictures, words and recipes that you, the reader, can experience for yourself. What did we learn along the way? Rock musicians like anything with chilli in it. America can put a man on the moon but they still can't make a decent cup of tea. Rock musicians really like sushi. A genuine and knowledgeable love of food can be found in the most unexpected people. And rock musicians really, really like curry.

LOVE MUSIC LOVE FOOD: INTRODUCTION

Above all, one truth stood out from meeting the subjects of this book – an extraordinary group of people who travel the world and live a life most of us can scarcely imagine, a strange mixture of relentless pressure and sudden boredom, bottomless adulation and accompanying loneliness – and it was rather a comforting one. No matter where you are in the world, no matter how far you've travelled from your roots and how much you've fulfilled the dream of becoming the person you always wanted to be, you will always remember the food you ate when you were a child.

The stars who graciously agreed to help out with this book can eat in the finest restaurants in the world. But when we asked them to name the best meal they ever ate, many of them gave the same answer: their mother's Sunday roast. That's what turns ordinary sounds into spectacular music and ordinary foodstuffs into the flavours of beautiful memory: love. We hope you enjoy the book.

Patrice de Villiers*—concept & photography*
Andrew Harrison*—interviews*
Sarah Muir*—recipes*

I WORKED WITH Patrice for approximately three years when I was writing a column for *The Sunday Times Style* magazine. Seemingly unbound by the regular rules of food photography, she was continuously pushing the boundaries of what was possible. The results were original and exciting and I have been a great admirer of her fearless and imaginative style ever since. I remember on one occasion wanting to balance a plate on a spring to make a Quaking Pudding wobble as it was eaten. It was an almost impossible photograph to take but Patrice persisted until she got the shot. The final picture was, of course, perfect and Patrice went on to win a Glenfiddich Food and Drink Award for her photography.

HESTON BLUMENTHAL *foreword*

The extraordinary photographs in this book are a testament to the relationships that Patrice establishes with each of her subjects. Who else could get a pop star to pose naked in a bath of noodles? Every picture is brilliantly constructed and beautifully shot but it is the sense of fun that is really striking. She makes you look at food in a completely different way and the combination of food and music makes for some really unexpected images. As a chef, I find other people's food memories really fascinating. Nostalgia plays a big role in the menu at The Fat Duck and I am constantly trying to tap into that sense of awe that we felt as children eating something for the first time. Discovering the favourite foods of the musicians in this book is a great insight into how we come to like certain foods and why dishes become important to us. Like the music of our formative years, it can be as much about the context as the food itself.

The *Teenage Cancer Trust* is such an important cause and I am honoured to have been asked to write this foreword in support of it. Every day, six teenagers or young adults will find out they have cancer and many of them will find themselves on adult wards to undergo treatment. But the *TCT* is steadily building special teenage cancer units at hospitals around the country so that young people can adjust to their illness in an environment that is suited to their needs. Firmly associated with music and comedy and now, thanks to Patrice, food, the *Teenage Cancer Trust* is making a clear difference to the lives of young people at the time they need support the most.

Heston Blumenthal
March 2011

'hai'd up: Tabita Bulmer of New Young Pony Club dives into noodles and chilli, page 40.

Beats and pizzas: Fun Lovin' Criminal Huey Morgan's American feast, page 80.

contents

Paul Weller 12
Buzzcocks 16
Brett Anderson 20
Gabriella Cilmi 24
Roger Daltrey CBE 28
The Feeling 32
Johnny Borrell 36
Flood 38
Tahita Bulmer 40
Erik Hassle 42
Madness 44
Sugababes 48
Professor Green 86
Back Stage at Oxegen 88
- *Kate Nash*
- *We Are Scientists*
- *Mystery Jets*
- *General Fiasco*
- *Kids in Glass Houses*

Mick Hucknall 92
Sparks 96
Tinie Tempah 100
James Walsh 104
Example 106
Francis Rossi OBE 52
British Sea Power 56
Hadouken! 58
Juliette Lewis 60
Sir Cliff Richard 64
Katie Melua 68
Sophie Ellis-Bextor 70
Noel Gallagher 72
Fairport Convention 76
Huey Morgan 80
Liam Fray 82
Ellie Goulding 84
Speech Debelle 108
White Lies 110
Luke Steele 114
Goldie Lookin' Chain 116
Feeder 118
Neil Hannon 120
Back Stage at V Festival 122
- *Eliza Doolittle*
- *Tiffany Page*
- *Diagram of the Heart*
- *Detroit Social Club*
- *White Belt Yellow Tag*

Lissie 124
Newton Faulkner 128
Brandon Flowers 130
Dexter Holland 134
Richard Hawley 138
Siouxsie Sioux 144
Coco Sumner 148
Biffy Clyro 152
Marina Diamandis 156
Tony Hadley 158
The Kooks 162
Mani 166
BT 170
VV Brown 174
Paul Oakenfold 176
Kasabian & Noel Fielding 178
Alex Kapranos 184
Rolf Harris 188
Melanie Blatt 192
Tony Christie 194
Brian May 196
Papa Roach 202
Bullet For My Valentine 206
Howling Bells 208
Kelly Jones 210
Rob Zombie 212
Peter Hook 216
Paloma Faith 220
Jo Wood 222

NORMAL
INPUT

'Music, food and sex are the most important things in life.'
—Brett Anderson of Suede

Espresso yourself: Paul Weller with his beloved lattes in Bar Italia, Soho.

ROCKY MARCIANO
heavyweight champion of the world!
OPPONENT DECISION ROUND
DON MOGARD...DECISION...10
HARRY HAFT.........KO.........3
PETE LOUTHIS.......KO.........3
OPPONENT
HAROLD MITCHELL
ART HENIE
REX LANE
FREDDIE BESHORE
JOE LOUIS
LEE SAVOLD
GINO BUONVINO
BERNY REYNOLDS
HARRY MATTHEWS
JOE WOLCOTT
JOE WOLCOTT
ROLAND LA STARZA
EZZARD CHARLES
EZZARD CHARLES
DON ROCKELL
ARCHIE MOORE

'Travelling to different places, meeting different people, eating what they eat… it's made the British better as a people.'

In 1982, The Jam were the biggest musical force to come out of punk rock, capturing British life in all its rainy, lass-ridden, weak-tea-and-chips detail. Then, out of the blue, Paul Weller broke up the band and announced that he was forming a new group – The Style Council – that would be based in a slick Europhile world of modern jazz and coffee bars. It caused a minor panic among fans. What was Weller playing at? Here was Britain's official spokesman for youth swanning around Paris in an Alain Delon mackintosh. Drinking 'coffee'.

At 30 years' remove, Weller's idea to plunge into the New Europe seems inspired. He first became interested in London's lost 1950s café culture after reading Colin McInnes's famous novel *Absolute Beginners*, the set text of the young soul rebel of the 1980s. 'It was such an intriguing, romantic, fascinating time,' Weller explains over coffee at Bar Italia on Frith Street in Soho, where he has come 'for years, at all hours'.

'Everybody forgets how horrible Britain was in the 80s,' says Weller. 'But look around you now and it's almost like we've got a new version of that *Absolute Beginners* world – the cafés and the cosmopolitan side of it.' OK, Starbucks and Costa don't exactly breathe the same demi-monde romance as the old Italian espresso places – but at least everyone can get a decent cup of coffee nowadays.

'It's travel that did it,' Weller continues. 'Seeing different places, meeting different people, eating what they eat… it's made the British better as a people. It's made us more open-minded, less xenophobic. It's made us happier people.' Travelling with The Jam and The Style Council, Weller saw, 'how dull and old-fashioned England was at that time. In Paris and Rome, it seemed like a freer, more broad-minded way to live. And it was there for everybody, not just the elite.'

The Jam were a working class band and Weller grew up in Woking on a working class diet. 'Egg and chips, beans on toast, nothing wrong with it,' he says with a smile. He didn't even see pasta until the end of the 70s. Now, with a cross-cultural self-education under his belt, it's still Italian food that he loves best. It's a pleasure playing in Italy, he says,

PAUL WELLER *loves* CAFFÈ LATTE

because even the motorway service stations serve fantastic fresh food. Give him a spaghetti pomodoro, just a basic tomato sauce, and he couldn't be happier. 'It's simple, but done right it's unbeatable. And it is the food that most Italians will eat, the diet of the ordinary person, but it's beautiful too. I like that.'

Weller is, he admits, no good in the kitchen himself: 'fish fingers and cheese on toast, that's about it,' but his girlfriend is a versatile cook and they eat well. For eating out, it's the exemplary fish and chips at the Golden Hind on Marylebone Lane or the vegetarian Indian place next door. Weller was vegetarian for 12 years until one day, travelling on the German Autobahn while on tour, he simply decided he was having chicken that day. 'I never got on well with the vegetarian thing,' he says ruefully. 'It really takes it out of you if you're on tour. I don't know how some bands do it.'

And the Weller coffee of choice? 'A latte,' he says. 'I like it milky. Can't do the espresso, it gives me the jitters.' He smiles again, drains his cup and sweeps off into Soho.

The Perfect Latte & Amaretti Biscotti

for the latte

Preheat your mug with hot water. Pour enough milk into a jug to almost fill your mug. Place the steam wand in the milk and steam for 10–20 seconds. Steam with the end of the wand partially out of the milk to aerate it – this creates a lovely velvety foam. After the first 10–20 seconds move the steam wand to the bottom of your jug and steam the milk until hot. Make 1 or 2 espresso shots depending on your desired taste. Pour into the warmed mug, then pour the milk on top, holding back the foam with a spoon. Fill the mug to about 1cm from the top. Gently spoon on the foam from the jug to top off your latte.

for the amaretti biscotti
makes 36

400g plain flour
2 tsp baking powder
125g butter, softened
200g caster sugar
2 medium eggs
2 tsp finely grated orange zest
1 tsp almond extract
75g almond flakes, toasted
1 large egg white, lightly whisked, to glaze

Preheat the oven to 190°C/Gas mark 5. Line a baking tray with baking parchment. Sift the flour and baking powder together into a bowl and set aside. In another large bowl, cream together the butter and sugar until light and fluffy. Beat in the eggs, one at a time, then stir in the orange zest and almond extract. Add in the flour and stir until smooth. Finally mix in the toasted almonds.

Divide the dough in half and shape each into a log, about 5cm in diameter. Place both on the baking tray and gently flatten. Brush the tops with egg white. Bake for 25 minutes until light brown.

Leave to cool slightly and then gently cut the logs diagonally into 1cm slices. Place the slices flat on the baking tray and bake for a further 10 minutes until crisp. Transfer to a wire rack to cool. Store the biscotti in a paper bag to help them soften slightly.

Pete Shelley (left) and Steve Diggle of Buzzcocks enjoy a champagne mini-supernova – with oysters.

MOËT & CHANDON

THERE'S A LOT to be said for punk rock but it wasn't exactly oriented towards good food and drink. The 1977 generation kept its energies up by other means, and when they weren't hammering illicit substances, they drank. Pete Shelley, singer with original Manchester punk band Buzzcocks, recalls that the most you could expect backstage in those days was a crate of pale ale or, more likely, a tray of pints that would go flat while you played.

Things were different when Buzzcocks reformed in 1989 on a wave of goodwill for their standard-setting songwriting – *Ever Fallen In Love, Everybody's Happy Nowadays* – and spreading reputation among new fans, including the young Kurt Cobain. The Buzzcocks' tour manager told Pete and guitarist Steve Diggle that they could have whatever they wanted now, so what would it be? 'Champagne,' they said. 'In plastic cups.'

'Champagne's perfect for us,' says Pete. 'Our songs are really fast and there are a lot of words, so you can't drink beer. You'd be in a right mess. Champagne's a bit more refined. And the bubbles stop you from drinking too quickly. The closest I'd ever got to it before was Babycham…'

'It's a nice instant way to have a drink,' says Steve. 'It's rock and roll fuel. Plastic cups are easier to grab when you're reaching for your drink onstage in the dark. It stops you spilling it and blowing up the amp.' They insist on Moët, he says. 'It's the right bubble size for singing. And we like an oyster every now and again. Pete's into the health thing now and they are very healthy.'

BUZZCOCKS

love MOËT & OYSTERS

The 1989 reunion has now lasted four times as long at Buzzcocks' first incarnation between 1975 and 1981, when they took the noise and anxiety of punk rock to a new level and became the first punk band to write genuinely moving love songs. 'It beggars belief doesn't it?' says Pete of their longevity. Buzzcocks now tour the world on a semi-regular basis and enjoy the food opportunities that this well-earned life affords. France, Italy, Malaysia, Australia, New Zealand, Singapore, Bangkok… 'It's a lot of good experiences,' says Pete. 'The best I've had is in Japan, especially the robotayaki where they cook it right in front of you. Eating out is one of the best reasons for going to Japan.

They've both had long periods of vegetarianism, Pete for nearly 19 years, 'but in Brazil the allure of sausages got to me,' he admits. 'After that, it was steak and everything. You tell yourself for years that meat's going to taste horrible,' he says, 'but then you give it a try and it's lovely. I realised I'd forgotten why I was a vegetarian in the first place.' At home they're each modest cooks – lentils, roasts, a bit of chicken soup. 'We were always very ordinary and we still are,' says Pete proudly. 'We have Marmite on the rider.'

Back in their early days Buzzcocks seldom experienced record company largesse, possibly because they stayed in Manchester as long as they could. Smorgasbord in the Danish food centre in Manchester, or a late-night dinner at one of the renowned Chinese restaurants, was as far as it went. It's an attitude that's stayed with them.

'We don't really enjoy the swanky fancy dining experience,' admits Pete Shelley, 'we never have. Maybe shows up our poor Northern upbringing.'

'What we really like,' he says, raising his glass of Moët with a smile, 'is value for money.'

'Champagne is rock and roll fuel. And Moët is the right bubble size for singing.'—***Steve***

Champagne & Oysters

serves 2

1 bottle of Champagne
12 fresh oysters
lemon halves, to serve

Place your Champagne in the fridge for 3–4 hours. Don't put it in the freezer as the aromas and flavours will be ruined. Younger and lively Champagne should be served at 8°C; vintage Champagne should be served at 10°C.

Rinse the oysters in cold water. To prepare, hold the oyster in a folded tea towel with the flat part uppermost and the hinge (tapered end) facing outwards. Hold firmly on a flat surface, push an oyster knife into the hinge and exert pressure. Twist the knife from side to side to prise open the shell – the hinge should pop. Lift off the top shell without piercing the oyster. Gently slide the knife under the oyster and cut through the muscle holding the oyster to the shell. Leave the oysters in the bottom shells and serve on a big platter of crushed ice.

Now open the Champagne. Undo the wire cage, hold the cork in the palm of one hand and use the other hand to hold and twist the bottom of the bottle until it pops open. Serve with the oysters.

Sassy's Dirty Oysters

serves 2

150ml soured cream or crème fraîche
¼ red onion, peeled and finely diced
juice of ½ lime
12 fresh oysters
2 tsp caviar

In a small bowl, mix together the soured cream or crème fraîche, onion and lime juice. Cover and chill in the fridge for an hour.

Meanwhile, open and prepare the oysters (as above). When ready to serve, spoon ½ tsp of the creamy dressing onto each oyster and top with a spoonful of caviar.

Blue sky thinking: Brett Anderson of Suede is energised by blueberries.

'**Music, food and sex** are the three most important things in life,' declares Brett Anderson, svelte singer with reunited glam-punk Britpop outrages Suede. 'You can't do without any of them.' He pauses and considers. 'Well, you can do without a couple of them. But you shouldn't.'

It is no secret that when Suede were at the height of their initial success Brett indulged himself in other, more illegal ways than eating well. An enthusiasm for chemicals and Byronic excess led to him echoing the extreme lifestyle of his hero David Bowie. 'In the 90s I had a phase of only eating brown rice for two months at a time,' he admits. 'I was very unhealthy and I had this idea that brown rice would somehow be very good for me. Basically all I was putting in my body was brown rice and cocaine, and that's not healthy. I was very bi-polar. Plus I was getting into meditation at the same time, so I was tri-polar. I was taking my body to extremes. It was an experiment. I didn't want to trudge in the middle lane.'

Brett kicked the drugs before Suede split up in 2003, but in 2007 he went to see a naturopath, 'and that changed my life.' A diet tailored to his individual metabolism (no mushrooms, corn, milk or wheat) has, 'really, really worked, to a startling degree.' His wife also studies naturopathic medicine. 'I feel a lot better and I'm very conscious of my diet now,' he says.

Hence the antioxidant blueberries that feature in his picture for *Love Music Love Food*. Brett makes his own muesli with oats, flax, and crushed pumpkin and sunflower seeds, and the blueberries go on top. 'I try to have them every day,' he says. 'I even used to have blueberry bushes, but they died. I got a year's worth of fruit but then a friend of mine kicked them when he was playing football, and that was that…'

This sort of healthy diet is a far cry from Brett's upbringing in Haywards Heath, Sussex, where his family were genuinely poor. 'I used to pretty much exist on crisps and Marmite on toast as a kid,' he says. 'I was a really reluctant meat-eater because we couldn't afford very good meat, so what we got wasn't very nice. Bits of liver and offal with veins in it. I spent a lot of my childhood crying into my steak and kidney pie and I became a vegetarian as soon as I could.' But he was an unhealthy one. 'The furthest I went was making toast, or spaghetti with nothing on it.'

BRETT ANDERSON of SUEDE *loves* BLUEBERRIES

Blueberry Fool

serves 4

450g blueberries
juice of 1 lime
425ml double cream
400g mascarpone
juice of 2 lemons
6 tsp honey
4 fresh mint sprigs
icing sugar, for dusting

Put the blueberries and lime juice into a food processor and blend until smooth. Whisk the cream in a bowl until peaking.

In a large mixing bowl, gently combine the mascarpone, lime juice, honey and three-quarters of the blueberry mixture, then fold in the whipped cream.

Spoon or pipe the blueberry fool into serving dishes and drizzle over the rest of the blueberry purée. Top with a sprig of mint and a dusting of icing sugar.

Brett's parents were strict about not wasting food and even now he's a little guilty to be smearing blueberries on his face. 'I feel like I should scrape them up and take them home.' He remembers having a fantasy as a child that one day he'd make enough money to buy a mountain of crisps. 'I had this vision of buying 150 packets of crisps and just rolling in them…'

Did this foreshadow the rail-thin rock beanpole that he became with Suede? Perhaps it did. Strangely Brett eats a lot of comfort food – pizza, or fish and chips. 'I'm actually obsessed with food,' he says. 'I've got a fast metabolism, so I'm thin but I graze all the time. I'll have double the portions as everyone else.'

In Suede, he admits, eating well wasn't at the forefront if their priorities. 'It was pearls before swine,' he says sadly. 'We'd be in Hollywood or Japan and we just wanted to have chips! You sort of wish we could go back in time and appreciate it…' But as the years went by they learned to appreciate what the touring lifestyle offers: ceviche in Peru, or amazing meals in Tokyo.

Now he and his wife live in Ibiza and they're particularly fond of a restaurant called Balafia. 'They do a simple, brilliant barbecue in a beautiful orange grove. It's amazing.' Brett cooks a lot at home: roast chicken ('free-range and organic – anything else would be hideous') or vegetarian sushi with brown rice, and a lot of fish which he cooks with tamari and an 'incredibly hot' samba with scotch bonnets, mangos and onions. 'A tiny bit of it will take your head off.' The best meal he's ever had, he thinks, wasn't a luxurious music business dinner but on his honeymoon in Capri. Brett had a simple ravioli alla caprese (ricotta, pasta and a napoletana sauce), 'and it was the most delicious thing I've ever had. Nothing flashy, just simple and gorgeous.'

He seems a long way from the haunted young man of *Animal Nitrate* and *Dog Man Star*. Perhaps he's expressing his Epicureanism in other ways? He laughs. 'Yes, that's it. It's my joie de vivre.'

'As a child I had this fantasy of buying 150 packets of crisps and just ***rolling*** *in them…'*

You want hands-on real cookery from your pop stars? Gabriella Cilmi, Australian teen phenomenon turned blossoming pop-rock artist, is of Italian descent. Every year her paternal grandma gets the family together to make vast quantities of their own tomato sauce. Gabriella's job is to peel the tomatoes, push them through the machine ('it's quite messy') and bottle up the sauce at the end. 'We put it in old wine and beer bottles that we've saved,' she says – a little mistily, because she's feeling homesick. 'You have to be careful round our place. If you open a bottle of beer you might get a mouthful of pasta sauce.'

Her other grandmother – her stepgran – makes pasta, gnocchi and ravioli. There's a big Italian community in Gabriella's hometown of Melbourne and they keep the old food traditions alive. 'It's funny,' says Gabriella. 'You go to Italy and everyone has moved on but the Italians in Melbourne are really proud of their past. I'd like to keep it alive myself if I can – if I ever get the time.'

Gabriella's family are Calabrese and Sicialiani, 'proper down-south culture,' and she visits Calabria every summer to stay in the house where her mum was born. 'My grandfather built the stairs himself – they're very rickety now,' she says. 'It's a crazy place but you'll never go hungry. I eat way too much when I'm over there.' Her favourite is her grandmother's pasta melanzane. Gabriella likes to watch her frying the aubergines and then drowning them in tomato sauce.

Even as a kid, Gabriella ate well. She remembers that her friends would bring simple peanut butter sandwiches to school while she would have a huge piece of schnitzel or a giant piece of piave ('my favourite cheese') in a ciabatta. 'I was always a good eater,' she says proudly, but her grandmother worried about the other grandchildren's appetites. She would give them a nip of a strange Italian alcoholic drink – Gabriella can't remember what it's called – that stimulates the appetite. 'She used to give it to all the grandchildren and skip me!' says a still-miffed Gabriella. 'She used to say, "You're all right," even though I really liked the taste…'

Her family's talent for cooking has only partly rubbed off on her, she admits. She can make a decent polenta and a good tomato sauce with cherry tomatoes. Top tip: 'Leave the skins on. They're sweeter when they're a little bit burnt.'

Where should we eat in Melbourne? 'It's a good food town,' she says, 'and there are so many Italians there that you can hardly go wrong. Try the fashionable, Roman-style Caffe e Cucina in South Yarra. *But*…' Gabriella adds, 'In Melbourne we have the second highest number of Greek people in the world outside of Athens, so the Greek restaurants are *incredible*. Souvlaki by the beach, that's what we like to do.'

For a singer travelling the world, there are plenty of chances to eat well. When she played at Hangar 7 in Salzburg, 'an amazing old aircraft hangar with planes hanging down', they laid on a Michelin chef who cooked, among other things, Gabriella's favourite dessert, a chocolate bombe. 'He gave me the recipe and it was the most complicated thing in the world,' she says. (She prefers Nigella's simpler version.) When she's in London she likes to visit the Japanese restaurant Tosa in Hammersmith. 'I'm not going to go out for an Italian, am I?' she smiles.

But really it's the taste of home she likes best. Her grandmother always made spinach and ricotta ravioli but for some reason the last time Gabriella went home it tasted extra-good. 'I was eating it for breakfast and lunch, waking up in the middle of the night with jet lag to eat it.'

'I'm not very good at cooking food,' says Gabriella Cilmi. 'But I'm very good at eating it.'

GABRIELLA CILMI *loves* PASTA & BASIL

Spaghetti with a Bloody Mary Sauce

serves 2

100ml olive oil
2 garlic cloves, peeled and crushed
1 onion, peeled and sliced
1 celery stalk, finely chopped
1 carrot, peeled and chopped
15 very ripe plum tomatoes
200ml vodka
6 fresh basil leaves
1 fresh bay leaf
sea salt and freshly ground black pepper
500g good-quality dried spaghetti

Heat the olive oil in a large saucepan and cook the garlic and onion until soft. Add the celery and carrot and cook for a further 2 minutes. Stir in the tomatoes, vodka, herbs and some seasoning. Simmer gently over a low heat for about 1 hour or until the sauce is thick. Discard the bay leaf.

Bring a large pan of water to the boil, add the spaghetti and cook for 10 minutes or until al dente.

Meanwhile, pour the tomato sauce into a food processor and whiz until smooth. Drain the spaghetti and place in a large warm serving bowl. Pour on the tomato sauce and serve immediately.

'You have to be careful in our house. If you open a bottle of beer you might get a mouthful of pasta sauce.'

'The love of a good pie is a powerful thing.'
—Suggs of Madness

YAMAHA
Batter 250

Aquaculture club: The Who's Roger Daltrey CBE set the rock'n'roll foodie template with his famous trout farm.

When you think of rock royalty and food, one image springs to mind: Roger Daltrey and his trout farm. The post-punk brigade roundly mocked Lakedown Trout Fisheries as the last word in rock star folly when The Who singer began work on it in the late 70s. 'I got ribbed rotten about the bloody trout,' is his good-humoured confession. Back then a fish farm seemed to symbolise the rock establishment's decadent desire to join the landed gentry.

But time has a way of correcting these harsh judgments. Yesterday's indulgence is today's agriculturally aware, low-mileage, community-friendly innovation. According to *Trout Fisherman* magazine, 'There can be no prettier fishery in this land' than Roger Daltrey's 26-acre place in the Wealden Valley area of Sussex, which offers wild and brown rainbow trout for the Zen-minded angler. And where would Alex James' bucolic cheese business be without Roger to point the way?

'I wouldn't mind all the ribbing,' Daltrey explains over tea and biscuits in a Shoreditch arts café, 'but I was a bit tongue-in-cheek about the idea myself in the first place. I never wanted to become a country gent. But I'd long had an interest in aquaculture. When I moved into the area I realised that this was a proper community suffering in a terrible recession, and the most valuable thing I could do was give someone a job. I didn't *care* about people taking the piss out of it. I'm very proud of what I achieved. I didn't buy my fishery, I built it – me, a mate and a couple of bulldozers – and it's *beautiful* now.'

'Food has shaped so much that we're unaware of,' he says, warming to his subject. 'The English countryside, our towns, they're completely shaped by what we eat. My local council classes my area as one of outstanding natural beauty. I've got news for 'em: there's fuck all natural about it. It's all created by the farmers: the fields, the patchwork. The only natural thing is the bumps in the bloody fields.'

ROGER DALTREY CBE *loves* TROUT

Born in 1944, Roger grew up at the tail end of food rationing. He admits that, even though The Who have sold millions of records over five decades, to this day he feels terrible guilt if he ever throws food away. He was raised on the traditional British menu: 'Meat and two veg that turned into something else the next day with the leftovers. A joint on Sunday, then shepherd's pie on Monday, and jam sandwiches for tea the rest of the week. Or bread and butter pudding with stale bread. Most blokes my age still love a bit of that.'

Though The Who took off in the mid-60s as the advance guard of Mod, with its infatuation with all things Italian, it wasn't antipasti and espresso that fuelled the band but Chinese restaurants. The band would finish playing at 11pm and the only places open would be the late-night dives of Chinatown. 'Thank God for them or we'd never have eaten at all,' he says. 'We were so used to the idea that food was scarce that it almost wasn't important to us. Then, when we first went to America and saw our first *real steak*… I mean, we thought a steak was a tiny bit of shoe leather. We used to wrap up the American steaks in tin foil and bring 'em back on the plane. One of them would feed a family for a week back here.'

As the British Invasion of the American charts turned into the stadium rock of the early 70s, The Who gained a reputation for excess. Drummer Keith Moon in particular was a key culprit. 'Every dinner would end with Moonie throwing cake at everybody,' says Roger. 'He liked *really* hot curries, maybe because he drank so much that he only realised he was eating if he was burning himself to death…' Roger laughs ruefully, for Keith's story famously ended sadly. The drummer died in 1978 after years of alcoholism. But when times were good they were very good, and The Who parties were legendary. For a West End after-show party for their musical *Tommy* in the 70s, they booked a juggler, a fire-eater and a snake-charmer – but the fire-eater set the stage alight and burnt the snake while the juggler was on. 'That was the kind of functions we had. You couldn't invent it. It was insane.' You get the impression that he doesn't miss it very much.

The best meal he's ever had in the course of his career? It wasn't with The Who, he says, but when he was filming the *Highlander* TV show in the early 90s. They shot a whole episode at the Cordon Bleu college in Paris. 'I've never tasted desserts like that before or since,' he says, still a little amazed. 'I'd highly recommend any film maker, write a scene in the Cordon Bleu college…'

Does Roger Daltrey eat out much? His favourite restaurant is Locanda Locatelli, the much-loved Italian in Mayfair. 'I love that place,' he says. 'The chef is a genius. The food's beautifully light and fresh, the wines are amazing… and they're not that expensive! Certainly not for the standard. I think it's the best Italian in London.' But really, he says, he's a bit over restaurants. He never got the whole nouvelle thing ('I thought the main courses were just hors d'ouevres') and he doesn't understand the fuss and contrivance of today's superstar chefs and their creations either. He'd rather have some friends around for dinner instead. He knows his way around a roast and a barbecue. 'I try to have at least one dinner party a week. I just like having the neighbours around, to eat and talk.'

'I mean,' says the rock star turned trout farmer, turned actor, turned founder of the Teenage Cancer Trust, 'what's the point of life if you're not spending time with people? That's what it's all about.'

'I didn't buy my fishery, I built it – me, a mate and a couple of bulldozers – and it's beautiful now.'

Hay-Smoked Rainbow Trout, Pickled Lemon & Pea Shoots

serves 4

You will need a bag of meadow hay for this recipe but it is easy to find in most pet shops. Setting fire to the hay should be done outside as it gets very smoky, but the delicate flavour it imparts to the fish is worth smoking the garden out a bit.

for the fish

4 fresh trout fillets, skin on
sea salt and freshly ground black pepper

for the pickled lemons

150ml water
100ml Chardonnay vinegar
50g sugar
2 Amalfi lemons

for the trout cure

50g unrefined caster sugar
50g table salt
20g finely grated lemon zest
10g finely grated lime zest
5g coriander seeds

to serve

450ml olive oil
a handful or two of pea shoots

For the pickled lemons, mix the water, vinegar and sugar together in a pan and place over a gentle heat. When the sugar has dissolved, remove from the heat and allow to cool. Thinly slice the lemons, discarding the seeds, and immerse in the pickling liquid. Place in the fridge for 48 hours before using.

For the trout cure, put the sugar, salt, lemon zest, lime zest and coriander seeds in a food processor and blitz to a fine powder. Sprinkle the mixture evenly onto a tray and lay the trout fillets on top, flesh side down. Set aside in the fridge for 30 minutes.

Rinse the trout fillets under cold running water to remove the salt mix and drain well on kitchen paper.

Heat up the barbecue, if using. Line a barbecue fish clamp with meadow hay. Place two of the trout fillets skin side down on the hay, then place the other two fillets on top, skin side upwards. Cover with more hay before closing the clamp. Either place on the barbecue and cook until the hay has burned, or set the hay alight and allow it to burn. When the flame has died down and the hay is cool enough to handle, remove the fillets, cleaning off as much of the hay debris as possible, and set aside.

Drain the lemon slices, reserving the pickling liquor, and place in the centre of serving plates. Season the trout fillets with black pepper and place on top of the lemon slices. Combine 150ml of the pickling liquid with the olive oil and mix well. Dress the pea shoots with this mixture, season with salt and black pepper and serve.

This recipe was supplied by Heston Blumenthal.

Food frenzy with The Feeling (from left) Kevin Jeremiah, Paul Stewart, Dan Gillespie-Sells, Ciaran Jeremiah, Richard Jones.

Bloody rock stars: everything seems to fall into their laps, doesn't it? 'I'm a rubbish cook,' admits Dan Gillespie-Sells, frontman with soft rock superstars The Feeling, 'but I live with a couple of chefs. It's brilliant! They can knock up something very sophisticated really easily. I'm completely spoiled, it's made me very lazy but I'm not great in the kitchen anyway. I panic or screw it up. I get performance anxiety.'

Before he moved in with the cooks – his friend Mike, a trained chef who Dan met when The Feeling were honing their skills as the modern 10cc house band at a French ski resort, and upcoming TV chef Anna Barnett – Dan had another stroke of luck. For a while he and his boyfriend lived next door to a pub, and the Italian owner would deliver whatever they wanted.

'Traditional Sicilian stuff that wasn't even on the menu, anything you like,' remembers Dan. 'He'd plate it up and bring it next door. It's terrible really, we couldn't even be bothered to walk a few yards to the pub and we hardly ever cooked ourselves. So I've lost any skills I ever had in the kitchen. But we did eat *very* well.'

Still, you can't say he doesn't appreciate it. 'I have become a proper foodie now,' he says. 'London's food culture has really taken off, plus I can actually afford to go to restaurants now…' These days The Feeling have a 'fairly expensive' rider for each show, favouring quality alcohol. 'Paul and some of the others like the smokier Jura or Hebridean whiskies but I like the lighter, lowland whiskies,' says Dan. 'The butterier ones that go down a bit easier. We want to have a certain quality of alcohol and food. We're too old for crisps and Haribos now.'

He relates how he and his band mates used to see how much money a label was willing to spend on dinner with The Feeling in order to get their signature. The record company people would favour 'pretty ridiculously expensive' places but The Feeling were older and wiser than most bands, and a bit harder to dazzle.

THE FEELING *love* A BIT OF EVERYTHING

Pork Sausage, Red Onion & Dijon Mayonnaise Door-stop Sandwich

serves 2

1 tsp Dijon mustard
2 tbsp good-quality mayonnaise
6 good-quality pork sausages
1 red onion, peeled and finely sliced
dash of Worcestershire sauce
1 tsp brown sugar
sea salt and freshly ground black pepper
4 thick slices of fresh white bread, buttered

In a small bowl, mix the mustard with the mayonnaise; cover and refrigerate.

Place a frying pan over a high heat, add the sausages and cook, turning frequently, until golden brown all over. Remove from the pan and cut in half lengthways. Return the sausages to the pan and fry cut side down until just crispy. Lift out of the pan and set on two of the bread slices.

Pour out any excess oil from the frying pan, then heat up the pan and quickly fry the onions until softened. Add the Worcestershire sauce, brown sugar and some salt and pepper. When the onions are browned, place them on top of the sausages.

Spread a big dollop of the Dijon mayonnaise on the other two slices of bread. Place face down on top of the onions and press together.

Serve whole with a big mug of builder's tea.

One major record label spent tens of thousands on a giant meal for the band and an entourage, and The Feeling didn't even sign with them. 'You used to get a lot of that sort of thing,' says Dan. 'Maybe less so now. There will be an awful moment when they order the most expensive Champagne – they always say Cristal – and you try to say no because it's a waste of money and everyone's hammered already anyway. And it'll only end up on our account.'

His choice for *Love Music Love Food* is a sausage sandwich, 'the perfect comfort food. Very traditional and hearty on a winter's day. It just makes you feel great.' And it's all about the quality of the banger. Dan's boyfriend comes from a butcher's family so they get their meat from his shop in Manchester. The homemade sausages in particular are very special indeed.

'If I got my housemates to cook these amazing sausages with a chef's touch,' Dan muses, 'then they'd probably be the best sausage and mash in the world, wouldn't they?'

Bloody rock stars!

'Nooo!' he says, and laughs. 'If I was a real rock star I wouldn't need to share a house, would I?'

'I'm a rubbish cook but I live with a couple of chefs. It's brilliant!'—***Dan***

Guitarist **KEVIN JEREMIAH** ***loves*** SOFT SHELL CRABS: 'Every proper studio has a takeaway menu with soft shell crab on. They don't taste anything like how they look, and for some reason that's appealing… The best meal I've ever had would be when Ciaran, Rich and I used to order the local dodgy pizza delivery, grab a few cans of cheap beer, and devour it while watching *Buffy the Vampire Slayer*. Do I need to explain why?'

Keyboards player **CIARAN JEREMIAH** ***loves*** MUFFINS: 'They're an indispensable part of my mid-afternoon routine. I love them because they're the perfect accompaniment to a sandwich. A sandwich is never enough, but stick it with the muffin and you're content. The best thing I ever ate? A battered Mars bar. I thought I was going to die afterwards.'

Drummer **PAUL STEWART** ***loves*** SAUSAGES: 'I couldn't be a bigger fan of the British banger if I tried. Being a simple drummer, it may just be that "banger" describes both my favourite food and my role in the band. A good sausage is all about well-bred livestock, close attention to the combination and quality of the ingredients, and cooking it all for just the right amount of time. Much like our band…'

Singer **DAN GILLESPIE-SELLS** ***loves*** SAUSAGES ***too:*** 'The perfect comfort food, very traditional and hearty on a winter's day.'

Bass player **RICHARD JONES** ***loves*** ROCKET, MOZZARELLA AND PARMA HAM: 'My favourite pizza topping, from Franco Manca in Chiswick, the best pizza in London. I love Italian food. Sophie (Ellis-Bextor, see page 70) and I got married in Umbria and had a traditional six-course Italian meal at our wedding. Simple food, great ingredients – yum. I love Italy. My favourite restaurant is the beach bar in Santa Maria, just south of the Amalfi coast, where they do perfect pasta for about five euros. Order a bottle of greco di tufo and spend the afternoon sitting by the beach, enjoying the gentle sea breeze...'

JOHNNY BORRELL of RAZORLIGHT *loves* SALMON

'Steve Hatt's is the best fish shop in North London, without a doubt – and maybe further afield too.' So says Johnny Borrell, singer-songwriter with Razorlight, Muswell Hill boy, dater of models and actresses (Edie Campbell, Kirsten Dunst), and aficionado of Good Living. 'You don't get to cook much when you're in a band, but when I get the chance I always come to Steve's,' he says. 'There's always queues out of the door, they really know their stuff and it's a fantastic vibe in here.' From behind the staff cheer him on as he wrestles with a salmon the size of a small dog.

Steve Hatt is part of what Johnny and his mates call the 'Four Pillars of Highbury'. There's high-end butcher's Frank Godfrey in Highbury Barn, cheese mecca La Fromagerie over the road, and the Newington Green Greengrocer's nearby. 'With those four things, you can make your weekend,' he says. 'We'll get the wagon out on a Saturday morning, stock up, have lamb's kidneys and cognac for breakfast… and then you're ready to go.'

Johnny likes to cook dishes that take plenty of time: 'Something with the quality of a grand project. Get a few cod fillets and leave them salting in your airing cupboard for a week, to get that scary, deep quality of flavour. Something epic.' He likes to cook with a large group of friends if he can. 'It's a proper bonding thing.'

He was a late-comer to the kitchen. In music you're either on tour or at a studio or you're sleeping on somebody's floor. 'But cooking's creative, it's the same impulse as writing or painting. If you've got that interest it will transfer to cooking. There's the macho gamesmanship aspect too. I've got at least three friends who reckon they are the best cooks in the world – as all blokes do. You're always shooting for that satisfying moment when you can put your dish on the table and think, "that was cooked to perfection".'

Though Johnny grew up on fish fingers, chips and pizza it's been a thrill for him to discover food by travelling the world with Razorlight. (They even chose to sign their deal with Universal in part because the label took them out for a better dinner than their nearest rival.) Most bands don't take enough advantage of the places they visit, he thinks. But Razorlight will consult the *Zagat* guide and try to go local – or he'll just step out of the hotel and see what he can find.

That's exactly what happened when he was staying in Tokyo at the Ritz Carlton. 'I needed a break and sushi is the kind of thing you really can eat on your own.' He found a little place nearby that offered *Omokase*, chef's choice. Johnny sat there for an hour, reading and eating sushi he describes as, 'next level, absolutely incredible. I had to work out ways to communicate with him to show my appreciation. For a moment I'd stepped out of the promotional nightmare into this little oasis, and it was a really magical little moment.'

At home he loves a pub called The Bell on the Ridgeway in Oxfordshire. 'They've got *the* best ale. I'll turn up starving and without fail they've got an incredible hot crusty roll with coarse Ardennes pâté.' And the Food Lab on Essex Road in Islington, near Steve Hatt, which does a unique and brilliant Italian English breakfast. Then there's the infamous temple of nose-to-tail meat eating, St John in Clerkenwell. 'You'll have four or five amazing moments in one meal. It's not for the squeamish, it's brains and hearts and tails – but I'm not squeamish. I'll go for the bone marrow, which is fantastic. There's nothing I wouldn't eat off their menu.' St John's founder Fergus Henderson once gave him a bit of advice: 'Just cook, and you'll learn.'

But the best thing he's ever eaten was a little less exalted. When Johnny was first trying to become a musician he lived on the dole in Hornsey with a friend, Rory, who wanted to become a writer. One week their benefits didn't come through and they applied for ('this sounds very dramatic') a Hardship Loan. They queued for three hours, filled in the forms and waited. 'We'd spent all our money on alcohol and cigarettes and we hadn't eaten in two days,' he admits. 'But that's what you do when you're trying to start a band. You know when you're out of fags and you make butt-rollies from the butts? We were on butt-rollies of butt-rollies of butt-rollies…'

When the £35 eventually came through, they ran straight to Safeway on Holloway Road, bought lamb chops and ran home. 'That feeling of just getting these lamb chops home was sheer delight,' he says. 'We chucked them on the pan, I think we only seared them for a minute on each side, and then we just *devoured* them. It's got to be the most satisfying thing I've ever eaten.'

'That's my Proustian lamb chop, the one I'll always remember,' he says with a smile. 'It'll never get better than that.'

Smoked Salt & Chilli Crispy Skin Salmon

serves 4

grated zest and juice of 1 lemon
1 tbsp smoked sea salt flakes
½ tbsp chopped fresh parsley
½ tsp dried chilli flakes
4 salmon fillets, about 150g each, descaled
oil, for brushing and frying
4 tbsp soy sauce

In a small bowl, mix together the lemon zest, smoked sea salt, chopped parsley and chilli flakes. Put to one side.

Check over the salmon for pin bones, removing any you come across. Lay the fillets skin side up on a board and score the skin with a sharp knife. Brush with some oil and rub in most of the salt mixture.

Heat a large frying pan over a high heat and add a little oil. Place the salmon fillets skin side down in the pan and fry for 3 minutes, then turn over and sprinkle with half of the lemon juice. Cook for another minute or two, until the salmon is ready.

Transfer the salmon to warm plates, drizzle with the soy sauce and finish with the remaining salt mixture and a squeeze of lemon.

'I like to cook something that's a grand project, something epic. And to cook it with friends. It's a proper bonding thing.'

4·80
3-30
OCEAN STICKS
(CRABSTICKS)
3-20 PER 32
5-99 PER 64
3-50
2-08
GREENLIP MUSSELS
(NEW ZEALAND)
1KG BOX
6-30 Kg.
17-50
PORTUGUESE CLEANED OCTOPUS
1 KG (approx)
9-90 Kg.
SEAFOOD COCKTAIL
1KG BAG
5-50
COOKED PEELED KING PRAWNS
1 KG BAG
11-90
PLEASE KEEP YOUR RECEIPT
REFUNDS WILL ONLY BE GIVEN WHEN THE RELEVANT RECEIPT IS PRODUCED
SQUID TUBES
3-90
PER KG
KING PRAWN
IN FILO PASTRY
5-40 PER 500gm BOX
BLACK LUMP ROE
3.99
KETA SALMON ROE CAVIAR
9.50
FRESH SMOKED MACKEREL

Flood, aka Mark Ellis, is one of the most prolific and sought-after producers in British music. He has collaborated with artists as diverse as U2, Nick Cave and The Bad Seeds, Erasure, PJ Harvey, Sigur Rós and The Killers, and he was instrumental in helping Depeche Mode develop their enormous stadium sound. And he really loves sushi and sashimi.

'When I eat certain foods there's a connection,' he says. 'The protein and cleanliness of sashimi and sushi just make my body very happy. It's a no-brainer – I'll eat any of it. I'm not a big fan of eel but everything else, I'm game for a laugh. And trust me, I've had a lot of weird stuff.'

Flood's brother works in the City. They'll often challenge each other to see who can find the best Japanese restaurant, and to order one thing they've never tried before. 'He took me to one place near the Old Bailey and we tried octopus balls with squid tripe,' he says with a grimace. 'Even the poor waiter was like, "Look, I'm Japanese, are you sure you want this?" So that was like a red rag to a bull.' The octopus balls were kind of chewy and saline, and the squid tripe was even stranger: 'a little cup of this thick grey liquid with black bits in it. It was like the fishiest, chewiest bike tyre I've ever had…'

The first time he tried sushi was in New York, when he was doing front of house sound on a Soft Cell tour in 1983. He was 22, he'd never been to America before, and when someone suggested Japanese food he did not fancy it at all. 'But we went to a conveyor sushi place nearby and it blew my mind. Once I'd got over the "Oh my God I'm eating raw fish" factor it was amazing and I've never looked back.'

Ironically for someone who loves the food, works with international bands and is fascinated by every aspect of Japan, he's never been there. 'I keep trying to persuade all these bands that they need to make a record there!' he says. 'Everything about the culture, the land, the ideology, the way of life, the spirituality really interests me. I want to know more about it. I'm going to pick the right time.'

In the meantime there are the quality Japanese places of London, New York and Los Angeles, familiar stops on the international producer's itinerary. Sushi-Say in Willesden Green is his local, and Tajima-Tei in Hatton Garden is 'one of those places where you only see Japanese people going in. I love places like that. You have to brace yourself but the food is fantastic.'

The best he's had, he suspects, is Nobu New York because of the mixture of new-wave combinations with exceedingly well-executed traditional sashimi and sushi. A close second is the place in Las Vegas that The Killers took him to a few times – but he never remembered to note the name. A real favourite is Sushi Nozawa in Studio City, Los Angeles, in a strip mall in the San Fernando Valley. On the door there's a notice that says the chef will supply you with what he feels you should eat. 'The food is unbelievable and it just keeps coming,' says Flood. 'I saw a guy ask for a California roll once and they chased him out.'

The subtleties of sushi are what fascinates Flood: the little things that take a proper sushi chef six or seven years to learn. A true sushi master should be able to prepare the correct size portion for you just by looking at you. 'He'll watch you and gauge it so it's right,' Flood explains. 'It's a non-verbal conversation. And of course they've got to be trained not to cut the liver of the blowfish the wrong way or you'll be dead…'

So, an internationally renowned record producer likes food that requires meticulous preparation and attention to detail. Why on earth would that be? 'I know!' he says, and laughs. 'It's the control freak in me.'

FLOOD *loves* SASHIMI

Tuna Tartare with Seared Pink Grapefruit Salad & Ginger Dressing

serves 4

2 pink grapefruit
2 tbsp brown sugar
3 handfuls of mixed baby salad leaves
450g sushi-grade yellow fin tuna, thinly sliced and diced
6 shiso Japanese mint leaves (or rocket), finely shredded
3 spring onions, trimmed and very finely sliced

for the dressing

juice of 3 limes
dash of tabasco sauce
2.5cm piece of fresh ginger, peeled and grated
2 tbsp groundnut oil
2 shallots, peeled and grated
1 garlic clove, peeled and crushed
freshly ground black pepper

First make the dressing. Mix all the ingredients together in a small bowl and leave to infuse in the fridge for 4 hours.

Peel the grapefruit, removing all white pith, then cut the segments free from the membranes. Dip the grapefruit segments in the brown sugar. Heat a small frying pan over a high heat and quickly fry the grapefruit segments on both sides until caramelised. Put the salad leaves into a bowl. Strain the dressing through a fine sieve and use to dress the leaves.

For the tartare, mix the tuna, shredded shiso mint leaves and sliced spring onions together. Place a 6cm metal ring, 4cm deep, in the centre of each serving plate and spoon the tuna into the mould, pressing down lightly.

Pile the salad on top of the tuna and arrange the caramelised grapefruit around the outside of the mould. Carefully lift off the mould and serve at once.

'Everything about the culture, the land, the ideology, the way of life, the spirituality, really interests me.'

'It was so spicy and it had such depth that you couldn't stop eating it. If you did, you realised your lips were on fire.'

TAHITA BULMER of NEW YOUNG PONY CLUB *loves* THAI NOODLES

New wave dance-punk band New Young Pony Club's first big hit was *Ice Cream*, and the video called for frontwoman Tahita Bulmer to roll around in piles of confectionery and dribble chocolate sauce in her mouth. It's no surprise then that she loves to eat. 'Food is one of my great passions, definitely,' she declares with enthusiasm. 'I'm always looking for new recipes and trying stuff out on my friends.' And chief among her obsessions is Thai.

'Thai – the food that first made me think, when I was a student, "I'd love to cook that,"' she says. 'Before I discovered it I was just living on tuna and tomato ketchup like all students do…' After a bohemian childhood spent in London, New York and Cairo, Tahita had gone to study at the University of Sussex in Brighton. 'It was very alternative, lots of lentil burgers…' She began working in a t-shirt shop where her boss's wife, who was Thai, would sometimes bring in her home cooking.

'I'd never had Thai food before and this was home-style stuff,' says Tahita. 'It was completely different from what you'd get in a restaurant. It was incredible.' She helped her boss's wife, Noi, with her English and in turn Noi taught Tahita basic Thai recipes: green curry, red curry, Massaman curry. Soon afterwards Tahita went on holiday to Thailand which 'kick-started the whole thing in a much more massive way. I love cooking Thai now.'

Her specialities are 'very sticky' drunken fish – a dry red curry that uses palm sugar instead of coconut milk, inspired by the drunken lamb Noi brought in for a Christmas party in the shop. 'It was so spicy and it had such depth to it that you couldn't stop eating it. If you did you realised your lips were on fire.' Tahita doesn't eat meat so she adapted it to suit fish like tilapia or haddock. 'Nothing too delicate, or the chilli and coriander will kill it.'

Tahita grew up pretty much used to heat. Her father was English, a photographer who was part of Rolling Stone Brian Jones's circle, and her mother was from Trinidad. Her mum's family was thoroughly Anglophile and the whole family would dress for Sunday lunch. Her mother would cook a full spread of a roast chicken plus a chicken curry on the side, and a huge apple pie or a 'bizarre' French tart with ice cream for dessert. 'I loved it because it was theatrical,' says Tahita, 'but there'd be Trinidadian soul food as well as traditional English. I grew up on curries so it set me in good stead for enjoying spicy food.'

Christmas dinner too would mean chicken or lamb curry and roti alongside the traditional roast turkey. And there was Trinidadian Christmas Cake, an adaptation of English Christmas pudding. 'You start making it in March and feed it rum 'til it's the most noxious, flammable substance on the face of the Earth. You can only eat a morsel about the size of a dice because it's so strong. But it's addictive.'

Tahita thinks her education in home-style Thai might have spoilt her a little. Even though London is full of good Thai restaurants, she's yet to find one that's spectacular. Or maybe it's the fact that she spends so much time in Shoreditch with its thriving, high-quality Vietnamese places. She prefers a Guyanese restaurant called 16 in Hornsey, near her home. It's a family place and the food has the same depth and hotness that reminds Tahita of real Thai. 'I've got high standards!' she says with a smile.

Luckily her band are adventurous too. On tour in Seville they let Tahita try out her rusty Spanish and order for the whole band and crew. 'There was a lot of *platos muy típicos*,' she says, 'but we ended up with this really fabulous poached cod, scrambled egg and potato thing.' She liked it so much she looked it up on the Internet so that she could try cooking it: *patatas con bacalao borracho y huevos revuettos.*

'It's quite common for first generation immigrants to believe that food is really important,' says Tahita. 'It's an expression of love. When you love someone, or if you've been separated from them for a long time, you feed them – and sometimes you overfeed them.' One day in the future, when her knees have given out from all the bouncing around, she thinks she might try to invent her own cuisine: Thai-Trinidadian fusion.

Lime Noodles with Spiky Vegetables, Basil & Mint Paste

serves 4

200g assorted vegetables, such as pak choi, peeled carrots, mangetout, sweet peppers, purple-sprouting broccoli
25g edamame beans
3–4 tbsp vegetable oil
8 garlic cloves, peeled and thinly sliced
juice of 10 limes
125g granulated sugar
25 Thai basil leaves
20 mint leaves
100g sesame seeds, toasted, plus extra to garnish
1 tsp sea salt
2 tbsp groundnut or corn oil
450g wide rice noodles
20g unsalted butter

Cut the vegetables into matchstick strips and put to one side with the edamame beans. Heat 1 tbsp vegetable oil in a heavy-bottomed frying pan, add the garlic and fry until golden brown, then remove and set aside. In a separate small pan, heat the lime juice and sugar until the sugar has dissolved. Bring to the boil, then take off the heat.

Bring a small saucepan of water to the boil, then add the basil and mint leaves. Remove with a slotted spoon as soon as the water returns to the boil and plunge the leaves into iced water. Drain and squeeze the leaves dry.

Purée the blanched herb leaves with the sesame seeds, garlic, salt and groundnut or corn oil to a smooth paste. Over a high heat, heat 2–3 tbsp vegetable oil in a frying pan, add the vegetables and toss until almost tender, about 10 minutes. Set aside and keep warm.

Meanwhile, bring a large pot of water to the boil over a medium heat and cook the noodles until tender, about 30 seconds. Drain, transfer to a wok over a high heat, add the lime syrup and butter and toss until well combined.

Place the noodles in a warmed bowl, drizzle with the basil and mint paste, top with the vegetables and scatter with sesame seeds. Serve immediately.

MAYBE IT'S THE HAIR. Electro-pop singer Erik Hassle grew up in rural Sweden on a hardy diet of 'classical Swedish food – lots of meat, potatoes and vegetables, like an English roast.' But since living and working in London he's developed a love of the Mediterranean fruit (not a vegetable) that's as vibrant as his crowning glory.

In the wake of well-received debut single *Hurtful* and a tour with Mika, Erik moved to London to stay for a year with his half-Italian friend and guitarist Viktor Paronitti. 'He cooks a lot with tomatoes and I really started to love them,' says Erik. 'He has a lot of energy and he likes taking care of the people around him. It's like having a proper Italian grandmother. They don't want anyone else to interfere with their cooking. Something as simple as spaghetti bolognese – when it's done well, it's really good.'

Where should we eat if we want decent Swedish food in the UK? You can do a lot worse than the Ikea café, Erik admits. 'It's good value! Honest food!' But in Stockholm, he says, you can trust pretty much any restaurant. The Swedes have a low tolerance for bad food.

His father, for instance, is from Gothenburg and cooks a lot of fresh fish. His mum specialises in Sweden's fabled meatballs and potatoes with lingonberry jam. 'It keeps you warm during the winter.' Erik's favourite Swedish dish is one of his dad's specialities, the giant traditional sausage called Falukorv. 'It's really big, you cut it in pieces and have it with mashed potatoes and a creamy horseradish sauce. It's really good.'

Sometimes the traditional stuff is all you need. A couple of years ago Erik learned to drive in an intensive week-long course that ended in the test. He went to stay with his grandma for the week and, to help him concentrate, she let him write a week's worth of menus – anything he wanted for dinner at the end of each stressful day. On the final day she made him a moose steak, from a moose that his grandfather had shot himself, with Madeira sauce, fried onions and a little garlic butter. 'A moose, straight from the forest,' says Erik mistily. 'Very Swedish. And it was just perfect…'

ERIK HASSLE *loves* TOMATOES

Swedish Meatballs with Tomato Sauce

makes 20 meatballs

140g breadcrumbs
150ml milk
55g butter
4 shallots, peeled and grated
2 garlic cloves, peeled and grated
1 tsp caraway seeds, toasted and ground
sea salt and freshly ground black pepper
500g lean minced beef
500g lean minced pork
1 large egg
handful of fresh parsley, chopped
handful of fresh dill, chopped

for the tomato sauce

1 small onion, peeled and finely chopped
2 garlic cloves, peeled and chopped
1 tbsp brown sugar
290ml V8 vegetable juice
225g tomatoes, chopped

Put the breadcrumbs in a small bowl, pour on the milk and set aside to soak for 10 minutes.

Melt two-thirds of the butter in a saucepan over a medium-low heat. Add the shallots, garlic and caraway seeds, season with salt and pepper and cook until the shallots are soft but not coloured, about 3 minutes.

In a large bowl, mix together the beef and pork. Add the shallot mixture, egg and chopped herbs. Squeeze the breadcrumbs to remove excess milk, then add to the meat. Using your hands, mix well until thoroughly combined.

Pinch off pieces of the mixture, the size of a golf ball, divide these in two and shape into balls – you should end up with about 20 meatballs.

Melt the remaining butter in a large frying pan over a medium heat. Fry the meatballs in batches, turning to colour evenly, for about 6 minutes in total. Set aside on a warm plate while you make the tomato sauce.

For the sauce, fry the onion and garlic – in the frying pan used to cook the meatballs – until softened. Add the brown sugar, vegetable juice, tomatoes and some salt and pepper. Cook until the sauce starts to thicken, then add the meatballs and simmer slowly for 20 minutes. Serve with pasta or rice.

'Something as simple as spaghetti Bolognese – when it's done well, it's really good.'

In crust we trust: Madness's two frontmen offer the finest Pie and Smash (and Suggs).

MADNESS!

If poets are the unauthorised legislators of the world, then Madness write London's unauthorised national anthems. In 30 years in the business, they've grown from Camden Town nutty boys into pop writers of unusual subtlety and perception. They're guardians of the tradition of music hall as working class entertainment, and unofficial historians of their home city. In their raucous live shows, much-loved sing-alongs from the old days like ***Baggy Trousers*** and ***Night Boat To Cairo*** rub along with more introspective songs from their recent masterpiece ***The Liberty Of Norton Folgate***, a concept album about one of London's strangest and most lawless pockets.

Madness grew up in cafés. 'We pretty much lived in them,' says frontman Suggs, AKA Graham McPherson. 'Everyone of our age did. It was the only place you could talk and hang out and eat for not much money. The demise of the Great British Caff is a disaster. Even the New Piccadilly has gone. That mixture of spaghetti bolognese and chips was part of growing up in London.'

Madness shot the famous video for ***Return Of The Los Palmas 7*** in the Venus Café off Portobello, where the owner was 'right grumpy'. Co-frontman and writer Cathal Smyth – the artist formerly know as Chas Smash – once asked if he could have his bacon crispy and the owner asked him, 'How d'you want your fackin' head, then?' They used to go to the San Siro Café on Highgate West Hill too, and the Cally Road Café over the road from their studio ('a proper good chicken curry') and the Hope Dining Rooms in Upper Street. 'The Hope was fantastic!' says Cathal. 'Something from a dying age, slightly upmarket, maybe with pretensions towards the sort of chap who had bought his suit in Dunn's

MADNESS

love PIE & MASH

20 years before. It was a bit threadbare but he still wanted a bit of class.'

'And you'd be able to see the mother through a little curtain,' says Suggs, 'making pies, chopping up liver and hearts…'

Madness loved cafés so much that they eulogised them in one early song. ***Don't Quote Me On That*** concerned misunderstandings with the press and stories about the unwanted right-wing followers who bedevilled Madness in their early days, a group that the band eventually shook off. The song suggests that we'd all understand each other a bit better if we sat down and ate together and accept that the woes of the world are 'all just eggs, bacon, beans and a fried slice.'

For its seven members Madness has been about discovering that freedom and the good things in life are available to all of us, not just the self-selected few. Cathal now lives in Ibiza where the pace of life suits him and London is but an EasyJet away. His favourite restaurants there are the 'wonderful' organic café La Paloma in San Lorenzo and JD's – Joe and Darren's – who do a great Sunday roast and proper lamb shanks.

'The meat there is fantastic, the Spanish have such high standards,' he says. 'I like the Catholic countries because they have such a welcoming, open attitude to food and they want kids to be part of it. You eat as a family. I can't stand the old-fashioned stuffy English thing.' At home he'll cook Japanese feasts, or Hugh Fearnley-Whittingstall's Shoulder of Pork 'Donnie Brasco' – the one where you can 'fugeddaboutit'. 'Cover it in five-spice, half-hour sizzle, then 14–16 hours on a very slow heat,' he advises. 'Falls off the bone.'

Suggs can prepare a decent steak and kidney pudding. 'My wife Anne helps with the suet,' he says, which makes Carl guffaw. He can also do a splendid pheasant stew. Suggs was visiting Norfolk once and the game birds were just lying around everywhere, a pound each. He bought a brace and chucked them in the pot with a few cooking apples, potatoes, red wine and carrots. 'You leave it there for days on end,' he says, 'and something delicious comes out at the end. It wasn't the food of my youth, put it that way. Mine was more stewed peasant.'

Their food of choice isn't just Suggs or Cathal's favourite dish but Madness's collective favourite: pie and mash, the national dish of London. 'It's a beautiful thing, a pie,' says Suggs. 'A singular delight.' These pies are from the Eel House Pie Company, a new supplier that uses proper ingredients, fresh parsley, no food colouring in the liquor… 'It's pie and mash as it should be,' says Cathal. 'A reminder of another age, of the working classes' need to be fed cheaply but well.'

'Pie and mash can be a cliché but when it's done well you can't beat it,' adds Suggs. He relates how their mate Steve Jones of the Sex Pistols came home to London from LA recently and went in search of a good pie. But Manzi's in Chapel Market in Islington was shut. 'He said he ended up licking the window…'

'The love of a good pie,' says Suggs, 'is a powerful thing.'

'The love of a good pie is a powerful thing.'—***Suggs***

Suggs, Cathal and guitarist Chrissy Boy Foreman dial a pie.

Pie & Mash

serves 4

for the pie filling

2 tbsp vegetable oil
1 onion, peeled and finely sliced
500g lean minced beef
4 tsp plain flour
50ml beef stock
100ml beer
sea salt and freshly ground black pepper

for the pastry lid

225g plain flour
pinch of sea salt
50g cold butter, diced
50g cold lard, diced
about 4 tbsp cold water

for the pastry case

butter, for greasing
350g self-raising flour
225g beef suet
sea salt and freshly ground black pepper
4 tbsp water

for the gravy

knob of butter
2 tbsp plain flour
400ml chicken stock
handful of fresh parsley, stalks removed and chopped
1 tbsp malt vinegar

to glaze

1 medium egg beaten with 1 tbsp milk

For the filling, heat the oil in a large heavy-based saucepan over a medium heat and fry the onion until soft. Add the mince and fry gently, stirring to break up the meat, until lightly browned. Mix in the flour and stir until thick, then gradually add the beef stock and beer to make a thick gravy. Season with salt and pepper and simmer gently for about 1 hour, stirring occasionally. Allow to cool before assembling the pies.

Preheat the oven to 180°C / Gas mark 4. Butter 4 individual pie dishes well.

For the pastry lid, sift the flour and salt together into a large bowl and rub in the butter and lard using your fingertips, until the mixture resembles breadcrumbs. Add enough water to bind the pastry and knead lightly until smooth. Roll out the pastry to a 2mm thickness and cut around the upturned pie dishes to make 4 lids for the pies.

For the pastry case, sift the flour into a large bowl and add the suet. Season and stir, then mix in the water to form a moist dough. Roll out to a 2mm thickness. Upturn the pie dishes on the suet pastry and cut the pastry 5cm larger all round than the dish.

Line the pie dishes with the suet pastry and spoon in the cooled meat filling. Brush the exposed pastry rim with a little water and position the pastry lids over the filling. Trim and gently pinch the two pastries together to seal. Brush the tops with a little egg glaze.

Stand the pie dishes in a roasting tin and pour enough boiling water into the tin to come halfway up the side of the dishes. (Using a bain-marie ensures the suet pastry steams and the tops bake evenly.) Bake the pies for 20–30 minutes, until the pastry lids are golden brown.

Meanwhile, for the gravy, melt the butter in a saucepan, add the flour and cook, stirring, for a minute. Gradually stir in the stock, then add the parsley and vinegar and simmer gently for 10 minutes.

Serve the pies with the gravy and some mashed potato.

The sweetest girls: Sugababes (from left) Jade Ewen, Amelle Berabbah, Heidi Range.

Sugababes are a savoury fusion dish that only the most ambitious chef would attempt: a Moroccan-Jamaican-Italian-Scouse crossover.

The curse of the modern kitchen is that we no longer hand down recipes from generation to generation but instead get them from recipe books and cookery TV. Heidi Range, proud Liverpudlian and the longest-serving member of pop's most modular band the Sugababes since 2001, remedied this by bringing her beloved grandma down to London to cook her fabled apple pie. 'Bless her, she drove me mad,' says Heidi. 'I'm ready to take down all the measures in my notebook but she's grabbing handfuls of flour saying, "Put about *that* much in… a little bit more… now let's have some of this…" I'm never going to be able to cook like that. It takes years of practice.'

Sugababes may have chosen candyfloss for their *Love Music Love Food* picture, but the band is a savoury fusion dish that only the most ambitious chef would attempt: a Moroccan-Jamaican-Italian-Scouse crossover. Heidi grew up in north Liverpool on a diet of her nan's unparalleled soups and roasts, only seldom eating the city's national dish of scouse. By helping her grandma out with the potatoes and pastry Heidi picked up a love of cooking which leaves her a little frustrated today, for the Sugababes are always travelling. At home she has all the can-do British cookery books – Delia, Jamie, plenty from M&S where her grandma used to work – and her idea of a treat is to pull one off the shelf, pour a glass of wine and get fiancé Dave to choose a recipe for her to attempt. Heidi is especially proud of her Thai prawn curry and her chilli. 'How hot? Eight out of ten,' she declares. She used to avoid spicy foods like Dave's Jalfrezi until a trip to India upped her tolerance for heat. 'Over there you can taste the fresh herbs and really pick out each flavour,' she says. 'It doesn't seem hot to me any more. I'm putting chilli in everything now.'

Though it's a full-time job maintaining the Sugababes' profile, the girls' favourite restaurants are not all on the celeb circuit. While Heidi plumps for The Wolseley ('it's so romantic. You feel like you're in a Hollywood movie') and Amelle loves Nobu, Jade has a weakness for the bustle and energy of Wagamama. This incarnation of the band did, however, bond over food. When the gossip magazines became aware of upheaval in the Sugababes' ranks, management hid potential new member Jade away for days at the Mondrian Hotel in Hollywood, where she went slightly stir-crazy. They sealed the deal that she would join the band and replace Keisha Buchanan over pancakes. Seasoned member Amelle just ate the fruit but Jade, full of nerves… Jade ate the lot.

S U G A B A B E S *love* C A N D Y F L O S S

Amelle Berrabah, who joined the Sugababes in 2005, is the daughter of Moroccan parents who ran a kebab shop in Aldershot. Though her mother lovingly cooked all the Moroccan classics – lamb, cous cous, merguez sausage – a shamefaced Amelle confesses herself a fussy child. 'My poor mum, she had to make separate dishes with the raisins on the side because I'd pick them out,' she says sadly. 'She made all these beautiful dishes and all I wanted to eat was beans on toast. Kids are terrible, aren't they? But now I absolutely love the lamb, the merguez… In fact I'm a bit obsessed with it.' She persuaded fellow Sugababe Jade Ewen to hold her birthday party at the celeb-friendly Moroccan restaurant Momo, and was proud to see Jade trying Moroccan food for the first time, and loving it. 'I like my meat falling off the bone,' Amelle says. 'That's the Moroccan way.'

Amelle can be charmingly ditsy. 'I love the black cod at Nando's… sorry, *Nobu*,' she says, and bursts out laughing. She cheerfully admits she's 'quite bad' at cooking. Though she can cook a decent steak, 'I can only do it on the George Foreman grill. I'm not exactly Gordon Brown.' She pauses and laughs, 'Gordon *Ramsay*.'

With a Jamaican mother and a Sicilian father, newest Sugababe Jade Ewen, recruited in 2009, has a culinary heritage that some would kill for. Food at home was always packed with flavour, be it her mother's jerk chicken, lamb curries and patties, or her paternal grandma's amazing repertoire of Italian-Sicilian food. Over the years, as Jade's mother started trying to cater to her father's tastes, she developed her own Jamaican-Italian fusion. Her variation on lasagne alfredo is a crowd-pleaser which has never failed to convert a sceptic, according to Jade. 'At Christmas, turkey never tastes English,' says Jade. 'It'll have a Scotch bonnet pepper in it.' Jade's mother has passed down to her the Jamaican essentials of carrot cake and banana cake, plus a love for experimenting with heat and curries. But it's hard to cook as much as she'd like. 'Being a Sugababe, you don't have a life,' she says, ruefully.

Rocky Road

makes 15 – 20

125g butter
200g dark chocolate, broken into pieces
3 tbsp golden syrup
200g rich tea biscuits
100g mini marshmallows
50g glacé cherries, halved
80g candyfloss

Melt the butter, chocolate and golden syrup in a saucepan over a low heat. Stir until the mixture is smooth and glossy, then remove from the heat.

Place the biscuits in a food bag and crush with a rolling pin until roughly broken. Add the marshmallows, glacé cherries and broken biscuits to the chocolate and mix well. Leave to cool slightly.

Line a brownie tin (about 25 x 20cm) with baking paper and pour in half the chocolate mixture. Cover evenly with all of the candyfloss. Top with the remaining chocolate mixture and gently flatten with your hand. Chill for 2 hours until set.

Turn out and cut into squares, then triangles.

Nigiri rollin' home: Francis Rossi digs into Status Quo's sushi quotient.

AN ITALIAN WHO LOVES food – whoever heard of such a thing? Status Quo's Francis Rossi, the denim-clad and once-ponytailed singer-guitarist with English rock and roll's most dependable and indestructible boogie band, might only be half-Italian (his mother was a Northern Irish Catholic Scouser) but there are no half measures about his love of fine things to eat. He's one of nature's talkers, an amiable, cheerful South-East Londoner with the gift of the gab. It sounds like he's found a healthier avenue for the legendary, illicit appetites that laid Status Quo low in the 80s and 90s. Now nothing gets him going like memories of beautiful things he's eaten.

For instance, a beautiful little antipasto that his Auntie Loretta used to do for Christmas Eve, always a massive night for the Italian side of the family. She'd cut a piece of regular bread into triangles, and on each piece was an olive, a gherkin, an anchovy and a piece of Milano salami. 'I cannot replicate it, I've tried and tried,' he says plaintively. 'It was the most delicious thing you could imagine.'

Or the time that Quo were recording in Montreux in a studio half-owned by Queen, and Brian May took them to a Mexican restaurant on top of the mountain. The shredded beef, the tortillas, the prawns with garlic and chilli… Francis had never had Mexican before and he was in transports of delight. 'That's what got me into Mexi food,' he says. 'I love the idea of getting your hands in the food.' Or the Italian fried green pepper sandwiches he often has at home ('got to be fried in olive oil or you'll get the gripes…'), or the melanzane sandwich – aubergine in oil with chilli and garlic – that he's going to have today. 'God, I'm going to enjoy it,' he says. You can actually hear him salivating down the phone.

His late-blooming love, however, is sushi, which he discovered in the early 2000s thanks to Quo's Chinese-Maori PA Lyane Ngan. 'The first time she mentioned Japanese food I was like, get out of it, raw fish, no way!' he says, 'But she knows what makes us tick and once I tried the miso soup, I was just *wow*, what else have you got? Sushi just immediately feels great inside you. It might be the texture, maybe the stickiness of the rice or the fact that it's a taste explosion, I dunno, but I just fell for it.' Tuna nigiri and prawn nigiri are his favourites, but Lyane's menus are pan-Asian and he loves her Thai tom yum goong soup too. 'I keep forgetting what it's called, though. I'll go, "You got that Todd Rundgren Soup, love?"'

FRANCIS ROSSI of STATUS QUO OBE *loves* OSUSHI SUSHI

He is, he admits, terrible for liking one thing and eating it every day. He's just come back from a six-week Quo tour where he had veal escalope Milanese and two veg for every dinner. Long touring experience has taught him that this is the way to do it. He and Rick Parfitt, his musical partner since 1965, when the band was known as The Spectres, will have the same meal every day while the rest of the band will go for the luck of the draw. 'Ours is always very good and theirs might be a bit chancy,' says Francis. 'I told them, have a fixed meal and then you know what you're getting. But we're fed extremely well on tour. You go to restaurants afterwards and it's crap in comparison. We live charmed lives in that respect.'

It's all a bit different from the old days of Quo, when their fondness for booze and other stimulants put the band in disarray. 'Food wasn't important to us at all back then,' he says. 'It was all alcohol. I don't even remember caterers. Eating well didn't become important 'til our mid- to late- thirties, and now we won't go anywhere without a chef. It just becomes more important as you get older.'

And he bridles a little when asked which food is the most rock and roll. 'I can't be doing with that rock and roll bullshit,' he says, 'People taking drugs, shagging everybody and smashing the place up is not rock and roll to me. It's just silly behaviour. Rock and roll is the music.

'But if you mean the attitude, in the way that a car or a pair of shoes can be rock and roll, then it's got to be hot dogs and fried onions. That lovely, fast-food American thing that was so new and so exciting, *that's* rock and roll.' Whenever his manager comes to the house for a meeting, ***that's*** what Francis's wife cooks: hot dogs with fried onions, the rock and roll repast.

Francis Rossi, 100 million selling guitar hero, ponytail donor (he chopped it off in 2009) and rock and roll survivor, have you anything else to say? 'Yeah, I hate music and I hate food. Ha ha ha!' You can tell he really, really doesn't.

'Sushi immediately feels great inside you. It's the texture, or the stickiness of the rice or the fact that it's a taste explosion.'

Kaibashira Ceviche with Wakame, Cucumber & Ume Boshi Dressing

serves 4

8 large scallops, shelled and cleaned
finely grated zest and juice of 2 limes
10g dried wakame seaweed
½ cucumber, deseeded and finely sliced
1 tsp sea salt
2cm piece of fresh ginger, peeled and cut into fine matchsticks

for the dressing

6 tbsp rice vinegar
4 Ume boshi or pickled plums, finely chopped
1 tbsp good-quality soy sauce
1 tbsp mirin
1 garlic clove, peeled and finely diced
1 spring onion, trimmed and finely sliced on the diagonal

Slice each scallop horizontally into 3 discs and lay the slices out on a plate, making sure they don't overlap. Mix the lime zest and juice together and pour over the scallops. Cover with cling film and chill for 2 hours.

Soak the wakame in warm water to cover for 15 minutes. Put the cucumber slices into a colander, sprinkle with the salt and leave for 10 minutes to soften.

Drain the wakame, cut off and discard any stems, then chop into 3–4cm lengths. Rinse the cucumber under cold water, drain and squeeze out excess water in a clean tea towel. Mix together the cucumber, wakame and ginger.

For the dressing, stir all the ingredients together in a bowl and use to dress the cucumber mixture. Divide between 4 bowls and serve with the chilled scallops.

BRITISH SEA POWER *love*

MINT, POTATOES & SAUSAGES IN A CUP

Kendal-born, Brighton-based British Sea Power are the most agrarian, Wordsworthian band in rock and roll. Their surging, heartfelt anthems on subjects as uncommon as Antarctic ice-shelves, the peril of light pollution, or aristocratic seabird the Great Skua have won them a Mercury Prize nomination and a following among those who like their rock and roll, well, different.

Is it therefore OK for singer Yan, AKA singer/guitarist Jan Scott Wilkinson, to choose a foodstuff he no longer eats because of his vegetarianism? Well, maybe it is.

'I chose the sausage maybe because sausages confuse me,' Yan admits. 'I used to be a big sausage eater before British Sea Power. The mystique and allure of the sausage is plain to see. Pour some homemade gravy on it and serve with creamy mash... lovely.' Though nominally vegetarian, Yan admits to a weakness for Black Pudding and pâté. 'I'm a coward and ethically confused,' he confesses. 'If you kill a beast you ought to use every bit. But vegetarian sausages have come on leaps and bounds. I'd rather have one of them.'

The minty potatoes are the choice of lead guitarist and keen birdwatcher Martin Noble – known only as 'Noble' – in tribute to the 'good Yorkshire diet' of his youth. 'Mint and potatoes is a heavenly mix,' he says. When Noble was younger, mint was just something chewing gum tasted of; real life mint was something he discovered later on. He is, however, a man who knows his spuds. He's grown his own Maris Piper and red King Edwards alongside two mint plants, one from Marrakesh. 'Your mash champions are Saxon, Rooster and Wilja,' he advises. 'Your boiled specialists are Osprey and Harmony. King of roasts are Desirée, King Edward and Maris Piper, and we all know Charlotte and Nicola make the best salad potatoes.' When BSP performed their soundtrack to the 1934 documentary movie *Man Of Aran* at the Branchage Film Festival, the organisers gave everyone who came in a bag of Jersey potatoes. 'They were delicious,' says Noble. 'You can really taste the earth in them. It's like they're flavoured with Jersey soil.'

The inevitable veggie-carnivore mix of the modern alternative rock band means that BSP must mix it up diet-wise, sometimes cooking giant communal stews in the farmhouses and other characterful buildings where they record their wind-blasted music, and sometimes resorting to Little Chef. Though band members favour everything from mature Cheddar cheese (drummer Wood) to Dunn's River nourishment drinks (bassist Hamilton) to Tom Yum Soup (trumpeter Phil) and Bavarian smoked cheese (violinist Abi), the typical BSP rider consists chiefly of tequila, vodka and nuts.

The band also favours more wholesome refreshments. One of its most popular items of merchandise is a mug emblazoned with the words 'British Tea Power'. The band have also offered BSP clotted cream fudge and Kendal mint cake for sale at gigs. British Sea Power remain the only rock band to have an Official Beer – the original, fiercely independent Budweiser Budvar of Ceske Budejovice – and in 2008 they released their own limited edition British Ale Power beer, a very drinkable 4% ABV tipple produced by Yorkshire's Dent Brewery under a slogan to warm the heart of BSP hero George Orwell himself: 'Four pints good, two pints bad.'

Heroes matter to BSP, be they the Czech poet Bohumil Hrabal who defined happiness as: 'To spend our days betting on three-legged horses with beautiful names' or snooker meteor Hurricane Higgins. Their food heroes include Gordon Ramsay ('He's sexy because he'd stick up for you,' says Abi), Keith Floyd ('the man who showed you could cook great food and get sozzled at the same time') and seafood superstar Rick Stein, who appears in the BSP song *Zeus*. In British Sea Power's world the chef, poet, sportsman and flâneur all join the same glorious war against boredom and mediocrity. 'We only live once,' say British Sea Power. 'So let's live.'

Yan puts it best when asked to name the best of all bangers. 'The best sausage?' he says. 'The best sausage is the next sausage.'

Saucisson & Menthe En Croute

serves 4

for the pastry

200g plain flour, plus extra for dusting
sea salt
100g cold butter, diced
1 tbsp fresh mint, chopped
a little cold water, to mix

for the filling

knob of butter
2 tbsp olive oil
1 red onion, peeled and finely sliced
1 garlic clove, peeled and chopped
1 apple, peeled and grated (avoiding the core)
250g potatoes, peeled and grated
freshly ground black pepper
1 tbsp fresh mint, chopped
400g good-quality sausage meat

to glaze

1 medium egg, beaten

*'The best sausage? The best sausage is the **next** sausage.'—**Yan***

What's for tea, BSP? Noble with the spuds, Yan with the bangers.

Preheat the oven to 180°C/Gas mark 4. To make the pastry, sift the flour and a good pinch of salt into a large bowl. Using your hands, rub in the butter until the mixture resembles fine breadcrumbs. Add half of the chopped mint and enough cold water to bind the pastry. Do not overwork, as the mint will turn the pastry green. Wrap in cling film and place in the fridge for 30 minutes.

Meanwhile, prepare the filling. Heat the butter and oil in a large frying pan, add the red onion and fry until soft. Stir in the garlic, grated apple and potatoes, and season with pepper. Cook gently over a medium heat until the potatoes are slightly browned. Transfer to a bowl, stir in the rest of the mint and set aside.

Roll out the pastry on a lightly floured surface to a rectangle, about 35 x 25cm. Transfer to a baking tray lined with baking parchment.

On a piece of cling film, flatten the sausage meat to a rectangle half the width and 5cm shorter in length than the pastry. Gently place the potato mixture in a strip down the centre of the sausage meat and, using the cling film to manoeuvre, roll the sausage meat over the potato until the potato is sealed within the meat. Remove from the cling film and lift the meat onto the centre of the pastry. Roll the pastry around the sausage meat until the two ends meet. Position so that the join is underneath and pinch the two open ends together to seal.

Brush the pastry all over with the beaten egg and bake for about 30 minutes until golden and crispy. Leave to stand for 5 minutes before trimming off the pastry ends and slicing into 4 portions.

Serve with a cucumber, dill and yoghurt salad.

Choc horror: Hadouken!'s James Smith and Alice Spooner.

'The Flake adverts were extremely erotic if I remember correctly...'—***James***

backstage at the READING FESTIVAL

Only the crumbliest, flakiest chocolate for the nu-rave-rock-rap band, as frontman ***James Smith*** *explains...*

'THE FLAKE ADVERTS were extremely erotic, if I remember correctly. Kind of like chocolate porn, if you will, and slightly better than the Cadbury's Caramel bunny. There was always a soft-rock soundtrack too, and I think Hadouken! could definitely do a modern version if we were asked. It'd have to be a collaboration with 10cc and Chris de Burgh, with Vangelis on production duties.

The Flake is great because you can't bite it as it crumbles; you have to use other methods to consume. The all-in-one-bite method may choke inexperienced consumers and I cannot vouch for the sucking method. You can, however, attempt to drink liquids through said Flake. And I believe it's against EU law to serve any other confectionery but a Flake with a Mr Softee ice cream.

HADOUKEN! *love* CADBURY'S FLAKES

Also the Flake has always been the Flake, with no strange varieties introduced into the shops. There's absolutely nothing wrong with wild card flavours, though – they are 85% of the reason to visit the USA. Wow! Skittles Wild Berry edition! OMG! Tic Tac's Wintergreen flavour! Grape Fanta! The wonders of consumer capitalism. May I suggest a few combos for Flakes? How about Garlic Flakes – you could have them with Spaghetti Bolognese – or Raw Salmon Sushi Flakes?

It's not all chocolate with Hadouken!, though. I've just moved in with Alice (Spooner, keyboards) and I have to say she can make a whole load of killer fresh soups. I'm quite good with Italian and I make my own fresh pasta too. When we first started rehearsing with the other boys, Nick (Rice, drummer) and Dan (Rice, guitar), they introduced us to the wonders of a Mars Bar and a choc-ice, cut up and put in the microwave for 30 seconds exactly. This, they considered to be a great way to serve dessert. That's probably a good summing up of their own culinary skills.

The best meal I've ever hard? One part of me says an epic meal out in Toyko with the band that consisted of sushi, sashimi and Kobe beef. The other part says Mum-cooked Christmas dinner each and every year.'

Flake Shake

serves 2

1 banana
2 tbsp caramel sauce
3 scoops vanilla ice cream
400ml milk
2 tbsp chocolate liqueur
3 chocolate flakes

Put the banana, caramel sauce, vanilla ice cream, milk, chocolate liqueur and one of the flakes into a blender and whiz until completely smooth.

Pour into 2 tall glasses and place a flake in each. Serve immediately, with a straw and a spoon.

'It's hard to imagine anything better for you. This is an instant vacation in your mouth.'

JULIETTE LEWIS *loves* COCONUT & PAPAYA

Music is a matter of dark and light, heaven and hell, good and evil, and all that sort of stuff. Thus the volcanic star of movies and rock and roll Juliette Lewis – who knows a little about such things, having starred in *Cape Fear*, *Natural Born Killers* and *From Dusk Til Dawn* – appears in *Love Music Love Food* in both sinful and redemptive modes. On the cover of the book she's slathered in chocolate; inside she presents a detox cocktail of cleansing coconut and papaya. 'It's yin and yang,' Juliette declares. 'I love the healthy stuff and I love chocolate and ice cream too. You have to balance it.'

She loves papaya: 'It goes with anything, it has natural digestive enzymes and the taste is wonderful.' But it's clear that coconut is her real passion. Oh, the flavour, the scent, the texture… she uses coconut hair and skin lotions and, when at home in Los Angeles, has a regular coconut smoothie from her favourite juice place at home.

'It's decadent and sensual and natural all at the same time,' she says. 'On a purely nutritional level, coconut water is pretty much the most hydrating thing you can drink, and much better than man-made sports drinks.' Nutrition fact: a cup of coconut water contains more electrolytes than most sports drinks, and more potassium than a banana. 'If you're an energetic, physical person like me it's hard to imagine anything better for you,' she says. 'Papaya and coconut are like instant vacations in your mouth.'

Juliette is possibly unique in the ranks of actors turned musicians because, unlike certain movie stars' vanity bands, her music actually stands up on its own – a raw but poppy garage-punk noise with the magnetic Juliette as its focal point. With her former band Juliette And The Licks, she supported the Foo Fighters and Muse, and she sang on The Prodigy's album *Always Outnumbered, Never Outgunned*. But how does one move from the comfortable world of movie-making to the grind of the touring rock band?

When you play rock festivals you're always 'pathetically grateful' if the catering is good, she says. You always remember who feeds you well, like the German festivals or Leeds, Reading and the Isle of Wight. 'If you're tired and you haven't had a shower in days you are so glad of any home comforts.' But she does love the touring life, only occasionally missing favourite restaurants at home in Los Angeles, like Little Dom's in Los Feliz or La Loggia in Studio City where 'everything is so tasty, the appetisers are just stunning. Even if it's a salad you can't believe the flavour.'

Movie versus rock and roll – who's got the best food? 'Oh please, do you even need to ask?' she says, and laughs. 'There's so much more money in the movie world for food. I make a nice living from my touring but half the time we live off bread and lunchmeat.'

'It is two different worlds, and artistically they're two different mediums. In movies there's a lot of waiting around but when you're acting it's pretty juicy, creative stuff. In music I'm like a lead actor-writer-director and I have to promote the band too.'

'Every night I'm trying to create the most exciting, visceral, interesting show I can, so it's much more creatively stimulating. I love every second of it – but you have to live on lunchmeat sandwiches.'

Virgin Detox Cocktail

serves 2

50g papaya
3 fresh mint leaves, shredded
juice of 1 lime
juice of 1 fresh coconut, chilled
4 cherries

Put 2 Martini glasses into the freezer to chill for 10 minutes. Meanwhile, peel and deseed the papaya, then cut into small cubes.

Spoon the papaya into the chilled glasses, add the shredded mint and squeeze over the lime juice. Pour in the chilled coconut juice and garnish each with a couple of fresh cherries to serve.

'An English Sunday roast is a special ritual all of its own...'
—Simon Nicol of Fairport Convention

Living dhal: Sir Cliff meditates on the majesty of Indian food.

VIDA NOVA

Harry Rodger Webb was born in Lucknow, India in 1940 and grew up on curries. His father Rodger managed a catering company for the sprawling Indian railways, and though the Webbs were experiencing the final days of the Raj they lived modestly, in Lucknow and then Howrah.

'Curry will always be my favourite food because it reminds me of my childhood,' Sir Cliff Richard says now, as he relaxes in the spacious converted farmhouse in the Algarve – bought with the proceeds of six decades of hits and 260 million records – the place where he likes to spend much of the summer. 'It's the most highly flavoured, the most vibrantly scented food there is. After we moved back to England in 1948 my mother used to hold back on the chilli but we always used to ask her for more.' He pauses. 'Well, I say we came back to England but I'd never been before. Neither had my parents. But we still talked about "coming back to Blighty".'

In India his father had been relatively wealthy but in England 'we had absolutely zero. We went through real poverty.' One of the standard meals of the day would be toast dipped in tea with sugar on it. 'It was that bad.' But a love of curry stayed with him over the years – not so much the heat as the spice.

'Spice is what gives curry all its dimensions. The cardamom seeds, the coriander, the cloves… Most Brits don't like the heat. I do but I like to taste the food too.' When Cliff orders a hot curry at a restaurant he knows it will be mild by his standards, so he orders a green chilli on the side and shaves it over the top. In particular he loves a chicken tikka masala, that peculiar, unbeatable, ever-changing but always dependable dish whose

SIR **CLIFF RICHARD** *loves* CHICKEN TIKKA MASALA

origins are lost in the past (is it Punjabi street food or was it synthesised in the Indian kitchens of Soho and Glasgow? Nobody knows). The late Foreign Secretary Robin Cook once called the chicken tikka masala 'Britain's true national dish' and if anyone has been our national pop star for the past half century it's Sir Cliff. Both are unique and unrepeatable products of the British colonial era.

Cliff doesn't often cook but then he seldom needs to. When he's in Portugal a hotelier friend provides him with a chef. 'He literally lends me one of his staff. I'm spoiled rotten.' Near Cliff's villa is Vila Joya, the boutique hotel and noted centre of slow food presided over by chef Dieter Koschina. 'You have to be prepared to settle down and spend at least four hours having lunch there, looking out across the sea,' says Sir Cliff. 'There's supposed to be seven courses but it's usually about nine with the various amuse-bouche. It is just spectacular. The food is always brilliant: foie gras, then a carpaccio of salmon, or cheese wrapped in a fig… It's an adventure of taste.' Elsewhere on the hills northwest of Albufeira is Cliff's own vineyard, Adego do Cantor – the Winery of the Singer. 'I'm a farmer now,' he says. 'I depend on the weather.'

When he's back in England, Cliff Richard's favourite curry places are School of Spice in Shepperton or a new favourite, the Tiger's Pad in Sunningdale. He doesn't like his Indian food too westernised. 'The Bombay Brasserie had the most fantastic starters,' he says, 'but I always thought the main courses were too posh. I like my curries to have a nice thick sauce, I like a good mound of lentils and rice. I like it traditional style, lots of everything.'

It's easy to satisfy a taste for spice nowadays. Not so when the young Cliff began his career in the late 1950s, when skiffle was giving way to rock 'n' roll and most of Britain still looked with parochial horror on 'foreign' food. Cliff had no such fear. He can still remember the first time he ate Chinese. After finishing a recording session, producer Norrie Paramor took him and The Shadows to a Chinese restaurant in Swiss Cottage. 'Although I didn't know what it was at the time, I had Singapore Noodles. I thought I'd died and gone to heaven – that experience of having something so new and different. My taste buds had never experienced anything like that.'

He and The Shadows rapidly developed a taste for Chinese. They would always eat after a show, often at the Lotus House on Edgware Road, London. Even if they were playing in Bristol they could just about get there by closing time if they drove fast enough. 'If you got there at five to two they would still serve you,' says Cliff, 'So we would drive like the wind – and this was before motorways, 1959 or so. It was a fantastic way to end a day.'

It wasn't always good, though. Years later, when Cliff had become an international star, a record company took him and his band out as guests of honour in Hong Kong. They insisted he try a Thousand Year Old Egg. 'You have to hold your end up,' he says, 'so I had to grit my teeth, take a bite, swallow and keep smiling. It did not agree with me.'

As well as his lengthy career – the longest of all the British rock 'n' roll generation – Sir Cliff's physical vigour continues to astound. He works out a bit ('I'll never look like Arnie Schwarzenegger but it seems to be working') and diet plays its role. Sadly this limits his beloved curries to special occasions, for Cliff's blood type does not suit tomatoes, aubergines, coconut and several other staples of the Indian repertoire. 'Every now and again I say to hell with it and have a chicken tikka masala.' A few years ago he discovered turmeric's beneficial properties as an aid to digestion and a potential anti-carcinogen. Without knowing it, his mother had given young Harry an uncommonly healthy start.

The other morning he woke up to hear a story on the radio about this year's new Cliff Richard calendar. The presenter said that Cliff had the body of a 45-year old and that all his former critics in the unforgiving rock world were either fat, bald or dead. 'I woke up laughing,' says Sir Cliff Richard, Knight of the Realm and rock 'n' roll survivor. 'I must have done something right.'

'A record company took us for dinner in Hong Kong and ordered me a Thousand Year Old Egg. I had to grit my teeth, take a bite and keep smiling.'

Chicken Tikka Masala

serves 4

4 skinless chicken breasts, cut into 3cm cubes

for the chicken tikka marinade

250ml plain yoghurt
2 tbsp lemon juice
2 tbsp ground cumin
2 tbsp paprika
2 tbsp freshly ground black pepper
1 tsp ground cinnamon
2.5cm piece of fresh ginger, peeled and grated
sea salt

for the tikka masala sauce

15g butter
2 garlic cloves, peeled and crushed
1 green chilli, deseeded and very finely chopped or grated
2 tbsp ground coriander
1 tsp ground cumin
1 tsp paprika
1 tsp garam masala
½ tsp sea salt
400g tin chopped tomatoes
250ml single cream
4 tbsp coriander leaves, chopped

For the marinade, mix together the yoghurt, lemon juice, cumin, paprika, black pepper, cinnamon, ginger and some salt in a large bowl. Stir well and leave for 15–30 minutes. Add the chicken and turn to make sure that it is well coated. Cover and leave to marinate in the fridge for at least 2 hours.

Preheat the grill to medium. Thread the chicken pieces onto skewers and grill, turning regularly, for about 15 minutes until the chicken is cooked through; when pierced with a knife, the juices should run clear. Place on a plate to rest while you make the sauce.

To make the sauce, melt the butter in a large saucepan over a medium heat. Add the garlic and chilli and cook for 1 minute, then stir in the spices and salt. Tip in the chopped tomatoes and simmer gently for 30 minutes. Stir in the cream to enrich the sauce and cook gently for about 5 minutes.

Pull the skewers out of the chicken. Add the chicken pieces to the sauce and place over a low heat to gently and thoroughly heat the chicken, about 5 minutes.

Garnish with the fresh coriander and serve immediately.

KATIE MELUA SPEAKS GEORGIAN, English and Russian, and eats Japanese, reflecting her diverse roots. Born in the former Soviet Republic of Georgia in 1984, Ketevan Melua – that's her full name – moved to Belfast and then London where she enrolled in the BRIT School, alma mater to Amy Winehouse and Adele. There she immersed herself in Bob Dylan, Joni Mitchell, Ella Fitzgerald and The Beatles and discovered her own musical voice.

Her debut album even crossed the species barrier: it was made under the tutelage of a *Womble*, the legendary songwriter/producer Mike Batt, who detected in Katie's music an antidote to the mechanically constructed pop of the time. Katie's memories of an austere upbringing in Kutaisi and Tblisi, where the Melua family were sometimes even short of running water, stood her in good stead during the tedious promotional grind. 'The toleration of hardship is in Katie's blood,' Batt once said. Co-writing with him, Katie went on to become the best-selling British artist of 2004 and 2005, and her debut *Call Off The Search* became the 87th best-selling British album of all time.

Why sushi? Katie admits that the first time she encountered traditional Japanese food, at the beginning of her career, she found it daunting. Business contacts had taken her to a very traditional Japanese restaurant, 'and I really didn't like it at all,' she says. 'The dishes were all very uncompromising, it was real sushi and they weren't trying to make it easy for you! The raw squid and things like that were just too much for me.'

Instead it was the nursery slope of Japanese food that won her over. Busy recording in London and no fan of cooking ('I'm terrible in the kitchen, I can't even cook rice') she began eating at Wagamama, the much-admired noodle chain. Edamame beans and bentos led to other, more adventurous flavours and when Katie finally tried sushi she was hooked. Now she eats it all the time, particularly from Feng Sushi in Notting Hill.

'The real beauty of sushi is that it is so pure,' she enthuses. 'I love the texture when it's done just right. There's very little fat and you can taste the purity. I'll eat it 'til I'm ready to burst but you always feel so healthy afterwards.'

KATIE MELUA *loves* NORI ROLLS

Given her choice she'll always go for a salmon and avocado 'uramaki' – an inside-out roll that's a cousin of the original East-West fusion sushi piece, the California Roll. 'I love the softer texture, that gorgeous "squidginess",' she says, 'And it's got to be inside out. You get a much smoother bite that way.'

Nothing connects you to home like food, though, and Katie's favourite dish from her childhood is khachapuri, the traditional Georgian cheese bread. 'It's basically a boat made of bread with a load of melted cheese in the middle,' she says, 'And an egg too. You tear the bread off and dip it into the melted cheese and it's just "mmmmmmm"... It's the anti-sushi, it's all fat and carbs but it's so delicious.' When she really wants proper Georgian she'll go to Mimino on Kensington High Street for khachapuri or khinkali. 'It's a massive dumpling the size of your palm,' she rhapsodises, 'with sauce and meat inside. You bite it and suck out the sauce, and it's "soooo" good...'

Nori-Maki

serves 4

½ cucumber, peeled and deseeded
2 standard sheets toasted nori seaweed
2 tbsp wasabi paste, plus extra to taste
1 tsp rice wine vinegar
3 tbsp water
4 cups cooked sushi rice
115g tuna, salmon or cooked prawns, cut into strips

Cut the cucumber into 10cm long matchsticks and set aside.

Cut the nori sheets in half lengthways. Place a strip of nori, shiny side down, on a bamboo mat, with the shorter edge of the mat and nori sheet directly in front of you. Place a weight, such as a knife, on the opposite short end of the nori.

Mix 1 tbsp wasabi paste with the rice wine vinegar and water and use this to moisten your hands. Using your fingertips, spread about 1 cup of sushi rice over three-quarters of the sheet in a layer about 5–7mm thick, leaving the end furthest away from you free of rice.

With your index finger, smear a thin line of wasabi paste across the width of the rice, about a third of the sheet from you. Lay the cucumber, tuna, salmon or prawn strips along the wasabi paste.

To roll, hold the line of ingredients firmly in place with your fingertips. With your thumbs push up and turn the end of the bamboo mat up and over the filling until the two ends of nori sheet meet and form a cylinder. Press the roll firmly and evenly inside the mat. The filling should be in the centre of the rice.

Place on a board with the exposed end of the nori sheet underneath the roll and remove the bamboo mat. Repeat the process with the other 3 nori sheets.

To serve, cut the rolls into 2.5cm rounds with a sharp knife, wiping the knife clean between cuts.

'The real beauty of sushi is that it is so pure... I'll eat it, til I'm ready to burst.'

'Fish and chips only tastes right in England. The rest of the world just can't get it right.'

'IT'S ALWAYS BEEN my favourite meal,' says Sophie Ellis-Bextor, English rose, pop beauty and fan of a humble plate of fish and chips. 'It's pure satisfaction, pure comfort food. You long for it when you're travelling. Fish and chips only tastes right when you're at home, in England. The rest of the world tries to do it, but they just can't get it right.'

The cut-glass voice of numerous pop-dance hits including *Groovejet*, Ms Ellis-Bextor is also, famously, the daughter of a *Blue Peter* legend. Janet Ellis instilled in her daughter a belief in the values of the proper sit-down family meal. But Sophie's father, film-maker Robin Bextor, was ultimately responsible for her love of fresh fish and potatoes fried to golden perfection.

'Actually it was gherkins that did it,' Sophie says, laughing. 'When I was a little girl and dad took me to the chip shop I'd always have a couple of gherkins. He would tell me, "You've got your gherkin workin". And I still *love* them. Chip shop gherkins are so much better than supermarket ones.'

Sophie is now married to fellow musician Richard Jones, bass player with sophisticated soft rockers and fellow *Love Music Love Food* participants, The Feeling. Sophie cooks sea bass and whole roast salmon, 'I'm an all-rounder. A fish all-rounder!' And Richard and their four-year old boy Sonny will prepare the manly dish of pizza. 'We take it seriously, me and my husband,' she says. 'We're real foodies. Our idea of a treat is, "Let's go and check out that new restaurant".'

Fine dining is all well and good but she reserves her strongest enthusiasm for, yes, the chippie of her West London neighbourhood. There's Chris's on Turnham Green Road ('excellent'), George's Portobello Fish Bar ('wonderful and quite famous – Jamie Oliver goes there. They keep it traditional, they don't do curry on noodles or anything silly') and Geale's in Notting Hill Gate ('lovely, a proper white tablecloths place with really good fish').

Does a love of our national dish square with the demands of the pop industry, with its excess on the one hand and an unpleasant obsession with body image on the other? She loves the lobster dinners too, Sophie counters. 'And I don't actually agree with the idea that to be a pop star, you have to be thin. What you want is to look healthy. There's a difference. A person who looks healthy looks confident. If you're dieting frantically or obviously worrying about the way you look, it'll be clear lacking in confidence. I enjoy my food. I think I've got a good balance with it.'

And what's the secret of perfect fish and chips? Naturally you need good, crispy batter and the freshest fish… 'But really, it's always good,' says Sophie. 'Fish and chips is all about the ritual for me,' she says. 'Vinegar on the chips, no salt, but a bit of tomato ketchup and mayonnaise. And a gherkin. Perfect.'

SOPHIE ELLIS-BEXTOR *loves* FISH, CHIPS & A GHERKIN

Traditional Fish & Chips with Gherkin Salsa

serves 4

6 large white potatoes
sunflower or vegetable oil, for deep-frying
4 pieces cod or haddock fillet, about 175g each
225g self-raising flour
¼ tsp bicarbonate of soda
300ml beer (or soda water), well chilled
sea salt and freshly ground black pepper

Preheat the oven to 150°C/Gas mark 2. Peel the potatoes and cut into thick chips. Rinse in cold water and pat dry with a clean tea towel. Heat the oil in a deep-fat fryer or a large heavy-based saucepan to 150°C. Check that it is hot enough by carefully placing one chip in the oil; if it gently fries the oil is ready.

When the oil is hot, fry the potatoes in batches for 10–12 minutes until golden. The chips will fry better if there is room in the pan so be careful not to over-fill it. To check that they are cooked, pierce one chip with a sharp knife; it should be soft and fluffy. Lift out with a slotted spoon, drain on kitchen paper and place on a baking tray lined with greaseproof paper. Place on a low shelf in the oven to keep warm while you cook the fish.

Increase the oil temperature to 180°C (use a thermometer to check if necessary). Meanwhile, to make the batter for the fish, sift the flour and bicarbonate of soda into a large bowl and whisk in the cold beer. The batter should be the consistency of very thick cream; add more liquid if it is too thick.

Cook the fish fillets in batches to stop them sticking together. Dip the fillets into the batter, ensuring that they are fully coated, then gently lower into the oil. Fry for 4–5 minutes until golden brown and cooked through. Remove with a slotted spoon, drain on kitchen paper and place on a baking tray lined with greaseproof paper; keep warm in the oven while you cook the rest. Wait for the oil to reheat before frying the second batch.

Season the fried fish with salt and pepper and serve immediately, with the chips and a dollop of the gherkin, lemon and parsley salsa on the side.

for the gherkin, lemon & parsley salsa

small handful of fresh flat leaf parsley, stalks removed and finely chopped
finely grated zest of 2 lemons
8 pickled gherkins, finely diced, plus 4 tsp vinegar from the jar
2 garlic cloves, peeled and crushed
4 shallots, peeled and finely diced
a little sugar (optional)

Mix all the ingredients together in a small bowl. Cover and leave to stand in the fridge for 2 hours. Taste before serving: if the salsa is a bit tart dissolve a little white sugar in a small amount of hot water and add to the salsa to sweeten a little.

YORKSH
TEA

Love, love me brew: Noel Gallagher won't go anywhere without Yorkshire Tea.

'It's got to be the exact same colour as a Quality Street toffee or it's going down the sink.'

'**I AM OBSESSED** with Yorkshire Tea,' declares Noel Gallagher, for 18 years the leader of Oasis and now forging a solo career. 'I even bring it on tour. It was always on the Oasis rider. "Tea – must be Yorkshire."'

Why does a man whose formative musical years were characterised by cigarettes and alcohol and champagne supernovas feel the pull of this most homely of English beverages? 'I'm a Northerner and it's part of our staple diet,' he says, 'plus I'm of Irish descent. The kettle always seemed to be on when I was growing up. It's part of the fabric of your life.'

Noel gets through about five cups a day now, but he used to have a debilitating twenty-bag-a-day habit. When he was younger and worked on the building sites Noel's standard brew was two bags, one cup. 'I liked it really strong,' he says. 'Then one day I saw how brown and manky the inside of the cup was and I thought "that's what my insides look like, better get off it".'

Like a true tea drinker, he's got rules that must not be broken. Milk goes in last. Put your sugar in first, with the teabag, then fill it up to about an inch from the top and leave it for a good while. And what colour should the tea be? 'You know the Quality Streets toffees in the yellow wrapper?' he says. 'It's got to be the exact same colour as them or it's going down the sink.' When in London he makes his own cuppa because: 'there's a lack of good tea-making down here. Paul Weller's tea-making leaves a lot to be desired. It's pretty watery and the colour's not right.'

And like a true connoisseur, Noel wonders about the mysteries of tea. How old should you be before you start drinking it? Why can't you get a decent cup of tea in America? 'Because the whole country runs on coffee, caffeine and people talking a load of shit.' And why, as Nicky Wire of the Manic Street Preachers has pointed out, do people in London never use teapots? 'Tells you a lot about London, that,' says Noel.

Most mystifying of all, where did all these bizarre tea varieties come from? His kitchen cupboards are full of partner Sara's fennel tea, camomile, green tea ('fair enough, that's Japanese'), Lady Grey with a hint of orange, ***nettle tea***? What's that all about? Years ago, when Oasis were in the first flush of success, Noel stayed over at a girl's place and in the morning she asked what kind of tea he wanted. 'I was like, what do you mean? There are different kinds of tea?' She made Earl Grey. Noel thought it was like drinking his mam's perfume.

Noel is of course a noted Beatles enthusiast and his love of a proper brew echoes that famous sequence in ***The Rutles*** movie where Eric Idle and Neil Innes's spoof Beatles – the Prefab Four – meet Bob Dylan and 'turn on' to tea. 'There's a great picture of The Beatles in Hyde Park,' he says. 'They're in full psychedelic gear but they're all drinking tea. I love all that. Nowadays it's all getting wrecked on Thunderbird and strangling swans, isn't it?' He's made his own contribution to the admittedly limited area of tea-related rock and roll by releasing the single ***Cup Of Tea*** by the Liverpool band Shack on his own record label. It tells of a landlord whose lodger spikes him with acid. 'She puts it in his tea,' says Noel, 'so it qualifies.'

Noel is, he admits, not a great cook, although his missus is. 'She's truly excellent, she could have made a profession out of it.' Noel can just about cook mince and tatties. 'I don't starve. I can do fish but I won't go near chicken in case I kill meself. I get impatient, I go 'Oh it's only a bit of pink' and next thing you're tripping for three days.'

He retains a taste for the things he loved as a kid, like fish and chips. With his mum raising three sons on her own, the Gallaghers were 'on the breadline. We were just eating to survive.' He never even went to a Chinese restaurant 'til he was about 21, and still rates his first ever Chinese, at the famously brusque Wong Kei on Wardour Street with Inspiral Carpets, as probably his favourite meal ever. 'It was like a whole new world,' he says. 'I used to live in that place in the 90s. Best hangover cure ever – that and a can of Coke.

And he's always found big record company dinners 'quite awkward'. As soon as the food turns up Noel just wants to shovel it down him. It drives Sara mad. 'She tells me I'm like a dustbin, but I grew up with two brothers. If I didn't eat it quick somebody else would have it.'

But the rock star life has afforded a few magic moments. The first time he ate at The Ivy, Malcolm McLaren and Vivienne Westwood were sitting at the next table, mere touching distance away. Here were two of the people who'd changed his life – and now he was among them like it was the most natural thing in the world.

'I was like, ***wow***,' he says, still thrilled at the memory. 'I couldn't concentrate on what I was eating. Most of it went in me ear.'

NOEL GALLAGHER *loves* YORKSHIRE TEA

Perfect Cuppa

serves 1

To start with, use water that has only been boiled once; any more than that and the level of oxygen in the water will be reduced, causing your tea to be a bit flat.

Pour the freshly boiled water directly onto your tea bag in the mug; this way the tea infuses better than if you add the tea bag to the water.

Leave to brew for 2–3 minutes, according to your taste. Remove the tea bag with a spoon, giving it just one squeeze.

Add milk, sugar or lemon, as you desire, and enjoy with a big slice of Yorkshire brack or York biscuits.

This recipe was supplied by Taylor's of Harrogate, the home of Yorkshire tea.

Harvest wallbangers: (clockwise from top left) Fairport Convention members Gerry Conway, Simon Nicol, Ric Sanders.

In rock and roll it's common to refer to any band that manages to stay intact for a decade as an 'institution'. Those who confer such easy praise might want to take a look at the real thing. Established in 1967 and still sporting many original features – singer-guitarist Simon Nicol, and multi-instrumentalist Dave Pegg who joined in 1970 – Fairport Convention are the great maypole around which British folk revolves.

Initially inspired by Bob Dylan and Joan Baez, they soon evolved a unique mixture of rock and traditional English music that still remains compelling. Among Fairport's alumni are the tragic genius of folk rock Sandy Denny, and world-renowned troubadour Richard Thompson. Current acts like The Memory Band, Tunng and the whole Green Man Festival all owe the Fairports a debt of gratitude.

There's a joke among the band members that Fairport have never been out of fashion because they've never been in fashion. But there is something almost punk rock about their love of music which has seldom had the support of the music industry – a set of genres that they've helped sustain themselves with their own Cropredy Festival, founded in 1979.

'Music that's on the periphery of the mainstream, folk- and jazz-type music, it doesn't toe the line,' explains violinist Ric Sanders, a fresh-faced newcomer who joined in 1985. 'But compared to 20 or 30 years ago, there are so many kids playing fiddles and mandolins now. It's actually become cool! When you go to see a band like the mighty Bellowhead, they are almost punk. They've got that energy.' The Fairports have survived in part because they're not closed-minded folkies. Ric loves The Prodigy and used to

FAIRPORT CONVENTION *love*
LAMB & A VEGETARIAN PLATTER

perform with the Albion Band whose show included punk Morris dancing, with bondage trousers and Mohicans.

The dish they chose for ***Love Music Love Food*** is very Fairport: a traditional English roast with quality organic lamb and vegetables. 'For me it's a family thing first and foremost,' says Simon Nicol. 'It's a very special little ritual that starts when you go to the butchers to select a piece of meat, it carries on when the house fills with that lovely cooking smell, and it all comes together when you're sat around the table with those close to you. There's something particular about a roast, it's a special event and it brings people together.' Simon is not one for barbecues but he does enjoy a classic roast.

But Ric has been vegetarian for 45 years and so is fellow member Chris Leslie, who could not appear in the photo (another rural hero and famous vegetarian, Shaun The Sheep from ***Wallace And Gromit***, takes his place). Ric wanted to represent for Fairport's vegetarian contingent because in his case there's a direct correlation between food and ending up as a professional musician.

He'd never been happy eating meat as a child and when he was finally able, at 13, to say he would no longer eat it, 'it was the first nonconformist thing I'd done in my life. It was really important to me.' Ric was a teenager just in time for the Summer of Love. '***Sgt Pepper*** and the ***Magical Mystery Tour*** changed my life,' he says. 'I wanted to be part of it. Being a musician was a good way to do that. But really it began with that moment when I thought, I'm not going to do what everyone else does.'

Fairport are custodians of a little piece of the English rural soul and so food matters to them, especially at the annual Cropredy Festival. Every August up to 20,000 people camp out in a village in Oxfordshire to hear Fairport and their guests, and the stalls offer everything from quality festival staples like pies and noodles to Mexican and Japanese food. Ric is especially keen on longstanding festival fixture Leon's Vegetarian Foods. Chef-owner Leon Lewis is so good that whenever Fairport play near him, say at Cambridge Corn Exchange or in St Alban's, they'll have Leon do the catering. Even the meat-eaters love it. And of course beer matters at Cropredy too, so much that they've had to install a W-shaped bar to fit more pumps in. 'The beer policy is sensational,' says Ric proudly. 'We have Wadworth 6x and everything you could wish for. To the Cropredy crowd, beer is one of your five-a-day.'

Cropredy might be a pilgrimage for electric folk fans old and new, but the Fairports have their own pilgrimage too. 'There's a place we've been paying homage to for many years,' says Simon Nicol. 'It's in Bradford, it's called the Kashmir and it's one of the earliest – if not the earliest – Pakistani restaurants in the country. I first went there in 1968 when your main meal cost four and sixpence, which is like 22p...' They still go there now and Simon goes for the keema dishes: minced lamb with spinach and a chaka dhal. 'It's not a tour unless we've found our way off the M6 to swing by for a feast...'

'It's not a tour unless we've swung by the Kashmir curry house in Bradford...' —***Simon***

Roast Rack of Lamb Glazed with Herbes de Provence & Lavender Honey

serves 4

3 tbsp finely chopped fresh herbes de Provence (marjoram, rosemary, thyme and bay)
1 tsp coarse sea salt
2 tsp freshly ground black pepper
2 French-trimmed 8-rib lamb racks
6 tbsp lavender honey

Preheat the oven to 200°C/Gas mark 6.

In a small bowl, combine the herbs, salt and pepper. Place the lamb in a roasting tray. Spread half the honey over the meat and sprinkle with the herb and seasoning mixture.

Roast in the middle of the oven for 20 minutes, then baste the lamb with the pan juices and pour over the remaining honey. Return to the oven and roast for another 10 minutes; the lamb should still be slightly pink.

Transfer the lamb racks to a warm platter and leave to rest for 5–10 minutes. Meanwhile, pour the cooking juices into a small pan and simmer until reduced slightly.

Cut the racks into individual cutlets and serve with the pan juices.

Butter Bean, Herb & Tomato Soufflé

serves 4

butter, for greasing
100g tinned butter beans
150ml milk
1 onion, peeled and finely diced
4 tomatoes, skinned and chopped
1 tbsp fresh parsley leaves, chopped
1 tbsp fresh thyme leaves, chopped
1 tbsp fresh sage leaves, chopped
sea salt and white pepper
4 medium eggs, separated

Preheat the oven to 180°C/Gas mark 4. Grease a 1.5 litre soufflé dish with butter.

Put the butter beans into a medium saucepan with the milk and diced onion and cook over a moderate heat until the onion is soft. Remove from the heat and roughly mash the onions and beans. Stir in the tomatoes, parsley, thyme and sage, and season with salt and pepper to taste. Leave to cool slightly and then mix in the egg yolks.

In a large, clean, dry bowl, whisk the egg whites until stiff. Stir a spoonful of the whisked whites into the bean mixture to loosen it, then gently fold in the rest of the whites, using a large metal spoon, being careful not to overwork.

Pour the mixture into the prepared dish and bake for 40–50 minutes until the soufflé is risen and lightly browned. Serve immediately.

Roasted Root Vegetables

serves 4

10 new potatoes, halved
2 red onions, peeled and quartered
4 small beetroot, washed and quartered
2 sweet potatoes, peeled and cut the same size as the new potatoes
3 carrots, peeled and cut into 1cm thick rounds
4 celery sticks, cut into 2.5cm pieces
3 fresh rosemary stems
3 fresh thyme sprigs
2 bay leaves
6 garlic cloves, peeled and finely sliced
sea salt and freshly ground black pepper
6 tbsp olive oil
2 tbsp vegetable oil

Preheat the oven to 220°C/Gas mark 7.

In a large bowl, combine the new potatoes, onions, beetroot, sweet potatoes, carrots and celery. Add the rosemary, thyme, bay leaves, garlic and seasoning and toss together in the olive oil until well mixed.

Heat the vegetable oil in a large roasting tray in the oven. When hot, carefully add the vegetable and herb mixture, making sure that the vegetables are in a single layer – otherwise they will steam rather than roast.

Roast in the oven for 20–30 minutes until tender, moving and turning the vegetables regularly to ensure that they brown on all sides. To check that the potatoes are cooked, once golden and crispy on the outside, prick to make sure that they are soft on the inside.

Transfer the vegetables to a warm serving dish, using a slotted spoon to drain off excess oil. Serve hot.

'The grilled cheese sandwich is an American institution that you just can't screw up. Anyone can make it and it will always be good.'

And how are you today, Huey Morgan – Fun Lovin' Criminal, BBC 6Music presenter, pizzeria owner and one-time wine columnist? 'Can't complain,' he replies cheerfully, 'nobody listens.'

A native New Yorker who grew up on the Lower East Side with an Irish-American mother and Puerto Rican father, Huey champions the melting pot aspect of his hometown with the perfect spread for poker night, movie night or just any night in. 'It's an environmental thing,' he says. 'You could be Irish-Puerto Rican or German-Scottish but if you lived where I did, you'd still grow up on grilled cheese sandwiches and pizza.'

The grilled cheese sandwich is, he says, an American institution – a cheese sandwich buttered on the outside, then slammed on the griddle. 'It's inside-out cheese on toast,' he says. 'It's one of those things that you just can't screw up. Anyone can make it and it will always be good. It's food for guys, especially single guys. All you need is a stove.'

And pizza is almost 'cheese on toast, Italian version. New York City is a pizza town,' he says, 'as opposed to LA which is a burger town, and like any kid there I grew up on pizza.' In fact he can remember his mother taking him to his first pizza parlour. He must have been six years old when she told him, 'It's time for you to start eatin' some pizza, boy.' For many years he co-owned two pizza places in Dublin. His tip for pizzeria management: 'You've got to put the love in it. Our chefs, they really did love pizza. It's an art form and those guys were dedicated to it.'

Completing Huey Morgan's perfect spread is his favourite San Pellegrino Limonata soda. 'I found it on vacation and I just fell in love with it. It's lemonade but it feels like mineral water. It will make you think you're being healthy…'

Huey grew up on the fringes of Little Italy and a stylised version of *The Godfather* aesthetic was a big part of Fun Lovin' Criminals' appeal when they appeared in the later 90s (their hit *King Of New York* paid homage to gang boss John Gotti). But there were echoes of the real thing in his old neighbourhood, like the bullet holes in the metal door at Umberto's Clam House on Hester Street from the shooting that killed Crazy Joe Gallo. People would travel to see it. 'There are a lot of places in New York with that kind of history,' he says. 'As a native New Yorker I have to say that, good bad or indifferent, that world is part of what makes New York what it is.'

HUEY MORGAN of FUN LOVIN' CRIMINALS
loves GRILLED AMERICAN CHEESE SANDWICHES

Having lived in London for so many years, does he agree that the capital has caught up with New York as a restaurant town? He has to admit it has, particularly British pub food. Because he works for the BBC he gets to review restaurants for *Olive* magazine. But it's hard for London to match up to New York's spontaneous culture clashes. 'Look at Chino-Latino crossover,' he says. 'You're only going to get a fusion of Spanish and Chinese in New York.' This gets him thinking about an impending trip back to New York, and the Cuba Café on Eighth Avenue. 'I just can't wait to get there…

'The best slice of pizza,' says Huey, 'is the very first slice when you get back to New York City.'

Grilled American Cheese Sandwiches

makes 2 sandwiches

3 tbsp softened butter
4 slices white bread
2 large slices cheddar cheese

Preheat a griddle pan or frying pan over a medium heat. Generously butter one side of a slice of bread and place, butter side down, in the pan. Top with a slice of cheese.

Butter a second slice of bread and place, butter side up, on top of the cheese. Griddle until lightly browned and flip over. Continue cooking until the cheese has melted.

Repeat with the second sandwich.

Serve with slices of pizza and a chilled San Pellegrino limonata.

backstage at the OXEGEN FESTIVAL

The award-winning Manchester band's singer-guitarist **can** *stand the heat... and he doesn't stay out of the kitchen.*

LIAM FRAY of THE COURTEENERS *loves* CHILLIES

'I FIRST STARTING eating chilli thanks to a close family friend who sadly passed away recently. She took me to Shere Khan in Rusholme and she was an extraordinary influence on me and the boys when we were growing up (The Courteeners have all known each other since they were 10 years old). She shaped the food we ate and the music we listened to, and the drink we drank, although we were only 15-ish... She was proper cool – loving and educated about the world, a bright shining star.

The main thing I like about chillies is the uncertainty when you've just bitten in – that perhaps you won't be able to breathe for a while. When the endorphins kick in, it's where you want to be. It's actually an addiction. I do love heat. I've not done the Scotch bonnet yet but I'm going to give it a go this year, definitely.

I've never accidentally ordered something that was too hot, but I have been given something that was insane. We were at this terrible Indian restaurant in London and I asked him to make it hot. I don't know what he put in there, but I do know that I managed three mouthfuls and there were these mirrored walls in there... Yes, I had gone purple. Couldn't speak for about two days. For me, chilli works with everything, though. I'm not into the chocolate but I did have a Chilli Cocktail in Soho House in Berlin and it was very good. By number five you're starting to feel it – or not feel it.

For me, the best chilli-based dish would be anything from the Monzil Tandoori in Barnes. We were in there with Stephen Street all the time whilst we were recording our debut album *St. Jude* – good times. The Painted Heron in Cheyne Walk, London is fantastic too. And they serve Kingfisher.

Chilli Cornbread

serves 4

- ***50g butter, melted***
- ***150g self-raising flour***
- ***1 tbsp caster sugar***
- ***1 tsp sea salt***
- ***2 tsp baking powder***
- ***½ tsp freshly ground black pepper***
- ***150g cornmeal***
- ***2 medium eggs, beaten***
- ***300ml milk***
- ***1 green chilli, deseeded and finely chopped***
- ***2 tbsp chopped basil***

Preheat the oven to 180°C/Gas mark 4. Grease a 20 x 10cm loaf tin with a little of the melted butter. Sift the flour, sugar, salt and baking powder into a large bowl and stir in the pepper and cornmeal.

Using a whisk, mix in the eggs, milk and the rest of the butter to form a smooth batter, then fold in the chilli and basil.

Pour the mixture into the greased tin. Bake in the oven until golden brown, about 40–45 minutes. To test, insert a skewer into the middle of the loaf – if it comes out clean the cornbread is cooked.

Transfer to a wire rack to cool down. Best served still warm, with crispy smoked bacon and a dollop of soured cream.

My own cooking is fairly easy. If I'm writing during the day I'll make a marinade of garlic, chilli, ginger and lime juice and stick a bit of chicken in there. Stir-fry a bit of red pepper, spring onion, bit of pak choi with ginger on the side, throw the brown rice in the rice cooker then throw it all in the wok and toss it around like a chef does on the telly. In my best Ramsay impression voice: *done.*

I love food. It's a very important part of life on the road. A lot of bands survive on sandwiches, crisps and Milky Ways but not us. We get the *Good Food Guide* out. Every meal I have with the band is special because whether we're in Tunbridge Wells, Texas or Tokyo, I'm reminded that I am very fortunate to be able to play music for a living and do it with people that I love, even though they constantly take the piss out of me – and will definitely do so for that soppy-arsed answer.'

'When you're eating chillies and the endorphins kick in, that's where you want to be.'

'I never used to eat fish a lot when I was young – but now it's like my body craves it.'

backstage at the OXEGEN FESTIVAL

The electro-popstress and Tinie Tempah collaborator on her love for tasty old ***Dicentrarchus labrax****.*

'I NEVER USED to eat fish a lot when I was young, but now it's like my body craves it. I try and order fish for every meal if I'm out, and sea bass is the best in my opinion. If you don't have fish often, you're more inclined to choose cod or tuna, but sea bass is light and delicious. Grilled sea bass with Thai vegetables is perfect.

I hated sushi when I first tried it and was quite intimidated by it. But curiosity kept getting the better of me and I kept trying it until it became my favourite thing. I used to have it every day on tour, until I got a bit sick of it! But it is really good for you, gives me a lot of protein and the oils keep your skin good. My favourite is spicy tuna or crab and I love squid, although I'm not so keen on scallop. I prefer the brown rice to the white though.

I like Itsu for sushi and even Wholefoods do great sushi, but Zuma is by far the best I have ever had. Everyone was just in awe of how good the food was there – the best sushi, beef and vegetables ever. And the dessert was so good I wanted to cry, literally.

I'm not an amazing cook, but I do love making a Thai curry and vegetable soup. I'm hardly at home and neither is my boyfriend, so we snack on things all the time like hummus and carrots, edamame beans, spelt crispbread, vegetarian meat, and a bit of cheese. We'll wrap a fish up in foil with lots of onion and mushrooms and things. Lovely…'

ELLIE GOULDING *loves*

Miso Glazed Suzuki (Sea Bass)

serves 4

2 tbsp sake
2 tbsp mirin
1 tbsp light yellow miso paste
1 tbsp brown sugar
1 tbsp light soy sauce
4 sea bass fillets, about 150g each, skinned
1 tbsp chopped spring onions
1 tbsp chopped fresh basil

In a shallow dish, mix together the sake, mirin, miso paste, sugar and soy sauce. Place the fish fillets in the marinade, turning them to make sure they are entirely coated. Cover the dish with cling film and refrigerate for 6 hours.

Heat the grill to medium. Remove the sea bass from the marinade and place on a baking tray. Grill, close to the heat, without turning, until the fillets are just about opaque in the centre, about 6 minutes.

Transfer to warm plates, sprinkle over the spring onions and basil and serve with sticky rice or soba noodles.

backstage at the OXEGEN FESTIVAL
The East London MC and grime king grew up with spicy Caribbean chicken…

'Being a Hackney boy I grew up surrounded by a diversity of cultures. There is a huge Afro-Caribbean community in the area and their presence is felt everywhere. It was hard to miss and I regularly enjoyed a Caribbean feast. It's good wholesome food with a kick. Jerk chicken, rice 'n' peas with a splash of stew sauce for good measure. Throw in a dumpling and you won't be going hungry.

I love cooking and I knock together a good roast and pasta dish. I just don't have the time to cook these days, so I tend to eat out more than anything. Of late I've eaten in some fantastic restaurants and I'm really into my food. From Nobu to Nando's I love it all. I've been to some amazing places recently and it's hard to pinpoint a specific standout meal. But Nobu a little while back was memorable, more for the sheer size of the tasting menu. I didn't eat for days afterwards. For me it's about enjoying good food with friends and family.

As for cooking jerk myself, I just don't have the cooking facilities or a secret jerk recipe. It's hard to beat shop-bought, especially in the Hackney area. My top choices in the area are In Ting and Peppers & Spice in Dalston, followed by Grannies on Downs Road if I'm Clapton way.

When I'm on tour it's a different story. I'll have mixed continental meats, hummus, Nando's of course, fresh fruit, premium lager, Sailor Jerry's rum, Jack Daniels and a selection of snacks. My tour manager recently updated the rider to make sure we get green towels. White is standard issue but this is a nice touch. Keeps the promoter rep on their toes!'

PROFESSOR GREEN *loves* JERK CHICKEN

Jerk Chicken Pizza

serves 4

for the dough

500g strong white bread flour, plus extra for dusting
½ tbsp fine sea salt
½ tbsp golden caster sugar
7g sachet easy-blend dried yeast
about 325ml warm water

for the topping

1 tbsp olive oil
2 garlic cloves, peeled and chopped
1 boneless chicken breast, thinly sliced
2 tsp jerk sauce
1 portobello mushroom, finely sliced
80ml pizza tomato sauce
75g hot pepperoni, sliced
115g mozzarella cheese, torn into pieces

To make the dough, sift the flour and salt into a bowl and stir in the sugar and yeast. Gradually incorporate the water into the flour mix until the dough starts to come together. Turn out onto a floured surface and knead until smooth and springy. Place in a clean, floured bowl, cover with a damp cloth and leave in a warm place until the dough has doubled in size, about an hour.

Preheat the oven to 190°C/Gas mark 5. Turn out the risen dough onto a floured surface and knead for about 5 minutes. Divide into 4 even-sized balls and roll out each one to a large round, the size of a dinner plate; this will create a thin and crispy pizza base. Place in pizza pans or on floured baking trays.

For the topping, heat the olive oil in a frying pan over a medium heat. Add the garlic and chicken and cook until the chicken starts to brown, about 10 minutes. Stir in the jerk sauce and mushroom and cook for a further 5 minutes. Set aside.

Spread each of the dough rounds with the pizza tomato sauce. Arrange the pepperoni and chicken mixture evenly over the sauce and top with the mozzarella. Bake the pizzas in the oven for about 10 minutes until the cheese is bubbling.

'For me it's about enjoying good food with friends and family.'

North London popstrel *Kate Nash* is a vegetarian who still loves *burgers – with meat*.

'I'm a vegetarian now but I still get cravings for cheeseburgers. I wake up in the middle of the night and just really want one. They're the most satisfying thing you can eat – and they look like they're straight out of the movies. A thin patty, a slice of really yellow cheese, a soft bun, plenty of ketchup, onion, gherkin, some salty fries… To be honest it's kind of awful but a cheap takeaway burger is probably best.

But I think my favourite meal of all is Christmas lunch. All that warmth and those smells, the presents and the TV… It's the best day for me. My sister makes cocktails and we drink piña coladas until we can't stay up any more. And I should mention my *second* best meal, Ms. Marmite Lover's supper club. She's a food blogger and her supper club in Kilburn is amazing. I took my boyfriend there for his birthday and she made the most delicious munchkin pumpkins and macaroni cheese and a sticky plum tart. You *have* to go.'

BACKSTAGE AT OXEGEN

Chris Cain of Brooklyn-based free-range indie experimentalists *We Are Scientists* chooses *soda bread, potatoes and wild Irish smoked salmon*.

'We travel quite a bit and we've found that when eating in a state of confusion, it's best to order what the locals have been eating for years – centuries, ideally. On a "foodie" scale, we're a six or seven. The restaurants in New York are of such high quality that you can't help absorbing a certain amount of annoying foodie selectiveness, but really they've strengthened our curiosity. So we're very slowly building a compendium of reviews at wearescientists.yelp.com.

We're based in Williamsburg where the food tends to be high-quality but restaurants seem to work hardest in establishing a unique menu and an interesting vibe. A place like Marlow & Sons is a good example of this – a very short, regularly changing menu, and wood-panelled, cosily-lit, vaguely-Mediterranean decor. There's a great Mexican place – tragically rare in NYC – called La Superior; reliably excellent pizza at Anna Maria; and a Michelin-starred dining room called Dressler that holds up well against any city's finest.

What else would I recommend? Blue Ribbon bakery for very fine bread and a tremendous French-American menu; Prune, a tiny gourmand's fantasy wedged between the East Village and the Lower East Side; Back 40, an East Village exemplar of locavore eating; Shake Shack in Madison Square Park, the best burger in all of New York City; Gramercy Tavern, if you want to spend a lot of money but without regretting it; and Per Se if you want to spend a *stupid* amount of money, but have one of the best meals of your entire life.'

Will Rees of fine-living indie rockers *Mystery Jets* on why they love *Irish cheese*.

'I like a good Tipperary Brie, nice and soft and buttery. Perhaps I'll eat in my bathing robe. I may put on some Ella Fitzgerald and languish in my easy chair, or nibble as I trim the posies... I do cook myself, but very badly. I like to think that my bolognese is very special but really it's quite ordinary. As a band, though, we eat a lot of sushi. Kapil will have a nato maki, Kai the salmon nigiri, Blaine a miso soup and me the unagi maki. We love going to Sushi Hiro in Ealing, which is London's best sushi place. You get lot of opportunities to eat brilliant stuff in this business. We had Mexican street meat by a go-kart track in Guadalajara and I think that's got to be the best thing I've ever eaten.'

Northern Irish indie band *General Fiasco* love *watermelon*, as frontman Owen Strathearn explains.

'A lot of food that you eat on tour leaves you feeling dirty, but watermelon is definitely the opposite. There's always a good fruit platter in catering with a nice bit of watermelon on it. It's refreshing and it tastes clean. We make a conscious effort to eat well on tour. Sometimes eating horrible food is unavoidable, and you've got to get the balance back. There's nothing better than a crisp fresh piece of watermelon, but you don't want it if it's been hanging about a little too long – it gets a little soggy and develops a weird texture.

When you're on tour you always end up having at least one meal a day from a service station, and an M&S box of prepared watermelon is a life-saver. I'll have it two or three times a week.'

It's the raw power of *sushi* for Welsh hard rockers *Kids In Glass Houses*, says frontman Aled Phillips.

'Short of open-mouth fishing there's nothing like sushi, is there? Healthy, good to share and it feels nice in the mouth. When we went to Japan, our label took us out to a very traditional restaurant, which was the first time I ate jellyfish. I can absolutely recommend it. The entire experience is really heightened in Japan.

Why do rock bands love sushi? Because we're self-important and we think it's dignified and gives us a sense of culture in the moral abyss that is the rock n' roll world. That's just me, though. Axl Rose probably just likes the taste...

In Cardiff there are two great independent sushi restaurants – Tenkaichi and Ichiban – good people and great menus. Could there be such thing as Welsh-Japanese fusion? Yeah, an entire leek wrapped in lambswool, with a Caerphilly cheese dipping sauce. It takes an informed palate to appreciate it.'

'Sometimes I won't even remember that we played a gig, but I'll remember what we ate that night.'
—Speech Debelle

Red tails in the sunset: Mick Hucknall of Simply Red with a lobster feast.

Reputations once earned tend to stick, and Mick Hucknall will always have a name as a lover of both food and women. The latter is a bit out of date – he is now happily married with a daughter – but the former passion remains intact. Mick Hucknall loves food and wine. He's been a vintner since the late 90s, producing wines under the name Il Cantante ('the singer') from grapes grown in the volcanic Sicilian soils of Mount Etna. He even talks eloquently on the subject on Twitter (follow @mjhucknall). But Mick tries to let his own offerings speak for themselves. 'It's all well and good being a pop star, but what does that have to do with wine?' he says. 'I've tried to avoid the celebrity angle.' Ironically he bought the vineyard as a way of putting an end to his own unhealthy drinking. Gabriella Wesberry, his long-term partner, mother of his daughter and since 2010 his wife, is a director of the company.

Mick has owned restaurants in the past. There was a minor stake in a bar in his native Manchester and then the Parisian restaurant Man Ray, which he co-owned with Johnny Depp, Sean Penn and John Malkovich, an experience he recalls with a shiver. They had wanted Man Ray to be a club but stringent French laws meant that they had to maintain it as a restaurant, 'And we couldn't fire anybody. It becomes a chain round your neck. I'd advise any aspiring pop star or actor to *never ever* invest in clubs or restaurants. You'll get screwed. Stick with what you're good at.'

A genuinely disadvantaged youth has made Mick appreciate the fruits of his success all the more. His mother left when he was three years old and his father, a barber, brought him up 'just above the poverty line'. It was mostly northern dishes on the table at home in Denton near Manchester: 'Lancashire hotpot, steak and cow-heel pie… it sounds like *Desperate Dan* food, doesn't it? But when they're made well, these dishes can stand up to anything in the world. My father wasn't a flashy cook but he was competent. He was always keen to stress the freshness of things, fresh eggs and so on, and I think I followed his lead.'

MICK HUCKNALL *loves* LOBSTER THERMIDOR

After Mick left home and moved into his first bedsit in Moss Side in the early 80s, he learned to cook by default, picking up a talent for Indian food from shopkeepers in Rusholme Market. When Simply Red took off he discovered a love of Italian, then French and German food.

'German food's very underrated,' he says. 'It's excellent, so beautifully simple. Roast goose or Schweinshaxe, a roast knuckle of pork deep-fried with crispy skin… it's so good. And Hungarian food too, because of all the various grades of paprika, although I'd have to plump for Italian food as my favourite in Europe.' The best meal he ever had, he says, was as a guest of one of the co-founders of Gambero Rosso, the Italian equivalent to Michelin, who took Simply Red to a restaurant in the back streets of Rome. 'We ate 'til about four in the morning,' says Mick, 'a beautiful array of Italian delicacies prepared with such skill and care that it was astonishing. The whole band were fainting because of its brilliance. The best meal I've ever had.'

Now he feels like he's come full circle with high-end cuisine. 'Having lived in Paris for a number of years, perversely I now loathe Michelin-starred food. To me it loses touch with what food should be. I like really good quality, fresh, well-bred food, cooked simply. The Michelin thing underwhelms me. You're supposed to be grateful for a three-inch piece of fish on a huge plate for fifty quid. It bores me. I've come to prefer brasserie, bistro, trattoria food, where you're getting an honest piece of meat, an honest whole fish that you can fillet yourself.'

Though he loves lobster, as seen in our photographs, he's just as happy with a good tricolore salad. 'Italian food is just *genius*,' he says. 'Tomato, mozzarella and basil or garlic, oil and red pepper on pasta – those things are timeless.' Tonight, he says, he's making *pollo alla cacciatore*: pan-fried chicken with tomatoes, peppers, onions, garlic and herbs. 'A simple dish, nothing hoity-toity. It's so satisfying to make those simple things well.'

Does Mick Hucknall's track record prove the old saying that a lad will never be short of a girlfriend if he can cook?

'It definitely helps,' he says with a smile. 'I mean, if you can't take her to a restaurant… well, you're either going to her place or yours, aren't you?'

'I'd advise any aspiring pop star to ***never ever*** *invest in restaurants. Stick with what you're good at.'*

Lobster Thermidor & Roasted Vegetables

serves 4

2 large lobsters, cooked
40g Parmesan cheese, freshly grated

for the sauce

60g butter
2 shallots, peeled and finely chopped
570ml fish stock
2 tbsp medium dry white wine
110ml double cream
½ tsp English mustard
1 tbsp chopped fresh parsley
1 tbsp chopped fresh chives
1 tbsp chopped fresh dill
juice of 1 lemon
pinch of cayenne pepper
sea salt and freshly ground black pepper
lemon wedges, to serve

Lay the cooked lobsters belly down on a board, hold firmly and cut lengthways in half. Remove all the meat from the claws, tail and head, saving any coral. Cut the meat up into small pieces and place back in the shell with the coral.

For the sauce, melt the butter in a large saucepan, add the shallots and cook until softened. Add the stock, wine and cream and bring to the boil. Let bubble until reduced by half, then add the mustard, chopped herbs, lemon juice and cayenne. Season to taste with salt and pepper.

Preheat the grill to high. Spoon the sauce over the lobster meat, sprinkle with the Parmesan, and place the lobster halves under the grill for 3–4 minutes until golden brown. Serve with lemon wedges.

for the roasted vegetables

8 tbsp olive oil
2 large red onions, peeled and quartered
10 asparagus spears, trimmed and cut into long diagonal slices
2 courgettes, trimmed, halved and cut into thick diagonal slices
1 fennel bulb, trimmed, halved lengthways and cut into 1cm thick slices
8 garlic cloves, peeled
1 tbsp fennel seeds, crushed
pinch of sea salt (ideally Fleur de Sel de Camargue)
4 trusses of baby plum tomatoes on the vine
drizzle of good-quality balsamic vinegar
1 tbsp chopped fresh basil
1 tbsp chopped fresh parsley

Preheat the oven to 200°C/Gas mark 6. Pour half of the olive oil into a large ovenproof dish and place in the oven to heat up.

Meanwhile, put the red onions, asparagus, courgettes, fennel, garlic, fennel seeds, salt and remaining olive oil into a large bowl and toss well. Carefully tip it all into the heated dish.

Cook in the oven for 15 minutes, checking after 10 minutes and turning down the heat if the vegetables are browning too quickly. Add the tomatoes on their vines and roast for a further 5 minutes or until the vegetables are caramelised.

Serve immediately, drizzled with balsamic vinegar and sprinkled with the chopped herbs.

Future food foundation: Russell (left) and Ron Mael of Sparks fly the flag for frozen.

Given the chance to pictorially celebrate the food you love above all others, most of us would go for either the epic and the decadent – an El Bulli takeaway served on the lip of a volcano, perhaps – or maybe the comforting tastes of home. Who would choose a bag of California frozen vegetables as the food that tells the story of their lives?

Sparks would. Two brothers from Los Angeles, Russell (hair) and Ron (moustache) Mael are forty-year music veterans who plough not just their own furrow but everyone else's too. When they performed the signature hit *This Town Ain't Big Enough For The Both Of Us* on TV in 1974, the sight of Ron's Charlie Chaplin moustache led John Lennon to exclaim that he could see Adolf Hitler appearing on *Top Of The Pops*. Since then Sparks have played glam rock, helped define the format of the impassive synth-pop duo, and enjoyed a late-career blossoming with a series of increasingly baroque albums culminating in a pop-opera about Ingmar Bergman.

SPARKS *love* FROZEN MIXED VEGETABLES

Polish Mixed Vegetable & Dill Pickle Soup

serves 4

1 litre beef or vegetable stock
150g frozen mixed vegetables
165g dill pickles, diced
100g potatoes, peeled and diced
15g plain flour
135ml milk
sea salt and freshly ground black pepper

Pour the stock into a large saucepan, add the frozen mixed vegetables and dill pickles and bring to the boil. Lower the heat and leave to simmer for 10 minutes, then add the potatoes and cook until tender, about 15 minutes.

Meanwhile, put the flour into a small bowl and gradually mix in the flour to form a paste. Over a high heat, slowly stir this paste into the soup and continue to stir until it comes back to the boil. Simmer, stirring for a minute or two. Season with salt and pepper to taste and serve immediately.

N.B. This soup is fantastic served with Polish dumplings and tiny meatballs.

True to form, their choice of mass-produced supermarket vegetables has a theory behind it. With its background in high technology, frozen food is the digital music to fresh food's earthy, organic analogue sound, says singer Russell Mael – the synthesiser to its acoustic guitar. And Sparks like to stand up for the future, even if it's the future as imagined in the past. 'And this really is what we eat,' says his brother Ron, writer of all of Sparks' songs. 'It's simple and easy and, you know, the less stuff that's on my food the more I like it.'

The brothers Mael grew up in Pacific Palisades in Los Angeles, the sons of a newspaper art director father and a library administrator mother who cooked, says Russell, 'real food for real boys.' One of her specialities was 'porcupines', giant meatballs with a rice filling which would cook all day in that touchstone of the 1960s American kitchen, the pressure cooker. 'That's something else we miss,' says Russell. 'The science fiction pressure cooker – kitchen equipment from the future, like an iron lung for your porcupine meatballs.'

Over the years their red meat, steak and chops all-American diet gently morphed into vegetarianism. But forty years in the music business has inevitably led them to eat in some unusual places. In 2009 Ron dined at a place called Umenohana in Kanazawa, northern Japan, which offered fifteen dishes of tofu done in different ways. 'I'm sure to someone who isn't a vegetarian it sounds awful,' he says, 'but it was astounding, the most amazing meal I've had recently.'

Russell, on the other hand, recalls one dinner in Malmo in the 1970s. The record company took them to a strange little seafood restaurant with its own little lake, where you remote-controlled your own tiny trawler boat to bring in your 'haul' of shrimp while piped foghorns played in the background. 'It was amazing – *Deadliest Catch: The Restaurant*,' he says. 'You know, we really should have shot a video there…'

'Frozen food is the synthesiser to fresh food's acoustic guitar. And we like to stand up for the future.'—**Russell**

BIRDS EYE
Steamfresh
Fresh Frozen Vegetables
Specially Seasoned
ASIAN MEDLEY
Steamy
VEGETABLES
CALIFORNIA
BLEND
VEGETABLES

Grand pasta flash: Tinie Tempah takes in an agreeable seafood linguine.

Life is good when you're Tinie Tempah. The Plumstead-raised artist, otherwise known as Patrick Chukwuemeka Okogwu Jr., has won a ton of praise for uniting the disparate music scenes of grime, underground rave and radio-friendly pop without selling any of them out. With two number one singles, a number one album and two Brit Awards at the age of 23, he has proved that you don't have to surrender your cool factor when success beckons. Tinie still gets massive respect as an MC and a relentless hard worker, but also as someone with an inquisitive mind and a mature attitude to success.

'My music is definitely saying that you can make it happen for yourself, if you work at it,' he says. 'That's how I felt for a long time, that success was almost unreachable. When it started to work out for me, I wanted my music to say, you know, this could be you if you put the hard work in.'

One of the fringe benefits to fame is that you get to discover new experiences in eating. Born in London to Nigerian parents, Tinie has always appreciated his food. He reminisces about an 'amazing' roast chicken with garlic and thyme jus that he had at the Salon Millesime in the Carlton Hotel in New York. 'They warned me it would take 45 minutes. After about 35 minutes they brought an almost-cooked chicken out and told me it was coming along nicely, and then 10 minutes later I ate the best chicken I've ever had.'

He talks about black cod at Nobu that just melts in your mouth, sushi at Katsuya in LA, trying surf 'n' turf in Australia for the first time ever, and a lovely and welcoming Italian place in Mallorca called Di Benedetto when he and his band were touring the holiday islands. 'It was so friendly, amazing food, and even though we were a gang of lads having fun in our shorts the owner was gently telling us dinner table etiquette. It was proper, I really liked it.'

When he visits a new country Tinie heads off the beaten track to try some traditional food – the old town in Dubai, or backstreet places in Australia. 'Didn't enjoy the kangaroo,' he admits. 'It was like a cross between beef and chicken, smoky but really chewy. It was so surreal, man.' He's kept a picture of the receipt on his phone: stubbie, stubbie, stubbie, kangaroo… and chips.

TINIE TEMPAH *loves* SEAFOOD LINGUINE & A GLASS OF MERLOT

Nigerian food is a fundamental part of his life, he says. It's what he grew up with and it builds up the palate because it's packed with flavour. The music lifestyle keeps Tinie out of the kitchen – he gets home at 2 or 3am most nights and falls 'flat on my face asleep' – but he used to cook a lot when he lived with his parents. He'd do chicken and steak, or help his mum with the rich West African rice dish called jollof. 'It's like a really good risotto,' he says. 'Nigerian food is lots of flavour, lots of tomato purée, rice, yam, beans… it's a whole load of stuff, really good.' His favourite would be pounded yam with egusi soup, a savoury soup with meat and spinach that exists in countless variants across West Africa.

He has a couple of favourite Nigerian restaurants, both on London's Old Kent Road: the classy 805 and the more home-style Presidential Suya. They're both family-run businesses, friendly and personal. Presidential in particular is one of those places where you feel like you're in Nigeria, he says. 'There is a real nice atmosphere. When I come back from travelling the world I do like to go there and chill. It's humbling, it's a nice experience. You might see the owner in there having a little Guinness.'

Oh yes, Nigerian Guinness, the mysterious variant on the classic Irish stout. 'There's only two Guinness breweries in the world,' says Tinie, 'one in Dublin and one in Nigeria. Ireland and Nigeria even have the same patron saint, St Patrick, but Nigerian Guinness is a lot stronger,' he says proudly. 'It's real tough and it puts lead in your pencil.' He starts laughing. He'll only have a Nigerian Guinness once in a while. He's more fond of liqueurs: amaretto with a bit of Coca Cola.

He's a recent convert to seafood, subject of his picture for *Love Music Love Food*. Tinie used to be apprehensive about shellfish and squid. Then he saw that his Maltese mate, who ate it all the time, was light on his feet and full of energy whereas a steak would wipe Tinie out. Then he tried a seafood linguine, 'and all my prayers were answered. It just felt right, it was light but it filled me up. I could still run around and do my thing.'

What does he say to people who praise his music as an antidote to US hip hop with its obsession with cars and material goods and luxury brands like Cristal? That's a cliché in itself, he retorts. Hip hop might have been like that in the 90s and early 2000s but it's changed. And in defence of the people in hip hop who used to make those videos and release those tunes, they grew up in the most impoverished backgrounds imaginable. 'I've spent time there and I've seen how you really can have it hard in a derelict project with no money at all,' he says. 'The minute they sign a deal and get a big cheque, it's very natural for them to splurge and show off what they've got.'

Tinie feels lucky. He had a pretty good upbringing with a mum and dad who worked hard in social work and the NHS. Success was less of a shock to him. 'You know how to deal with it,' he says, 'if you know who you are.'

'Seafood linguine answers all my prayers. It fills me up but I can still run around and do my thing.'

Seafood Linguine

serves 4

325g linguine
sea salt and freshly ground black pepper
75ml olive oil
knob of butter
2 garlic cloves, peeled and crushed
1 red onion, peeled and finely chopped
200g raw prawns, peeled and deveined
4 large scallops, shelled, cleaned and halved
4 langoustines, cleaned
tail of 1 small cooked lobster, peeled and sliced
4 ripe plum tomatoes, peeled, deseeded and diced
8 fresh basil leaves, finely chopped
100g clams, cleaned
lemon juice, to taste (about ½ lemon)
pinch of dried chilli flakes
lemon wedges, to serve

Three-quarters fill a large saucepan with water and bring to the boil. Add the linguine and a good pinch of salt and cook over a medium heat for about 10 minutes, or until just cooked.

Meanwhile, heat a large frying pan over a medium heat. Add all but a dash of the olive oil and the butter and gently fry the garlic and red onion until soft, about 5–7 minutes. Now add the prawns, scallops, langoustines and lobster tail slices and fry quickly for about 2 minutes.

As soon as the pasta is cooked, drain and toss with a dash of olive oil. Add the cooked linguine to the frying pan, along with the tomatoes, basil, salt, pepper and clams. Pop the lid on the pan for 1 minute or until the clams open, then remove from the heat.

Divide between 4 warm pasta bowls and finish with a squeeze of fresh lemon, a little sprinkling of chilli flakes and salt to taste. Serve with a good wedge of lemon on the side.

'Cheese on your chips? Cheese in your ***gravy?*** *That's just not right.'*

WHEN YOU WALK through a storm… you need a bag of chips to keep your hands warm. James Walsh, long-time singer with intergalactic North Western rock band Starsailor and now a burgeoning solo artist, combines two of his great passions in his photograph for *Love Music Love Food*: fish and chips and his beloved Liverpool FC.

'I chose fish and chips because of the number of times I've had it on the way home from a game,' says James. 'There's some good chippers round Anfield. It's like Americans and coffee shops round there.' Born in nearby Chorley, Lancashire, James has been going to watch Liverpool since he was about 13. He's played more than a few events for the fans, including making a Hillsborough benefit single with Anfield legends Kenny Dalglish and Bruce Grobbelaar.

And fish and chips was a Friday night institution at home, too. Family Walsh would eat reasonably healthily in the week but come the weekend it was a blow-out of fish, chips, mushy peas and curry sauce ('although I wouldn't mix 'em together'), plus a few cans of Tizer from the local old-school chippy. 'I'm sure they used lard not oil,' says James, ''cos lard makes the best chips. And it always had to be cod.'

Travelling with Starsailor took him to some unusual places, including a fantastic Chinese in Tokyo. 'It was my first experience of posh Chinese,' he says. 'Before that I'd only had sweet and sour, but this was sweetbreads and dumplings, and everything. And a lot of sake.' They served him cod balls, cooked right in front of him: 'I didn't even know cod *had* balls,' he says, not entirely seriously. More recently he recorded a solo EP in Norway and his hosts took him for elk burgers. 'They were quite nice!' he says. 'Staple diet over there, although they reminded me of the sort of burgers you used to get for school dinners…'

For the past few years James has split his time between Belfast, where he lives with his partner, and London. The fish and chip traditions are very different. 'They have garden peas, not mushy peas in Belfast,' he says with mild incredulity, 'and you can't get decent mushy peas in London. It's all about gravy. And they do weird stuff like cheese on your chips, or cheese in your *gravy*.'

This guardian of traditional fish-and-chip ways shakes his head.

'That's just not right.'

JAMES WALSH of STARSAILOR *loves* FISH & CHIPS

Tempura Whiting, Shoe String Fries & Pickled Onion Sauce

serves 4

8 whiting fillets, skinned and checked for pin bones
groundnut oil, for frying

for the batter

85g rice flour
1 tbsp cornflour
½ tsp sea salt
200ml ice-cold mineral water
2 ice cubes

For the batter, mix together the rice flour, cornflour and salt together in a large bowl. Pat the fish fillets dry. Heat the groundnut oil in a wok or deep frying pan. Meanwhile, quickly mix the ice-cold water and ice cubes into the flours, but be careful not to over-mix.

When the oil is hot, fry the fish fillets in batches. Dip the fish fillets into the batter one at a time to coat, and then gently lower into the hot oil. Move the fillets around with a slotted spoon to ensure they do not stick together. When the fish is crispy and golden, lift out and place on a plate lined with kitchen paper. Let the oil heat up again before frying the next batch. Repeat until all the fillets are cooked. Serve with the fries and pickled onion sauce.

N.B. Prepare the pickled onion sauce ahead and cook the fries before or at the same time as the fish.

for the fries

4 large King Edward potatoes, peeled
vegetable oil, for deep-frying
pinch of sea salt

Cut the potatoes into ultra-thin fries and soak in a bowl of very cold water until ready to use. Rinse in fresh water, drain and dry pat dry with a tea towel or kitchen paper. Heat the oil in a heavy-based, deep frying pan or deep-fat fryer until hot.

Gently lower two handfuls of the potatoes into the hot oil and fry until golden brown. Remove from the pan with a slotted spoon and turn out onto a plate lined with kitchen paper. Let the oil heat up again and repeat to cook the remaining potatoes. Toss the fries together in a large bowl with the salt.

for the pickled onion sauce

4 pickled onions
½ lemon, roughly chopped, pips removed
200ml crème fraîche
sea salt and freshly ground black pepper

Put the pickled onions and chopped lemon into a food processor and pulse until roughly chopped; do not overwork – the mixture should have some texture. Turn out into a small bowl and mix in the crème fraîche. Season with salt and pepper to taste, cover and refrigerate until ready to serve.

West London rapper Example, AKA Elliot Gleave, worked his way into the Top Ten via releases on Mike Skinner of The Streets' own record label, and has recorded with dubstep producer Skream and Hackney rap superstar Professor Green. He's also a trained film editor, an attempted stand-up comic – he gave it a try for the BBC's *Culture Show* – and a former Royal Mail Young Poet Of The Year (1992). But his claim to fame in the food world is that hip-hop-friendly peri-peri chicken chain Nando's created a loyalty card specially for him.

'I've been going to Nando's since I was 12 or 13,' he says. 'One of the first Nando's that opened was in Putney near my school so we used to go there for lunch. I am one of Nando's original gangsters.' He bigged up the critic-baffling chicken outlet so often that they got tired of giving him money-off vouchers and instead, at Example's suggestion, made him a Black Nando's card, conferring free chicken for life on the holder. 'It's not some high-tech swiping system, it's just a card with your name on it,' he says with a smile, but now other MCs including Tinchy Stryder and Dizzee Rascal are part of the exclusive Nando's inner circle. Example repaid the favour by launching his album *Won't Go Quietly* with a world tour of London's Nando's.

So why did he choose Jaffa Cakes for his *Love Music Love Food* picture? 'I love them too,' he says, 'and I feel like I've given a lot of love to Nando's. They're doing well. Jaffa Cakes are a different obsession. There's nothing that tastes like them. You don't feel guilty eating them 'cos they're not high calorie. And there's a bit of orange in there so you can tell yourself you're being healthy. It's one of your Five-a-Day, really.'

As if Example isn't lucky enough on the food front, his girlfriend works in restaurant PR so he has eaten at a lot of the best restaurants in London for free. 'Yep, all the poncey places where the celebrity chefs hang out,' he says. He's done Michel Roux Jr.'s magisterial Le Gavroche but is just as at home at the unpretentious barbecue mini-chain Bodeans. 'Give me a pulled pork sandwich or some burnt ends and beans and I'm happy.' Oh, and he had alligator in Florida. 'It's like salty chicken. When in Rome...'

Man cannot live on Jaffa Cake alone, though. Does Example have other biscuit favourites? He will on occasion stray to a custard cream, he says, and when he's in Australia – he worked in the film industry there before the music career took off – he likes a Tim Tam. A *Tim Tam*?

'Yeah, it's like an Australian Penguin.' David Attenborough, we need you.

EXAMPLE *loves* JAFFA CAKES

Jaffa Cake Semifreddo

serves 4–6

125g Jaffa Cakes
400ml double cream
300ml mascarpone
4 tbsp Cointreau, or other orange liqueur
85g caster sugar
2 tbsp diced candied orange peel
50g dark chocolate chips

Spread the Jaffa Cakes out on a plate and place in the freezer until frozen.

Line a 1kg loaf tin with cling film. Take the Jaffa Cakes from the freezer and dice into small pieces.

In a large bowl, whisk together the cream, mascarpone, liqueur and sugar until soft peaks form. Fold in the candied peel, chocolate chips and Jaffa Cake pieces. Pour into the loaf tin and smooth the surface.

Freeze for 1½ hours, then cover with cling film. Freeze for at least a further 24 hours before serving.

To unmould, dip the tin briefly into warm water, then run a knife around the semifreddo and turn out onto a board. Cut into slices with a warm knife. Serve immediately, with whipped cream or chocolate sauce if you like.

'A Jaffa Cake? It's one of your Five-a-Day, really.'

'You need Scotch bonnet pepper, you need the sweetness of allspice and you have to cook it over a fire – or it's just not real jerk.'

ANY RAPPER DEPENDS on their good memory – there are many more lyrics on the average hip hop track than on its pop equivalent – but a near-photographic recall of the meals you've had over the years is surely a bonus. 'I swear, I remember events in my life through food,' says Speech Debelle, Londoner and 2009 Mercury Prize-winning British rapper. 'Sometimes I won't remember that we played a gig but I'll remember what we ate that night.'

For instance, Glasgow was where she and her band had the best salmon she's ever tasted. Poland? Some amazing fried potato thing, completely unlike anything else she'd ever had. In Australia where she recorded her award-winning debut *Speech Therapy*, she discovered cinnamon poussin, salmon and mascarpone pizza – 'best pizza topping ever!' – and Belgian chocolate pizza too. 'I could list everything I ate in Australia, I'm so glad I went there.' A major band meeting? 'Le Chardon in East Dulwich. I had foie gras, a beefsteak with dauphinois potatoes and a crème brûlée.' And the Mercury Prize itself? She didn't eat that much, she admits. She got there too late.

'Actually,' she begins to remember, 'it was fish and it was no good! It was *overcooked*.'

As befits her Anglo-Caribbean heritage, Speech – real name Corynne Elliot – is a fish girl at heart. She has no room for fussy little fillets. It has to be the whole fish, fried and served straight up, stewed down with seasoned gravy or in a proper fish tea, a watery soup with fish and potatoes, thyme butter and onion. Jamaican food is the perfect takeaway, she says, and recommends The Humming Bird in Thornton Heath.

Then she rhapsodises about the steamed kingfish with bammy (the Jamaican cassava flatbread) and cabbage, which she had at a harbour restaurant in Jamaica. Or the fried parrotfish with just a little Scotch pepper vinegar, 'that is *super-hot*,' and fried bammy she had nearby. On the last day of a recent visit to St Lucia she and her friends caught a fishing boat, went to a little island and collected eel, snapper ('best fish ever!'), kingfish ('second-best fish ever!') plus lobster, eel and something with a really rock-hard shell on it whose name she never got. 'The fisherman cooked it up for us right there, and that was probably the nicest meal I've ever had. We even had the eel raw and it was delicious.'

For *Love Music Love Food* Speech represents Jamaica's other great contribution to the international arms race of heat in food: jerk spice. What makes great jerk, Ms Debelle?

'Got to be Scotch bonnet pepper, obviously. A lot of other chillies are heat without flavour, but the Scotch bonnet has a very particular scent to it. You need sweetness, but the sweetness of allspice, not sugariness. You need plenty of herbs and you have to cook it over a fire or it's just not real jerk. Fire gets you a completely different flavour.' She looks sadly out of the window at rainy London. 'It's never the season for it here.'

Speech Debelle's dream? To go on *Come Dine With Me*, the show with which she's obsessed. 'I'd start with a goat's cheese tart and pear tart and then take it from there...'

SPEECH DEBELLE *loves* JERK SPICE

Roast Jerk Shoulder of Goat

serves 4

1kg shoulder of goat
200ml pineapple juice
100ml water
100ml dark rum
olive oil, for roasting

for the jerk marinade

1 tsp coriander seeds
2 tbsp black peppercorns
3 tsp allspice
2 tsp fresh thyme leaves, chopped
small bunch of fresh coriander, stalks removed and finely chopped
2 cinnamon sticks, roughly chopped
1 tsp freshly grated nutmeg
4 garlic cloves, peeled
4 Scotch bonnet chillies, halved and deseeded
2.5cm piece of fresh ginger, peeled and chopped
grated zest of 1 lime
juice of 2 limes
140ml olive oil

to serve

plain yoghurt
lime wedges

For the jerk marinade, grind the coriander seeds, peppercorns and allspice together, using a pestle and mortar.

Put the thyme, fresh coriander, cinnamon, nutmeg, garlic, chillies, ginger, lime zest and juice, ground spices and olive oil into a food processor and blend to a smooth paste.

With a sharp knife, score the goat skin diagonally, then turn the shoulder around and cut across the diagonal to create a diamond pattern on the skin. Rub 6 tbsp of the jerk marinade evenly over the scored skin, making sure that it permeates the cuts. Then turn the goat over and repeat on the underside, rubbing the marinade into the skin, meat and around all the bones, using a little more if necessary. Place the goat in a dish, cover and leave to marinate in the fridge overnight.

Preheat the oven to 180°C/Gas mark 4. Place the goat in a roasting tray and pour in the pineapple juice, water and rum. Drizzle a little oil over the meat and loosely cover with foil. Roast on the middle shelf of the oven for 1 hour, basting the meat frequently to ensure it remains moist. Remove the foil and return the meat to the oven. Roast until the skin is crisp, about 1 hour.

Lift the goat onto a warm platter and leave to rest in a warm place for 20 minutes. Spoon off the fat from the roasting juices, then pour the juices into a small saucepan. Place over a medium heat and let bubble until reduced to a thick gravy.

Cut the meat into chunks and serve each portion with a dollop of yoghurt and lime wedges.

Pizza delivery courtesy of Domino's fans White Lies. From left: Charles Cave, Harry McVeigh, Jack Lawrence-Brown.

TAKE A FRESH LOOK
Domino's
Pizza

ROCK AND ROLL isn't just about the distant and mysterious. It also celebrates the magic in everyday life and the majesty of simple pleasures. For their *Love Music Love Food* picture, *Mojo* and *Q* Award-winning West London alternative rockers White Lies step out of one comfort zone – the atmospheric interzone of Joy Division and The Teardrop Explodes – and into another as they pay homage to the dependable Domino's pizza.

'You can trust Domino's,' declares drummer Jack Lawrence-Brown over a table-full of lager in a Shoreditch pub. 'You finish a show late, you're going to need a bit of energy but you might not want to chance a local pizza place. With Domino's, you know it's going to be good. We keep it simple with just a pepperoni or a couple of plain cheeses. You can't beat it.'

'Our keyboard player Tommy will go for a hot and spicy 'cos he thinks he's a bad boy,' says lead singer Harry McVeigh. White Lies' Domino's habit is a serious one. There's been inter-band tension when Jack has placed his pizza crusts on Harry's video game boxes on the bus.

'There's a line that you don't cross,' says Harry gravely. 'I think that was one of our most genuine fights…' admits bassist Charles Cave.

To some rock bands, food is just fuel. Not White Lies. 'We're definitely, properly into our food,' says Jack, and the band fall into rhapsodies of the restaurants they love. They've got a favourite fusiony-sushi place in LA, Fat Fish (on North Robertson, north of Melrose), which is 'absolutely amazing', and they love transplanted gastro-pub The Spotted Pig in New York and the sumptuous traditional-Belgian-with-a-remix restaurant Belga Queen in Brussels.

There's a drive-by Mexican called the Cactus Taqueria in Los Angeles (on Vine between Santa Monica Boulevard and Melrose) that they try to visit whenever they're over there for 'really good street food, quick stuff in your hand'. And they often go to Mel's Drive-In in LA. It's touristy but who cares when you can get a full breakfast at 2am? In Milan they had a sort of calzone-style pasty with mozzarella and tomato sauce. 'It was almost like a doughnut,' says Harry, followed by what their hosts told them was the best ice cream in Italy. 'Every Italian says that,' says Charles 'but in this case…'

WHITE LIES *love* DOMINO'S PEPPERONI PASSION PIZZA

And then there's pizza, pizza, perfect pizza. 'There's Vinny's Pizzeria in Brooklyn,' says Charles. All nod astutely. 'Not as good as Escape From New York in San Fran,' counters Jack. They all nod again. Harry loves the numerous Ray's Pizzas in New York – some original, some not – although Charles isn't sure about the sesame seeds on the crust. 'No', says Harry, 'that's Rocket Jones that does that.' They're obsessed, it's like they're playing pizza tennis.

Naturally they all cook. Jack does a mean Parmesan and pancetta risotto. 'I enjoy it because it's such a labour. You have to stand there stirring for 30–40 minutes to get a good consistency. It's almost hypnotic.' Charles' specialities are fresh tagliani with double cream, brandy, lemon and Parmesan: 'it's really subtle, great as a starter.' Or Gruyère and spinach muffins. All laugh at this. Who thought we'd see the day when rock bands are making Gruyère and spinach muffins? 'They're bloody good!' the bassist counters.

Frontman Harry goes for a bloodier, more brutally manly option. 'I like to spatchcock a chicken myself – I remove its spine, by hand – then make a piri-piri sauce, brown the chicken and then chuck it in the oven. You have to basically mallet it flat. It's *so* good.' They begin debating cooking techniques.

Charles: 'If you take less than 30 minutes to make scrambled eggs you're doing it wrong. Really low heat, patience, take it off the heat and let it cook a little more on its own… it should come out the consistency of porridge. I can't stand these gelatinous, microwaved scrambled eggs that you get.'

Jack: 'A spoonful of mustard in there makes a difference.' These are surprising levels of culinary sophistication for a rock band, are they not? Jack says that White Lies would love to appear on a rock and roll edition of *Come Dine With Me*. 'I'd love to cook with Sir Cliff…' he muses.

The touring lifestyle can be an anonymous whirl of hotels, but food has become a way for White Lies to remember the places they've visited. When they toured America with Kings Of Leon they became obsessed with the Travel Channel's show *Man Vs Food*, in which iron-gutted presenter Adam Richman eats enormous dishes such as the 7.5lb 'Sasquatch Burger' or a metre-long bratwurst. Stopping off to play in Midwestern cities where there's nothing to do but eat, they would seek out that town's episode of *Man Vs Food* on YouTube and try to track down the restaurant where it was shot.

They only managed one: the Iron Barley in St Louis, famous for its Monte Christo Dog – consisting of two giant grilled hot dogs cooked in chicken stock with melted Swiss cheese, inside a fried bun with strawberry jam on top. Only their drum tech was up for the challenge. 'And it was absolutely delicious,' says Charles. 'I shared it round – you had to, really. Definitely not the classiest meal I've ever had, but it was the most awesome.' Then they reminisce about the restaurant next door to the Black Cat venue in Chicago, and its 'strawberry cheesecake chocolate fudge brownie'. 'So big they had to write it over two lines on the blackboard,' says Charles. 'It was the most stoned-munchie dessert I've ever had and it was intense.'

Many a band will claim they look for new experiences. White Lies really do. Charles relates his visit to Tibet with his dad. They had read up and braced themselves for 'virtually inedible' food and when they arrived they tried yak butter tea, 'basically rancid milk with melted butter, very much an acquired taste'. Their guide gave them a Tibetan peach which looked like a shrivelled raisin but felt like a rock. 'All their food is rock hard,' says Charles – even the cheese. Then he took them to a traditional hotpot place where they'd dunk a whole duck, head and all, in boiling broth. 'You just had to gnaw at it and pull bits off with your chopsticks. Very frustrating. He offered me the head at the end but I let him have it.'

It takes nerve to eat this stuff but White Lies are up for it. From delivery pizza to Tibetan boiled duck, you've got to try it all. As Jack says: 'The search continues.'

*'Leaving pizza crusts on my video game boxes? That's a line that you don't cross.'—**Harry***

Pepperoni Pizza With Monterey Jack, Jalapeño & Sour Cream

serves 4

for the dough

500g strong white bread flour, plus extra for dusting
½ tsp sea salt
½ tsp caster sugar
7g sachet easy-blend dried yeast
2 tbsp extra virgin olive oil
about 320ml warm water

for the topping

100ml milk
1 tbsp plain flour
400g Monterey Jack cheese, grated
1 tsp English mustard
1 tbsp Worcestershire sauce
120ml beer
80ml pizza tomato sauce
12 slices of hot pepperoni
1 medium egg, plus an extra yolk
10g jalapeño pepper
25ml soured cream

White Lies vocalist Harry McVeigh dons the Badge of Honour.

To make the dough, sift the bread flour and salt into a large bowl and stir in the sugar and yeast. Add the olive oil, then gradually incorporate the water into the flour mix until the dough starts to come together. Turn out onto a floured surface and knead until smooth and springy. Place in a clean, floured bowl, cover with a damp cloth and leave in a warm place until the dough has doubled in size, about an hour.

Preheat the oven to 230°C/Gas mark 8. Turn out the risen dough onto a floured surface and knead for about 5 minutes. Divide into 4 even-sized balls and roll out each one to a large round, the size of a dinner plate; this will create a thin and crispy pizza base. Place in pizza pans or on floured baking trays.

For the topping, heat the milk in a saucepan and whisk in the 1 tbsp flour. Gently bring to the boil. Reduce the heat to low and add the cheese, mustard, Worcestershire sauce and beer. Leave to cook gently for 4 minutes. Remove from the heat and set aside to cool slightly.

Meanwhile, divide the pizza tomato sauce between the dough bases and spread it out to the edges. Cover with the slices of pepperoni.

Stir the egg, jalapeño peppers and soured cream into the cheese mixture until well combined. Gently smooth over the pepperoni.

Bake the pizzas in the oven for 10 minutes or until the bases are crispy and the topping is golden. Serve immediately.

Australian purveyors of celestial electro-pop Empire Of The Sun make music that traverses the outer reaches of outer and inner space. You might imagine, then, that frontman and songwriter Luke Steele would choose for his favourite food something from the intergalactic cookbook: maybe bantha steaks, spiced krynoid pie, or perhaps a healthy triffid ratatouille?

But cosmic wonder can be found closer to home in the shape of the great American hamburger, the 1950s' harbinger of consumerism, rock and roll, and the very Future itself. 'The Americana aspect of burgers is definitely part of the appeal,' says Luke, also of woozy psychedelic rockers The Sleepy Jackson. 'You can't pass up a burger served by a babe on rollerskates. And Elvis was a pretty rad ambassador too...'

He loves the versatility of the good old burger. A quality burger needs love. The meat can't be dry, and your additions must be carefully balanced with generous sauce and cheese. 'It's the temptation,' he says. 'You know you shouldn't really have it, but once you've got your hands wrapped around that bun there's no going back.'

When he got his first gigs, they'd play at a bar for four hours and get paid $50 AUD each. After they'd bought some beer and filled up the car, there'd be $10 left for a 'kitchen sink' burger on the way home. 'We might as well have been paid in burgers,' he says. Now Luke is a well-travelled man and gives 'international patty respect' to quality outlets Burger Man in Sydney, the Five Guys chain across the US and Wild Hogs in New Zealand. At home he makes sliders – the bite-sized miniburgers that just slide down – for his two-year-old daughter, which she loves. 'They're cute and not too heavy.'

When he's not cooking burgers he specialises in Australia's fantastic fish resources, cooking snapper and gurnard ('But I've been making fish into burgers – fishgers'). And like Empire Of The Sun's music, his tastes do veer into the surreal. At dreamlike London restaurant Archipelago he had a starter of rabbit soup, a main course of zebra meat and then chocolate scorpion for dessert. It was all topped off with the nightcap called 'The Doctor'.

'A waiter comes out dressed as a doctor with a medicine case full of absinthe and other wild alcohols,' Luke explains. 'You drop a pill into a bowl of boiling water, and just as it turns into a plastic snake you have to shoot the absinthe. Very weird and original...'

Still, all of those chocolate scorpions and psychoactive digestifs can't compare with the best dinner he ever had, which came at the end of a lengthy US tour. He'd spent months broke, eating whatever he could afford, but finally he walked into his parents' house and smelled a succulent lamb roast sizzling in the oven. They served it with all the trimmings – cauliflower cheese, butter-fried potatoes, sweet pumpkin, gravy, mint sauce, crisp white wine – and there was apple crumble and vanilla ice cream for dessert. And Luke Steele was finally back on Planet Earth.

LUKE STEELE of EMPIRE OF THE SUN *loves* BURGERS

Burger & Truffle Mayonnaise

serves 4

2 tbsp olive oil
2 shallots, peeled and finely chopped
2 garlic cloves, peeled and crushed
1kg lean minced beef
2 tbsp fresh flat leaf parsley, finely chopped
2 tsp Dijon mustard
1 tsp Worcestershire sauce
sea salt and freshly ground black pepper
½ tsp dried chilli flakes
1 large egg, beaten
8 rashers bacon, derinded
4 brioche burger buns, split in half
4 slices Gruyère cheese
lime wedges, to serve

for the truffle mayonnaise

1 small black truffle
2 tbsp good-quality mayonnaise

Heat 1 tbsp of the olive oil in a frying pan over a medium heat. Add the shallots and sauté for a few minutes, then add the garlic and sauté for another minute or so. Remove from the heat and set aside to cool.

In a large bowl, gently mix together the beef, parsley, mustard, Worcestershire sauce, salt, pepper, chilli flakes, shallots and garlic until well combined. Finally mix in the beaten egg.

Divide the mixture into four portions. Shape into burgers, place on a board, cover and refrigerate for 30 minutes to firm up so they'll keep their shape.

Meanwhile, for the truffle mayonnaise, shave the black truffle into the mayo and mix together. Fry the bacon in a dry pan until crispy. Remove from the pan and drain on kitchen paper.

Heat the remaining oil in the frying pan over a medium heat, then add the burgers and cook for 3–4 minutes on each side. In the meantime, lightly toast the burger buns for a couple of minutes.

Put the burgers on the bun bases, top with the Gruyère cheese, crispy bacon and a dollop of the truffle mayonnaise. Pop on the burger bun tops.

Serve with a wedge of lime and an ice-cold beer.

'You can't pass up a burger served by a babe on rollerskates. And Elvis was a pretty rad ambassador too...'

'That's an actual jar of Patak's Bengal pickle relish. I eat so much curry my missus says I smell like a jar of it.'—***Rhys***

backstage at the V FESTIVAL

The Welsh rappers' main man Rhys AKA P. Xain explains why GLC go for the old skool flava.

'CURRY AND CHIPS is a great way of turning a classic into the food of the 21st century. I love sauces and spice, and you can't go wrong with potato cut up and boiled in oil at 200°C for 5 minutes. And that is an actual jar of Patak's Bengal pickle relish held aloft in the picture. Serious, I eat so much curry my missus says I smell like a jar of it. Chilli, ginger, aubergine, I love all the pickles. I'll mash 'em together, eat it with cheese and crackers and watch a whole season of *Dexter* because I'm too lazy to leave the house.

If you're looking for the best curry and chips, there's a chip shop in Newport called Vacara's, and another great one in Blackwood, up in the Valleys, called Lui's Plaice. For the best Chinese curry sauce, you should go to the Slow Boat on Risca Road in Newport. It's not open Mondays though. Newport is the gateway to many beautiful and wonderful places. Stay at the Knoll Guest House, it's right near the centre of town. From there you can walk down Stow Hill on to Charles Street, have a coffee in the Secret Garden Cafe, then go across the road to Diverse Records which is always worth a look. After that you can just hang out at the Job Centre all day. Most people do.

GOLDIE LOOKIN' CHAIN *love* CURRY & CHIPS

I like to make my own curry sauce too. It's not that hard to turn a good supermarket sauce into your own personal version. Add whatever you want to it, like apple, ginger, chillies or onion, then wazz it up in the food processor and cook on a low heat for 5–10 minutes. It goes with anything, especially leftover roast potatoes (always cook more than you need when making roast potatoes).

I go pretty hot myself. I get my chillies off this guy called Chris at a farmers' market. He grows his own in a polytunnel and I get about 10 different types. You can freeze them and just cut off a tiny bit off the hot ones and then bang them back in the freezer. I'm into Hot Diggity Dog sauce too. I mix it with ketchup – it's really good on everything.

In the band, Billy Webb and Adam Hussain are the real hot curry heads. I like a madras – I still like to be able to taste the curry – but Billy will have a phall curry for breakfast. He actually does! *And* I've seen him put fresh chillies on them. He knows no bounds. Adam can cook a good curry and 2Hats follows Madhur Jaffrey's *Ultimate Curry Bible* so he makes a good one too. Who's the best cook in Goldie Lookin' Chain? I am. I'm probably the best cook in Newport.

And I want to be clear about this: I love curry.'

Prawn Curry – in a hurry

serves 4

2 tbsp groundnut oil
1 red onion, thinly sliced
2 garlic cloves, peeled and crushed
4 tsp fresh ginger, grated
½ tsp chilli flakes
200g tomatoes, chopped
150ml water
300g raw prawns, peeled
4 tbsp garam masala
6 tbsp yoghurt
sea salt and freshly ground black pepper
handful of coriander leaves, to garnish

Heat the oil in a heavy-based medium saucepan. Add the onion and fry until gently browning. Stir in the garlic, ginger and chilli, cook for 5 minutes. Add the tomatoes and water and leave to simmer for 2 minutes.

Mix in the garam masala and cover, cook for a further 10 minutes. Stir in the prawns, simmer for 5 minutes and then add the yoghurt and seasoning.

Scatter the coriander leaves over the curry and serve immediately, in a bowl over some chips.

'The weirdest I've ever had? Strawberry sushi...' —***Taka***

backstage at the V FESTIVAL

Bass player Taka Hirose knows his stuff – he was born in Mizuho, Gifu Prefecture, west of Tokyo.

'TO BE HONEST I don't know why bands love sushi so much, but they do. When I came to London nearly 20 years ago, people in the UK didn't like the idea of eating raw fish. It makes me laugh 'cos it's so popular these days. It's true that the bands love it but they still end up at the kebab shop after gigs.

When I was a kid, we were told that sushi was for special occasions and we had to appreciate it. So, whatever I ate, I thought "This is special!" Sushi is simple, healthy and tasty. Obviously I love authentic sushi in Japan, but since I started to tour and travel around the world I've appreciated all different styles of sushi, especially in the US – and the way that people in different countries can create their own sushi.

But the best I've ever had was in Tokyo. My friend took me to a long-established sushi bar and this old chef made me an incredible Edo-mae style sushi. Everything in the preparation, cut, size and temperature for fish and rice was perfect. There must be more around in Japan so I'd love to do a sushi tour of the country. Anyone? And the weirdest I've ever had? Has to be strawberry sushi...

People outside Japan think that sushi is simply fresh raw fish and rice, but fresh raw fish is not necessarily the best for sushi. Proper sushi chefs know how and when is best to prepare the fish, and there are so many different kinds of fish that it's incredibly hard to learn. I have a friend who is a sushi chef and he told me he would be happy if he could have really great quality tuna two or three times a year. That means that even if you have ten years of sushi chef experience, you have the best of the best quality tuna only 20–30 times. A sushi chef needs good eyes for fish!

Where should you eat sushi? Wherever you see Japanese eating sushi, it should be good.'

FEEDER

love

GIANT CRAB SALAD

Giant Crab Salad Nigiri with Wasabi Tobiko

makes about 20 pieces

2 cups sushi rice
2 tbsp rice wine vinegar
1 cooked giant crab, freshly prepared, white meat only, shell reserved
good-quality mayonnaise, to taste
sea salt
4 nori sheets
2 tbsp wasabi tobiko (flying fish roe)

Rinse the rice well under cold water, drain and cook in 4 cups of water until tender. Drain well. While the rice is still hot, mix in the rice wine vinegar. Leave to cool.

Meanwhile, using your hands, squeeze the excess moisture from the white crabmeat; it should start to flake. Roughly chop the meat and place in a small bowl. Mix in the mayonnaise, 1 tsp at a time, until you get the consistency you want, then season with a little salt. Place in the fridge.

Clean and remove all of the flesh and other bits from the crab shell and then wash the shell thoroughly.

Cut each nori sheet into 5 strips. Using slightly wet hands, form the rice into 20 small balls and then flatten slightly. Wrap a nori strip around each flattened rice ball and seal the ends with a little water. Place the parcels on a plate so that one side of the exposed rice is facing upward, and the other is to the plate. Cover the top of the rice with the crabmeat and add a little wasabi tobiko to each.

Serve the nigiri on the back of the giant crab shell.

backstage at the V FESTIVAL
Ireland's answer to Scott Walker extols a sandwich fit for Elvis himself...

'MY DEEP LOVE OF the peanut butter and Marmite toasted sandwich is a curious thing, I know. I'm sure, like most food cravings, it has more to do with association than actual taste sensation. It dates back to my secondary school days. By the Sixth Form I was merrily defrauding my parents of the fiver they gave me every Monday to buy school meal tickets. This aided the procurement of booze at the weekends, but left me completely starving by home time. The situation was cruelly exacerbated by the 20-mile bus ride home.

It started with Bovril, a mug of which would often accompany a hastily prepared round of toast. I was just too hungry one day and simply smudged the brown yeasty substance upon the toast itself to save time. This revelation was soon followed by the addition of peanut butter. The thing people misunderstand about peanut butter is that it is not a substitute for butter! In fact there is nothing so fine as applying peanut butter to already semi-melted butter. The effect is moderately orgasmic.

From these two great achievements it was but a small leap of the imagination to the unified sandwich. And lo, it was a fabled alchemy!

In later, more animal-conscious years I replaced Bovril with Marmite, which only seemed to improve my creation. And it is my creation isn't it? Or are you reading this now and saying, "How dare he take credit for my Mar-Nut Butties?"'

NEIL HANNON of THE DIVINE COMEDY
loves PEANUT BUTTER & MARMITE

Peanut Butter & Marmite French Toast
serves 2

4 slices brioche loaf
Marmite, for spreading
peanut butter, for spreading
2 medium eggs
100ml full-fat milk
20g butter
freshly ground black pepper

Spread two brioche slices with a small amount of Marmite and the other two with a generous amount of peanut butter. Press a slice of the Marmite bread and a slice of the peanut butter bread together to make a sandwich. Repeat to make a second sandwich.

In a large bowl, whisk the eggs and milk together. Immerse the peanut butter and Marmite sandwiches in the egg mixture until well coated.

Melt the butter in a large non-stick frying pan over a medium heat. Gently lift the sandwiches out of the egg mixture and place them in the frying pan. Fry for 2–3 minutes on each side until golden brown.

Remove the sandwiches from the pan and drain on kitchen paper. Slice in half and serve immediately, seasoned with black pepper.

'There is nothing so fine as applying peanut butter to already semi-melted butter. The effect is moderately orgasmic.'

KP

Eliza Doolittle, THE POP PRINCESS FORMALLY KNOWN AS ELIZA CAIRD, ON HER LOVE FOR *baked beans*.

'I'm a vegetarian so my mum has always filled me up with beans to give me my protein. I'm a rubbish cook myself, but beans on toast has always been so easy to make. I eat it whenever I cook at home 'cos I don't know how to make anything else (*laughs*). I do like to cook the beans slowly then they get super-mushy and sweet, then overload some standard white toast with butter – you got to get this shit right.

I'm a Camden girl so I like to go to the Lock Tavern, Sushi Waka, Cottons and of course Nando's. I'm a home girl when it comes to food, and I love my mum's cooking. I'm a sucker for her Christmas dinner. Even though I don't eat the meat, my mum makes a yummy nut roast…'

BACKSTAGE AT V FESTIVAL

SUGAR OVERDOSE ALERT: BLUES-ROCK-POP QUEEN *Tiffany Page* HAS A WEAKNESS FOR *chocolate brownies with ice cream*.

'What's not to love about this? Ice cream makes me happy and chocolate brownies make me *super* happy. If they're on the dessert menu I'll go for that over anything else. Monkey Nuts in Crouch End, London, make the best brownie I've ever had. My favourite ice cream is Green and Black's White Chocolate. I like to keep it simple. I don't go for weird variants. I'd never fit into my jeans if I ate all the stuff that's out there, and I've never been one for too much sweet stuff anyway, so White Chocolate it is.

The best meal I've ever had? I had bread sauce with my roast for the first time ever quite recently and it was amazing. I was like, "Why has no-one ever fed this to me before?!" Can I cook myself? Only one dish, really: a Thai green curry, as of last week. Although it is *mmm*…'

Marmite and mash? KYE SONES OF ELECTRO-POP DUO *Diagram Of The Heart* EXPLAINS THEY LOVE WHAT OTHERS HATE.

'I've always loved Marmite as a kid and they've brought out Marmite recipe books now so thought I'd try it. And it's good! There's just something really comforting about it. I need a Marmite binge at least once a week, and it just makes your boring old mashed potato more interesting all round. Marmite and mash is the kind of thing you'd eat when you're struggling and poor, but even if I had all the money in the world I'd still make it. It's classless.

Anthony (Gorry, bandmate) is a great cook but when I cook it's more of a 'chuck everything in and see what it comes out like' situation. I made a cottage pie last night which was pretty epic. With Marmite of course…

Is it possible for a Marmite lover to go out with a Marmite hater? I think so. I've had girlfriends who hate Marmite and ones that love it. It's not the first thing I ask when meeting someone. It is the second, though.'

THE SUNDERLAND INDIE BAND *Detroit Social Club* LOVE *fresh fruit* ACCORDING TO FRONTMAN AND 'VIBE CREATOR' DAVID BURN.

'We're not really health-mad. Our first choice was the lager that was in our hands already, but we felt the fruit would balance it up. Our mams and dads could have seen that photo… Anyway, fruit's the easiest meal to make as well, isn't it?

It's not that hard to get your Five-a-Day on tour. Our standard rider has plenty of oranges, apples and bananas, sticks of celery and carrots to dip into some hummus. And then there's always the Bloody Marys…We're quite partial to a good carvery too, so that's about ten of your Five-a-Day right there. And of course there's always Marks and Spencer. Service stations have improved dramatically in the last few years, mostly down to the touring bands that use them.

What's the king of all fruit? Got to be orange. Makes a damn good juice for any occasion and sorts you right out for loads of vitamin C.'

NORTH-EASTERN EPIC GUITAR BAND *White Belt Yellow Tag* SAY A *gourmet burger* A DAY HELPS YOU WORK, ROCK AND PLAY. JUST ASK CRAIG PILBIN…

'The gourmet burger is a matter of preference, finely-tuned over years of consumption. My choice would be a medium-to-well-done organic homemade beef burger with a layer of Monterey Jack cheese, crispy bacon, ketchup, mayo, American mustard and a lettuce leaf. I once had an Elvis Burger that was laced with peanut butter; it wasn't good.

But when a burger is good it's unbeatable. The cheese steak-burger with fries and a Blue Moon chaser at Epstein's Bar (82 Stanton Street, New York) is the best I've ever had. And we're not burger snobs. We rely on the King when travelling up and down the country and we've forged a special relationship with the XL Bacon Double Cheeseburger at Trowell Services between Junctions 25 and 26 on the M1. As J. Wellington Wimpy said, "These are difficult times. Burgers can't be choosers." The burger should be the staple diet of any self-respecting musician – just ask Elvis. As Justin always says, "A burger a day helps you work, rock and play".'

backstage at the V FESTIVAL

The folk-rock-pop phenomenon on why she's devoted to red hot chilli peppers.

'I LIKE SPICE and I like beans! A vegetable chilli is filling and comforting but can still be healthy. You need cumin, apple cider vinegar, masa harina and you've gotta have several kinds of fresh peppers like jalapeño, serrano and a touch of habanero – if you like spice, that is. It's different every time I make it and maybe that's why I love it so much. I actually entered a chilli cooking competition once, although I didn't win…

I cook all kinds of things. Just this morning I made huevos rancheros and fresh squeezed orange juice, last night I made veggies with rice… I cook as often as possible when I'm home. There's a great farmers' market down the street from me in Ojai, California where I get fresh produce on Sundays. Ojai's a great food town. One of my favourite restaurants, The Farmer And The Cook, has their own farm. They sell their produce and they make healthy and organic Mexican food. I like Osteria Monte Grappa too, which is authentic Italian and real close to my house. I have the mussels and a glass of Casa Barranca pinot noir – it's a local vineyard.

I'm not entirely vegetarian but I do eat veggie a lot. I try to only eat meat rarely, when my body actually is craving it. Growing up in Illinois we ate a ton of meat and dairy. My mom would make cheesy chicken and rice with lots of cream. It's comforting and rich and it's still one of my favourite dishes although I've tweaked it to include broccoli.

The best meal I've ever had? It might be when my uncle took me to the Gramercy Tavern in New York. It's like an eight-course meal, really fancy, and everything was made just perfectly. Luckily I didn't have to pay the bill. Watch out though, they serve a glass of wine with every course…'

LISSIE *loves*

Triple Bean Chilli

serves 2

3 tbsp oil
1 red onion, peeled and sliced
1 red pepper, cored, deseeded and diced
1 green pepper, cored, deseeded and diced
1 chilli pepper, deseeded and finely diced
4 garlic cloves, peeled and crushed
100ml lager
400g tin chopped tomatoes
100g tinned black beans
100g tinned kidney beans
100g tinned haricot beans
1 tbsp ground cumin
2 tsp chilli powder
1 tsp hot sauce
1 tsp sea salt
200g bag of tortilla chips, for dipping

Heat the oil in a large saucepan over a medium heat. Add the onion, peppers, chilli and garlic and cook, stirring frequently, for 3–5 minutes until soft. Pour in the lager, tomatoes and beans and stir gently.

Once the tomato mixture starts to get hot, add the cumin and chilli powder, the hot sauce and salt. Simmer for 5–10 minutes until thick.

Serve hot with the tortilla chips.

Tequila Salsa

serves 2

500g unripe green tomatoes, roughly chopped
½ onion, peeled and cut into chunks
2 garlic cloves, peeled and halved
small handful of fresh coriander
2 fresh jalapeño peppers, deseeded and roughly chopped
juice of 2 limes
50ml tequila
1 tsp sea salt
1 tsp ground cumin

for dipping

tortilla chips or vegetable sticks

Place all of the ingredients except the tortilla chips in a food processor and pulse briefly until finely chopped; do not overwork. Pour into a bowl and chill. Serve with tortilla chips or vegetable sticks for dipping.

'It's different every time I make it and maybe that's why I love it so much.'

Jose Cuervo
Especial
Reposado

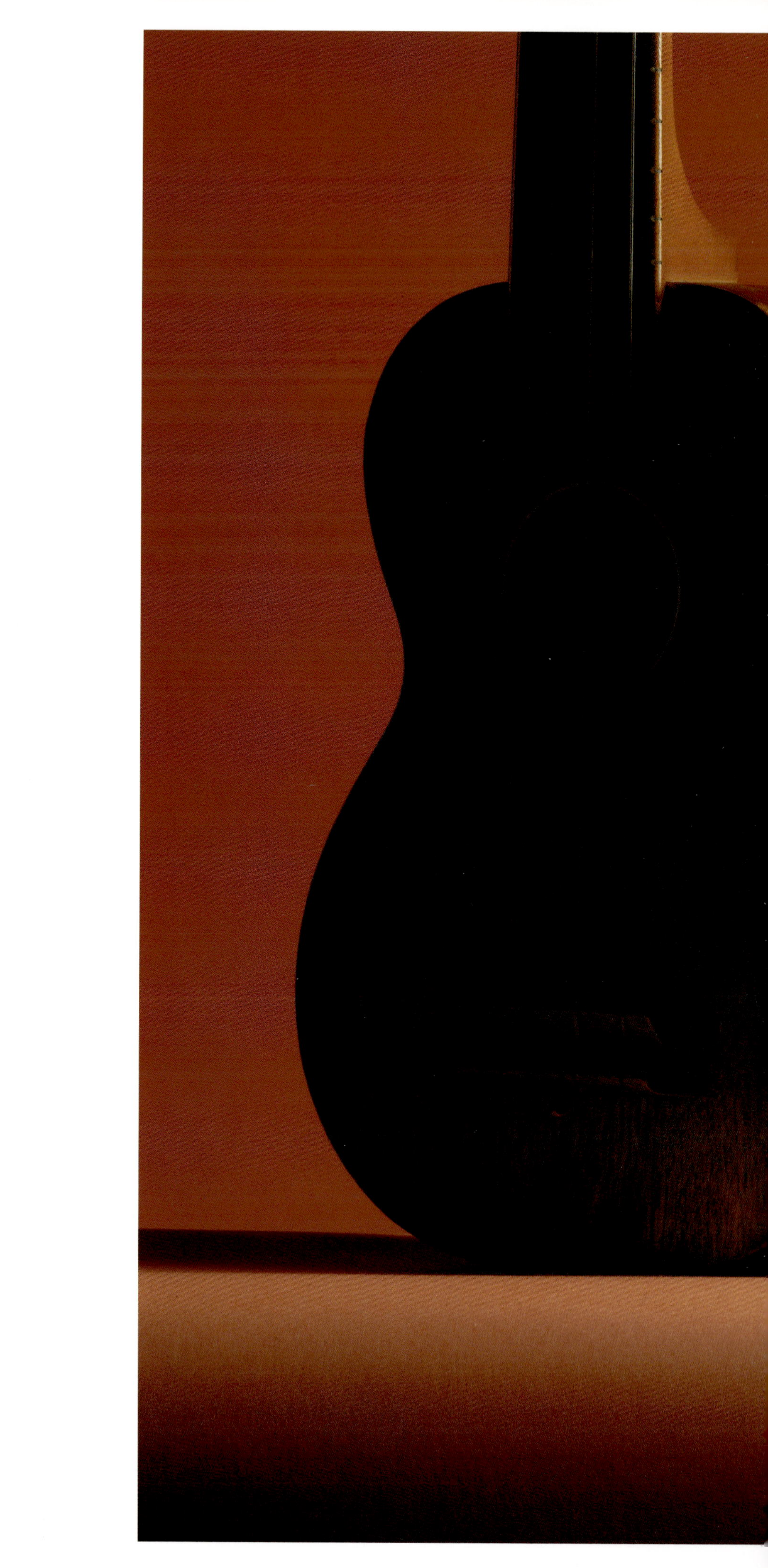

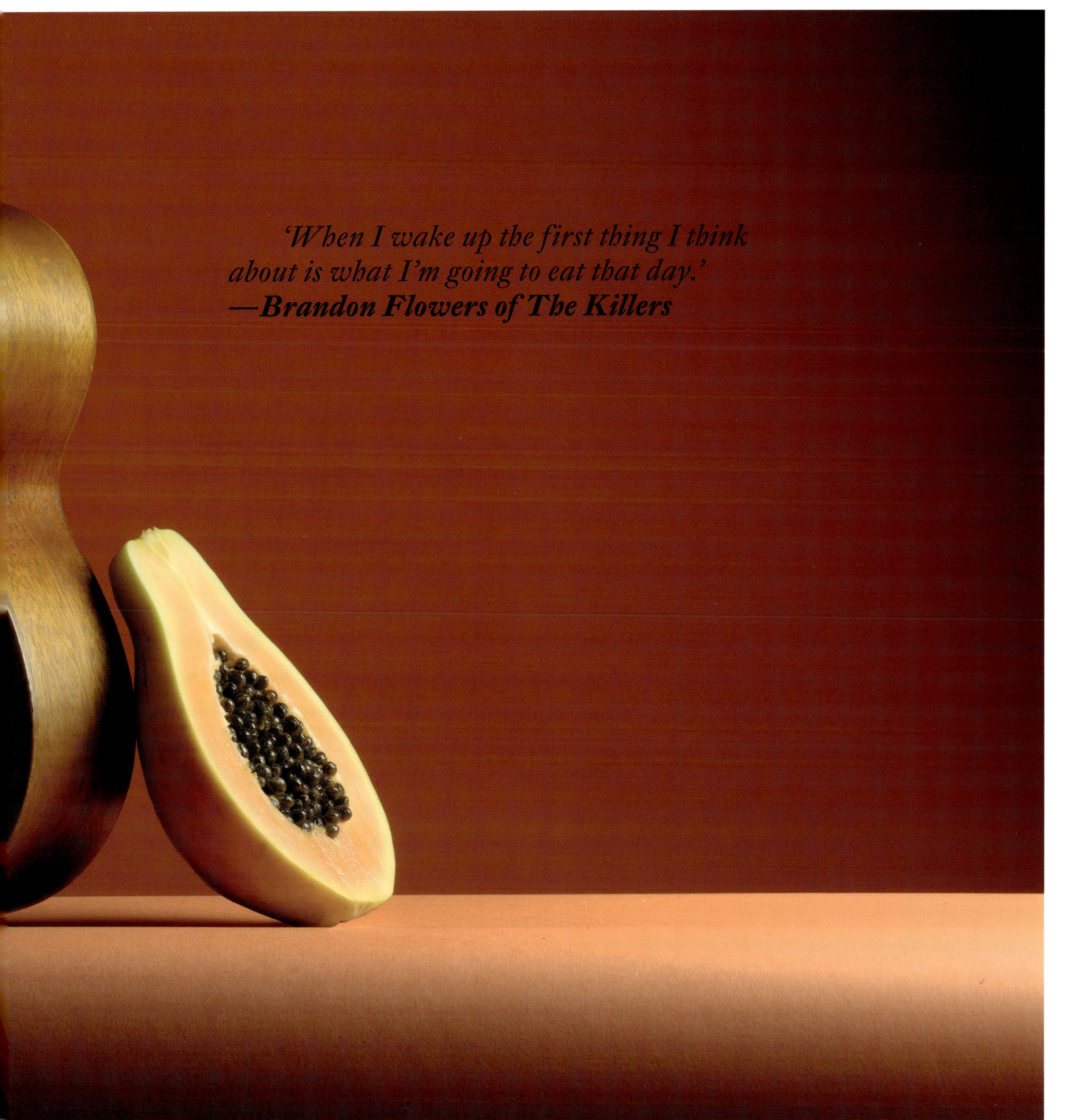

'When I wake up the first thing I think about is what I'm going to eat that day.'
—Brandon Flowers of The Killers

'I chucked peanut butter into pasta to see if it would work – it didn't. But that's how we discover what **does** *work.'*

'IT'S THE COLOUR!' DECLARES dreadlocked purveyor of left field, acoustic pop Newton Faulkner, with regard to his choice of the rich winter squash for his *Love Music Love Food* picture. 'I do eat butternut squash and I like it, in fact I eat *everything*. But I tried to think of a food that would go with me best, and I definitely have kinship with anything that's orange…'

Surrey-born Newton has won many fans with unique guitar-driven pop songs in which masculine geekiness opens up into surprising compassion and warmth. He is, he admits, an enthusiastic rather than an accomplished cook. 'I get a bit too experimental,' he confesses. 'The other day I chucked some peanut butter into pasta to see if it would work – it didn't. But that's how we discover what does work, isn't it?'

Newton wishes he was a better cook, and for a while he lived near London Bridge, opposite world-famous foodie mecca Borough Market. It was temptation on his doorstep. 'I just about managed to avoid spending myself into poverty,' he admits. 'There's so much amazing stuff there, especially the booze. There's a brilliant beer stall, Utobeer, that has some thoroughly evil, dark brews that I just can't resist. I'm quite ale-y and Porter-y. In terms of drinking I'm about 80 years of age, I like proper old man drinks: whiskey and dark ales and no fizzy lagers.' He's got a fondness for the Flying Dog Brewery's Gonzo Imperial Porter, which was named in honour of the late Hunter S. Thompson and offers a 'particularly evil' 7.8% ABV. Then there's the Belgian beers, the Chimays and the Rochefort Ten… 'Is it bad that I can talk more about beer than I can about food?' No. No, it isn't.

Actually he can talk about food, and with great enthusiasm. Newton becomes very animated when he recalls all the great places that his touring schedule has taken him. In Argentina he did the 'mega steak' and mounds of meat for breakfast, dinner and tea. Stranded in Hong Kong by the Icelandic volcano, he and his band toured the city's restaurants. 'Asian breakfasts can be a bit tricky,' he says delicately. 'It's a bit too textural for first thing in the morning. But everything else, I'm right in.'

He loves Japanese food and has visited many times. 'I've been thoroughly spoiled in Japan,' he says. 'Top-notch sushi, incredibly friendly people and at least one totally surreal restaurant that was beyond anything I'd ever experienced. There was dry ice everywhere, and you more or less have ninjas dropping from the ceiling with menus. It was Japanese turned up to 11. I felt like I was eating in a mixture of a Japanese pop video and *Blade Runner*.'

Back home he did the famous 17-course tasting menu at Heston Blumenthal's Fat Duck in Bray, including the infamous snail porridge. 'It was both hilarious and amazing,' he says. 'The snail porridge was just wonderful, so original and beautifully different. I do know how lucky I am to be doing this, and the chance to try different foods is a big part of it.'

In our picture we are also proud to present the rare sight of Newton Faulkner with a moustache. 'I don't usually do that,' he says with a smile. 'I had it for a week and everyone was like, what is *that?*' But every man must grow a moustache once in his life. 'If you'd waited 'til the end of the week you'd have seen it in its full waxed glory…'

NEWTON FAULKNER *loves* ANYTHING ORANGE

Butternut Squash, Almond & Goat's Cheese Rissoles

serves 4

1 small butternut squash
2 garlic cloves, peeled and finely chopped
1 red onion, peeled and thinly sliced
6 fresh thyme sprigs, leaves picked
1 tbsp olive oil, plus extra for frying
100g soft goat's cheese
100g fresh white breadcrumbs
50g flaked almonds, toasted
1 large egg yolk
25g plain flour
sea salt and freshly ground black pepper

to serve

crème fraîche
finely chopped fresh mint

Preheat the oven to 200°C/Gas mark 6. Peel, halve and deseed the squash, then cut into 2–3cm pieces. Place in a roasting tin and add the garlic, onion and thyme leaves. Drizzle with the olive oil and toss to mix. Roast in the oven, turning occasionally, for 30 minutes or until the squash is tender. Allow to cool. When cool, put the roasted squash mixture into a food processor and add the goat's cheese, breadcrumbs, 2 tsp of the toasted almonds and the egg yolk. Pulse until well mixed, but still a little chunky.

Divide the mixture into 4 or 8 portions and shape into balls, then flatten slightly. Roughly crush the remaining almonds and mix with the flour and some salt and pepper. Roll the rissoles in the flour mixture and place on a baking tray lined with baking parchment. Refrigerate for 30 minutes to firm up slightly.

Heat a little olive oil in a frying pan over a low heat and gently fry the rissoles on both sides until golden brown. Place them back on the baking tray and bake for 10 minutes.

Serve with a dollop of crème fraîche and a sprinkling of chopped mint.

Holy guacamole: Brandon Flowers of The Killers in Mexico City.

'I'M GENUINELY NOT just saying this because it's in the picture,' says Brandon Flowers, lead singer of The Killers, 'but if I could have any food of any kind, anywhere in the world, it would be these tacos al pastor right here, from this exact food stand in Mexico City. It's *twelve cents a taco* and it's so good that whenever we play in Mexico City we go to this place, like, twice a day.'

He'll order six or seven tacos and a bottle of Coke and he knows it will be just beautiful. The irony is, neither Brandon nor the rest of the band can ever remember the name of the stand. They'll just say, 'Let's go to the taco place' and their tour manager knows exactly where to take them.

As a Las Vegas native, Brandon was raised on Mexican food. 'It's kind of been adapted and absorbed into American culture,' he says, 'which I guess is what American culture is about, especially in the South West. Mexican food is a staple for us. It's always been in my life and I've always loved it.'

BRANDON FLOWERS of THE KILLERS *loves* TACOS AL PASTOR & ELOTES

But there are some things that haven't come across the border yet. You can't just go anywhere and get tacos al pastor – literally 'shepherd's-style' tacos – with chilli-marinated pork cooked over an open flame with onion and pineapple to tenderise it, much in the manner of the mighty doner kebab. Not legit, anyway. Or elote, a boiled corncob on a stick coated in mayonnaise and then rolled in cheese, with chilli powder and lime juice on it. Brandon goes into a little daze when he talks about these unparalleled street snacks. 'I've got to admit, I love food,' he says. 'When I wake up, the first thing I think about is what I'm going to eat that day.'

He can remember the first time he tried elotes, back when The Killers were struggling. Guitarist Dave Keuning used to live in a set of apartments in a predominantly Mexican area. 'We were very poor at the time and out in the street, tradesmen would bring carts of elote around.' Brandon and Dave used to get a piece of corn for $1.50. 'It was a feast for us, and so exciting to find something completely new. You can't get that at a restaurant.'

Many people think of Las Vegas as a shallow, transitory place dedicated only to gambling, but you can tell that Brandon loves his hometown. In the past decade it's become a magnet for great chefs because of the hotel boom. The fantasy city built in the desert has become a world-class restaurant town. 'That was just starting to happen when we got our record deal. They waited for us to leave first,' says Brandon wryly.

He eats on the Strip a lot but there are plenty of good places off the beaten track, like the Mexican restaurant Chapalla's on Tropicana and Pecos. 'Have the enchiladas verde and the albondigas soup, which is meatballs. It's really good, that's been my staple since I was young.' They just got a branch of Grimaldi's, the Brooklyn pizza legend where Sinatra used to eat. The original is at the base of the Brooklyn Bridge and always has a queue. 'I've queued myself and it is totally worth it,' says Brandon. But there are no lines at the Las Vegas branch. It's an entertainment town and service has to be fast and efficient.

Brandon should know. He worked as a bus boy at Wolfgang Puck's Spago's in Las Vegas when he was 18, and in a French restaurant in town. His first job, at 15, was at a branch of Taco Time. 'I do appreciate a good meal or good service,' he says. 'Las Vegas was built on that idea of service and it became part of me. It's all about hustling for tips and making people happy.'

'And if you can do that, you can be an entertainer.'

'Mexican food has been absorbed into American culture. It's always been in my life and I've always loved it.'

Tacos al Pastor & Elotes

serves 4

for the elote (Mexican corn)

4 corn-on-the-cobs, husks removed
55g butter, melted
60ml mayonnaise
65g Cotija or Parmesan cheese, grated
lime wedges, to serve

Preheat the grill to high or heat up the barbecue. When ready, grill the corn until lightly charred all over, about 7 minutes.

Roll the corn in the melted butter, and then spread with mayonnaise. Sprinkle with the cheese and serve immediately, with a wedge of lime.

for the tacos al pastor

1kg boneless pork leg or loin, very thinly sliced
225ml white wine vinegar
5 dried guajillo chillies
5 dried pasilla chillies
2 dried ancho chillies
1 tomato, peeled and deseeded
2 onions, peeled and finely chopped
6 garlic cloves, peeled
1 tbsp ground cumin
5 cloves
225ml pineapple juice
sea salt
2 tbsp vegetable oil
40 small tacos or corn tortillas

to serve

6 limes, cut into wedges
handful of fresh coriander, finely chopped
250g fresh pineapple, peeled, cored and diced

Put the pork in a dish, pour on the wine vinegar, cover and leave to marinate for 2 hours. Remove the pork and drain well.

In a small saucepan, boil the chillies in about 500ml water until soft. Drain the chillies, then halve lengthways and remove their membranes and seeds.

In a food processor, blend the chillies with the tomato, half the onions, the garlic, cumin and cloves until smooth. Add the pineapple juice and season with salt to taste. Heat 1 tbsp of the oil in a frying pan over a medium heat. Add the sauce and bring to the boil. Simmer for 5 minutes, then remove from the heat and leave to cool.

Pour the cooled sauce over the pork and set aside to marinate for 30 minutes.

Heat the remaining 1 tbsp oil in the frying pan over a medium heat. Add the rest of the onion and cook until softened, then add the pork and marinade and simmer until tender, about 15 minutes. Meanwhile, warm the tortillas.

Pile the tortillas with the pork. Serve with the lime wedges, coriander and pineapple.

N.B. The dried chillies can be replaced with 1 tsp hot chilli powder.

I fought the law: Dexter Holland of The Offspring with his Gringo Bandito Hot Sauce.

GRINGO BANDITO
BANG

'It's hot but I didn't want it to hurt you. My sauce is not the stuff you kill bugs with.'

DEXTER HOLLAND of THE OFFSPRING *loves* GRINGO BANDITO HOT SAUCE

When you've sold 17 million albums in the US alone, learned to fly your own planes and written working software for the Blackberry, you might be looking for a new challenge in your life. 'I was born and raised in southern California so Mexican culture and food were always a big part of my life,' says Dexter Holland, singer-guitarist with LA punk band The Offspring who are best known in the UK for *Pretty Fly For A White Guy* and *Come Out And Play*. 'Hot sauce was like a daily essential and one day I really did ask myself, why don't I have a hot sauce? The cosmos kind of lined up and it all made sense.'

Thus began a couple of years of experimentation, trial and error until he arrived at a recipe he was happy with. At first it was just for fun. He made little labels on his computer and gave bottles to friends at Christmas. But then people started to tell him that they didn't just like his hot sauce. They *really* liked it. 'I thought they were just being nice but they were like, "You should sell this!" So I did.'

An illustrator friend, Hugo Morales, drew a cartoon of Dexter for the label, 'I thought it would be fun to have a picture of me dressed up like Pancho Villa.' And Gringo Bandito sauce began to sell by word of mouth. It is now available in supermarkets across southern California and also online. Not that he makes a fortune from it. 'I'm not buying a yacht yet,' he says, 'It's a labour of love. But I do meet people who say things like, "Hey, I'm friends with Panic! At The Disco and they *really* like your hot sauce." To hear that stuff is just cool, it's nice. Metallica asked for a case for the tour bus and a case for the jet.'

The sauce itself is Mexican-style, hot without being punishingly so, designed to complement other dishes without blasting them out of existence. 'I didn't want it to hurt you,' says Dexter. 'A lot of people are like, "Hey, check this sauce out, you won't be able to breathe afterwards!" That's not what I wanted. It had to taste good so you can put it on everything.' On the Scoville Units heat scale, which measures chilli strength, Gringo Bandito comes up to a robust but tolerable 2,000 units, similar to Tabasco. There are however certain 'crazy' sauces that go up to a million Scoville units, he explains. 'Mine is not the stuff you kill bugs with.'

Gringo Bandito Hot Sauce Buffalo Wings

serves 4–6 as a starter

60g plain flour
½ tsp paprika
½ tsp cayenne pepper
½ tsp sea salt
24 chicken wings
vegetable oil, for deep-frying

for the sauce

100ml tomato ketchup
100ml Gringo Bandito Hot Sauce
100g butter, in pieces
3 tbsp honey

Put the flour, paprika, cayenne pepper and salt into a small bowl and toss to mix. Place the chicken wings in a large plastic food bag, add the seasoned flour and shake to coat. Refrigerate for 1 hour.

To make the sauce, in a medium saucepan over a low heat, gently bring the ketchup and hot sauce up to a simmer. Add the butter and melt, then pour in the honey and stir until well combined. Keep warm.

You will need to cook the chicken wings in several batches. Heat the oil in a deep-fat fryer or heavy-based saucepan. When the oil is hot, lightly shake a batch of chicken wings to remove excess flour and lower, one at a time, into the oil. Deep-fry for about 10 minutes until the wings are cooked through and golden brown. Remove from the oil and drain on kitchen paper; keep warm while you cook the rest.

In a clean bowl, toss the hot chicken wings with the sauce and serve.

Dexter cooks it up in a professional kitchen in batches of up to 200 gallons, with the aid of a Mexican friend called Florencia Arriaga. 'She's sort of the master chef,' Dexter says. 'When I was developing the sauce, she was the one who'd say, "Hmmm, nice but it needs more paprika." She's the sounding board.' They book time in a giant kitchen and cook up Gringo Bandito in huge vats. 'We're literally dumping in whole bags full of spices. It's amazing. And it's handmade stuff.'

As an aficionado of Mexican food, can he recommend any good restaurants if we're visiting LA? Javier's in Newport Beach is a nice upscale place with really excellent food, he says – a good place to take a date. On the other end of the scale there is El Tepeyac in East Los Angeles, 'It's the ultimate hole-in-the-wall Mexican place, it's like going to a dive bar in the worst part of town. But once you get inside the food is incredible, very authentic.'

Dexter admits he's not much of a cook himself. He's a macaroni and cheese, Hamburger Helper kind of guy. But you can put Gringo Bandito on anything and it will taste good. His sauce is, in fact, an example of instinctive, punk rock cookery made good. Once, after seeing a TV show about the arcane science behind the McDonald's McGriddle sandwich, Dexter wondered if a food science lab could help him tweak his sauce to improve the flavour. He found one and worked with them for a month or so… 'And it was terrible!' he says. 'Didn't taste good at all. It ended up being me back in my kitchen adding a little bit of salt and a little bit of chilli – doing it the old-fashioned way.

'But doesn't it always work out that way? DIY always wins.'

Atomic rooster: Richard Hawley with the ingredients for the perfect roast dinner.

RELISH

Spatchcock Roast Chicken with Smoked Bacon, Mushroom Soy, Marsala & Henderson's Relish Sauce

serves 4

1 free-range chicken, about 1.5kg
groundnut oil, for brushing
sea salt
1 tbsp Szechuan peppercorns, crushed
4 rashers of smoked bacon, cut into small strips
1 red onion, peeled and finely sliced
50ml Marsala wine
150ml chicken stock
1 tbsp tomato purée
50ml mushroom soy sauce
3 tbsp Henderson's Relish, plus extra to serve
2 tbsp arrowroot

Preheat the oven to 200°C/Gas mark 6. Using kitchen scissors, cut along the backbone of the chicken, then press firmly on the breastbone to flatten it. Place the chicken in a roasting tray lined with baking parchment. Brush with groundnut oil and sprinkle with salt and Szechuan pepper. Roast for 30 minutes or until the juices run clear and the skin is golden brown. Set aside in a warm place to rest, saving any juices.

Heat a saucepan over a medium heat, add the chopped bacon and fry gently for 2 minutes. Add the onion and fry until softened and browning at the edges, then add the Marsala. When it is gently simmering, add the chicken stock, tomato purée, mushroom soy, Henderson's Relish and the juices from the resting chicken. Bring to the boil, turn down the heat and leave to simmer for 5 minutes.

Meanwhile, in a small bowl, mix the arrowroot with a little cold water to make a smooth paste. Skim off any fat from the surface of the sauce. Now add the arrowroot a little at a time (you may not need all of it), stirring as you do so, until your sauce is the desired thickness.

Remove the chicken from the baking tray, and portion into four. Serve with the sauce.

'I poured the Hendo's onto my dinner and I just burst into tears. It meant that I was home.'

RICHARD HAWLEY *loves* HENDERSON'S RELISH

When was the last time a bottle of table sauce brought you to tears? Many years ago Richard Hawley – later guitarist with Pulp, then a solo artist who blossomed into our modern Roy Orbison in the 2000s – arrived home from a gruelling American tour with his band The Longpigs. He had barely seen his wife or daughter in nine months and mentally he was, 'like a sausage frying in a pan. I was all over the place.' His wife Helen sat him down and made him sausage and mash with peas, onion gravy and cabbage. Beside it she set a bottle of Henderson's Relish, the fabled elixir of Steel City.

'I poured the Hendo's out,' says Richard, an otherwise controlled and undemonstrative man, 'And I just burst into tears. I was home.'

Henderson's Relish is a Sheffield tradition. Any café or chippy in the city will have a bottle of this spicy condiment on the table. Richard says he's even seen local restaurants offering 'compôte de Henderson's'. When Sheffield United met Sheffield Wednesday in the FA Cup Semi-Final in 1993, Henderson's produced a batch in commemorative bottles: red and white for the Blades, blue and white for the Owls. Richard's own merchandise stall sells bottles of Henderson's after gigs, and to expatriate Sheffielders it is as precious as memory itself.

'Hendo's do a good export business with these huge tubs that look like they've got anti-freeze in them.' says Richard. 'The drummer out of Def Leppard gets it posted to him in LA. And I carry a card with me that says: 'In case of accident, please put some Hendo's in me instead of blood.'

'It's older than Worcestershire sauce and it's got no anchovies in it, so it's vegan. We don't say the "W" word in Sheffield,' he continues. 'There's a bit of a patriotic thing about it but at the end of t'day it just tastes rare good. On sausage and mash or any British food there's nowt to beat it. It's a local tradition and we're really proud of it. You wouldn't go to those extremes to get it if it wasn't that good. And if you don't like the taste you can always clean car windows with it.' He's at pains to point out that Hendo's may be ordered online at www.hendersonsrelish.com and sent worldwide.

Richard first tasted Hendo's at his granddad's table at Sunday dinner when he was maybe two years old. Now his picture's on the wall of the factory among the Friends of Henderson's Relish. 'Jarvis (Cocker) in't up there and he's always got a face on about it. I told him, just ring 'em up and ask!' Richard and his band were the first to play a gig at the factory, balancing on wobbly pallets and inhaling the aroma of the city's history.

For Richard, food goes hand in hand with good times and family gatherings. A Sunday dinner with everyone sat together was important because his family worked hard, his granddad sometimes putting in 14 hours a day at the steelworks, so Sunday lunch mattered.

'Families don't sit down to eat any more, but the point of a family is to spend time together,' he says. 'Food should bring you together. Proper family dinners are even harder for me now because things are so irregular in my life. The kids and our lass, they've got a routine. I'm the random one.' His children are aged 17, 10 and 8. 'You can spot when I've been on tour…'

He admits he's not the world's greatest cook himself. The kids know that if dad's cooking it will be pasta surprise, the surprise being: it's pasta. But he'll eat anything. 'I'm not a stick-in-the-mud, meat and two veg bloke, me. I've circumnavigated the globe at least 14 times and I've eaten all kinds of food. The only food I've ever struggled with was sushi. You can't trust any cuisine that comes with a hammer to make sure it's dead.'

Complementing the legendary Henderson's in our picture is a yet-to-be-roasted chicken, 'I love me meat but I fell in love with that bird,' says Richard wistfully – plus that other pillar of the Sheffield diet, the Yorkshire pudding. Someone once told Richard that the Pud was actually invented in France. He says they nearly got stretchered out of the pub. 'Let's leave that to urban myth, eh? They are ***Yorkshire*** and if you can make a good one your house will never be empty.'

There used to be free Yorkshire puddings and onion gravy on the bar at the Firth Park Hotel in Sheffield where Richard played his first ever gig on his 14th birthday, January 17th 1981. His dad used to run a little folk club upstairs during Sunday dinners. Anybody with a guitar could get up and sing. But Richard spent more time at the bar with the Yorkshire puddings than upstairs. His grandmother too was a dab hand at making the pudding, and unafraid of getting the fat so hot that it burned her hands when she made them. Her secret: refrigerate the batter overnight. 'Me sister used to have jam on them,' Richard remembers, incredulously. 'I thought that was rare wrong.'

Family, food and rock and roll – they are all about togetherness with those we love, and so they are all part of the same thing. Somewhere at home Richard has got a picture of his grandparents, his parents and all the kids sat round the table for Sunday dinner. Some are still around now and some are gone. The only thing in that picture that hasn't changed over all those years is the bottle of Henderson's Relish.

CLASSIC
Classic
FM 88 90 92 94 98 102 104 106 108 MHz
AM 54 60 70 80 100 120 140 160 x10kHz
POWER/FUNCTION
OFF
PHONO TUNER
BAND
FM
FM-ST AM

'I love the kitsch appeal of Americana...'
—Marina Diamandis of Marina & The Diamonds

That yolk isn't runny any more: Siouxsie Sioux with a luxury vegetarian breakfast.

In social science there's the concept of 'patterning', which suggests that once a sufficiently large number of people have placed you in a certain category it's almost impossible for you to get them to change their minds. By that token we should expect Siouxsie Sioux – formerly Susan Ballion of Chislehurst and since the advent of punk rock the Lady Mayoress of the Dark Side – to subsist on a diet of raw meat and red wine, if she eats at all. But no.

'Beans on toast for tea, that was my childhood,' she enthuses. 'You usually grow out of what you loved as a child but I don't think I'll ever grow out of this. The nearest I've got to making it a bit more sophisticated is to add some Worcestershire sauce or HP. I love pasta, cauliflower cheese, I love a beautiful mozzarella, tomato and fresh basil salad. And pizza – Pizza Express Fiorentina, or a Margherita with garlic and extra mushroom. I do *love* garlic. I love hummus. Waitrose hummus! You can't get it in France (where Siouxsie now lives), only tzatziki. I love eggs! Boiled eggs, fried eggs, omelettes, scrambled eggs, the full veggie breakfast…'

Hence her picture for *Love Music Love Food*, in which the components of the humble British breakfast meet Siouxsie's fetish aesthetic. 'You know,' she says, regarding a boiled egg balanced vertically on her upraised black vinyl stiletto heel, kept supple by the yoga exercises she's performed since she was 15,'There's an awful a lot to be said for simple British tastes.'

Siouxsie moved to South West France in the early 1990s 'because London began to feel too cramped' and has managed to find a compromise between her ardent vegetarianism and the bloodier French diet. 'It's all cassoulet and foie gras where I live,' she says glumly, 'which can be… difficult.' This means much cooking for oneself: smoked tofu with sesame seed and almond, chillies in carne or soya mince shepherd's pie. 'Real shepherd's,' she says, 'but no sheep.'

Siouxsie has, however, fallen in love with the local red wines, breads and cheeses – 'a good ripe, runny Brie with cornichons, mmm' – and the Armagnac brandy of the region. The latter proved yet again that the English and French are separated by more than the Channel when Siouxsie brought her band, who were then rehearsing in her 18th century farmhouse, for a tasting at a local distillery. Though their hosts were practised in tasting rather than swallowing, the musicians took a very British attitude and refused to waste a drop. 'It started off very civilised but ended up very *Ab Fab*,' she says drily, 'with English musicians reeling about all over the place.

Armagnac is lovely. It's such a part of the region that if you ask them for cognac they give you a terrible look. But it's a killer. There's nothing like an Armagnac hangover.'

SIOUXSIE SIOUX *loves* BREAKFAST

Granary Toast with Baked Beans & a Poached Egg

serves 1

1 small tin baked beans
2 slices of granary bread
butter, for spreading
pinch of sea salt
dash of white wine vinegar
2 large organic eggs (preferably 2 days old)
freshly ground black pepper

Three-quarters fill a small saucepan with water and bring to the boil.

Whilst waiting for the water to boil, put the beans into a small saucepan and heat gently, stirring occasionally so that they do not stick to the pan. Toast the bread slices, place on a plate and spread with butter.

When the water has come to the boil, add a pinch of salt and a dash of wine vinegar, which will help to bind the eggs. Turn the heat down to a simmer. With a spoon, gently swirl the water around the pan then break the first egg into the centre – the white will wrap around the yolk to form a perfect poached egg. Add the second egg straight after the first. Gently turn up the heat, keeping the water moving until the eggs are ready, about 2 minutes.

Tip the hot baked beans over your buttered toast, lift the eggs out of the water with a slotted spoon to drain off the excess water and serve on top of the beans. Finish with a twist of freshly ground pepper.

In the late 70s food mattered less to a touring punk band than drink, and the Banshees did not eat well. Siouxsie's decision to go vegetarian in the mid-80s was considered completely bizarre. She hated playing Germany in particular: 'It was all knuckle of pork and schinken. They'd put bacon bits on your salad and look at you as if you were mad when you complained, "That's not meat." "Yes it bloody is."' Today she sets her own schedule and eats better for it.

There were, however, the occasional memorable meals in the Banshees days. They found themselves in Hong Kong in 1982, guests of the record label, which took them to the obligatory fine dining establishment. Lazy Susans groaned with dishes that Siouxsie found inedible – duck, chicken, chicken's *feet* – but holding court on the next table, with full entourage, was Kirk Douglas. 'The real Kirk Douglas, not the son,' she says, 'with the real dimple! We were thrilled to bits.'

And does she remember what the great Hollywood figure made of the pale and beleathered post–punk band seated nearby? She pauses to consider.

'If I recall right,' she says, 'he seemed to think we were a right bunch of idiots.'

'You usually grow out of what you loved as a child but I don't think I'll ever grow out of this.'

The eating rifles: Coco Sumner dips for victory.

'The toast has to be mildly burnt. It's got to have crunch.'

THAT ANCIENT AD slogan must have lodged in the British subconscious. Coco Sumner – musician, model, daughter of Sting and Trudi Styler and now an electro-pop star in her own right as I Blame Coco – likes to go to work on an egg. 'I've had egg and soldier for breakfast pretty much every day of my life,' she says. 'I love it, it never bores me and it's healthy. It sets me up for the day. Three and a half minutes for the right consistency, and the toast has got to be brown bread, and "mildly" burnt. You really don't want a limp bit of white bread. It's got to have crunch.'

You might be surprised at such an unpretentious choice given her rock royalty parentage, but as Coco explains, she didn't exactly spend her childhood jetting around the resorts and fine restaurants of Europe. Born Eliot Paulina Sumner but quickly nicknamed Coco, she grew up in rural Wiltshire, with her younger brother Jake at home and three older siblings away at school. 'We didn't eat in too many show-off type places,' she says. 'My parents would get in lots of stuff from local farms instead, and I really liked that.' In fact, as a child Coco would eat only plain pasta and salad 'even in restaurants'.

COCO SUMNER *loves*

She started learning to cook when she was seven. Her first dish: eggs. Now she loves a proper fillet steak, 'nice and rare – I'll eat meat three times a day if I can.' She cooks every day, partly to wind down, and prides herself on her carbonara. She's just discovered oysters and has gone on a major seafood bender, eating clams, mussels, anything in a shell. Her album *The Constant* came out in November 2010 and the pace is hotting up for I Blame Coco: more travel, more meetings, more foreign places.

The record – a hectic synth-rock collection that sits between Friendly Fires and Florence And The Machine – was written and recorded in Sweden. When there, inevitably, Coco found herself eating reindeer. 'You do feel a bit weird eating this animal that's a byword for cute,' she admits, 'but it was *very* tasty…'

Soft-Boiled Egg, Soldiers, Beluga Caviar & Crème Fraîche

serves 2

3 tbsp crème fraîche
10 chives
4 large eggs
4 slices of brioche or brown bread
good-quality butter, for spreading
2 tsp beluga caviar

Put the crème fraîche into a bowl. Using scissors, finely snip the chives into the bowl, stir and put to one side.

Gently put the eggs into a saucepan, cover with cold water and place over a medium heat. When the water comes to the boil, turn the heat down until simmering and cook for 3½ minutes.

While the eggs are boiling, toast the brioche or brown bread and spread with butter. Cut two of the slices diagonally and the other two into soldiers and divide between two plates.

Remove the now soft-boiled eggs from the pan, peel and cut in half. Place on the toast triangles, add a dollop of chive cream to each egg, and top with ¼ tsp Beluga caviar. Serve immediately.

Biffy Clyro's Caledonian feast. From left: James Johnston, Simon Neil, Ben Johnston.

God only knows

Is this both the most Scottish and the most metal photograph ever taken? Stripped for action and ready to rock, Kilmarnock post-hardcore new-prog proper-metal trio Biffy Clyro brandish actual claymores upon which are impaled haggis – a sheep's stomach stuffed with heart, liver and lungs plus onion, oatmeal and seasoning: how metal is that?... plus their natural accompaniments – neeps and tatties – known among Sassenachs as swede and potatoes.

These are the components of the traditional Burns' Night supper and the diet on which Caledonia will surely one day rise up and be a nation once more. Haggis is so metal that it cannot be imported into the United States (regarding food with sheep's lungs in it, America is *feart*). Not for the fainthearted, haggis is practically a dish of mass destruction.

Biffy Clyro, what is the appeal of the noble haggis?

'Quite simply, it's the taste', says bass player, co-singer and co-writer James 'Jimbo' Johnston. 'It's just so moreish. It's spicy and has a great texture. It really isn't as unpleasant as rumours would suggest. And it's our national dish. We're proud Scots and we love any chance to live in the traditions of our culture. Part of the allure is the fact that most people find the very idea of it repulsive, and it's fun to rub people's noses in it...' Robert Burns' poems stir something in the soul, James explains, and none more so than *Address To A Haggis*, 'great chieftain o' the puddin' race!' Here Scotland's bard calls for gratitude for the food we receive, and respect for the animals we eat – which is best expressed by using all the parts. Hence, the haggis.

Having grown up in Ayrshire the three members of Biffy – James, his twin brother and drummer Ben, and singer-guitarist Simon Neil – always had haggis on

BIFFY CLYRO *love* HAGGIS, NEEPS & TATTIES

Burns' Night. They heard all the tall tales from their elders, including the one that insists that haggis is the wild offspring of the Loch Ness Monster.

Now Biffy seize any chance to eat their national dish. It plays a central role in Ben's 'ridiculous' two-plate breakfast alongside bacon, sausage, black pudding, beans, eggs, mushrooms and tattie scones. The band ensure there's haggis on the menu at least once a week if they get catering on tour – that's how you find out which crew members have an adventurous palate. And eating haggis expanded the band members' own tastes at a young age, which comes in handy when travelling. In Japan they had raw chicken liver and chicken stomach: 'the most unpleasant thing in the world', James grimaces. And in Estonia they had bear, which was 'surprisingly tender'.

But little compares with the mighty haggis. 'Don't get me wrong, neeps and tatties do have to play a strong supporting role,' says James, 'but if the haggis is hitting the high notes then it really doesn't matter.' Against the usual run of things, he recommends tinned haggis, especially from the small manufacturer Grant's not far from their own Kilmarnock home.

What is the most rock and roll foodstuff in the world, we wonder? Rock bands tend to have a taste for hot sauce, James says. Once everyone's had a few drinks, a bottle of hot sauce will appear and a competition starts. Biffy had a meal to celebrate mixing their last album, which ended up with a special weapons-grade hot sauce being liberated from a locked container in the back office. 'It got pretty messy. Combine that scene with a mechanical bull in the restaurant and you've got a fairly vivid picture of the evening's events.'

You need a strong stomach in rock and roll, even if it used to belong to a sheep. Biffy Clyro, we salute you, O power of Scotland.

*'Part of the appeal is the fact that most people find the very idea of haggis repulsive. It's fun to rub people's noses in it...'—**James***

Haggis, Tatties & Neep Timbale with Whisky Sauce

serves 4

¼ swede, peeled and very thinly sliced
100g potatoes, peeled and thinly sliced
sea salt and freshly ground black pepper
knob of butter
2 tbsp oil, for frying
1 red onion, peeled and finely sliced
4 large cabbage leaves
200g good-quality haggis, cut into 4 slices
150ml Stag's Breath whisky liqueur
2 tbsp demerara sugar

Place the swede and potatoes in a large saucepan and cover with cold, salted water. Bring to the boil and simmer until tender but still holding their shape, about 10 minutes. Drain, add a knob of butter and season with salt and pepper to taste. Set aside.

Heat the oil in a frying pan, add the onion and fry until well coloured and crispy, but not burnt; set aside.

Preheat the oven to 180°C/Gas mark 4. Half-fill a saucepan with water and bring to the boil. Submerge the cabbage leaves and blanch for 30 seconds, then remove and plunge into a bowl of very cold water to refresh. Drain and pat dry with kitchen paper.

Butter 4 ramekins. Cut out the main vein from the cabbage leaves. Line each ramekin with a leaf, making sure the outside of the leaf is facing down and covering the base and sides completely; leave the excess overhanging the rim. Layer the sliced swede, potato, onion and haggis in the mould. Fold the edges of the cabbage leaf over the mixture to enclose it completely and make a parcel. Stand the ramekins in a shallow baking tin and pour enough hot water into the tin to come halfway up their sides. Cover the tray with foil and place in the oven to steam for 30 minutes.

Meanwhile, heat the whisky liqueur in a small pan and add the sugar, stirring to dissolve. Simmer gently until slightly reduced and thickened. Remove the haggis parcels from the oven and take off the foil. Leave to stand for 4 minutes, then carefully turn out onto warm plates. Serve with a drizzle of the whisky sauce.

Marina Diamandis is a mercurial entertainer and the tastemakers can never quite pin her down. Is she an indie singer with an instinct for pop melody, or the most idiosyncratic pop singer around? Whichever, it's certainly true that she's the most successful Welsh-Greek crossover ever. Born in Abergavenny to a Greek father and a Welsh mother, she grew up in Monmouthshire and moved to Athens with her father when she was 16 after her parents separated. This, strangely, accounts for her fascination with American pop culture – and food.

'My dad was very traditionalist, very Greek,' she explains. 'He was quite against commercialism and American pop culture, so I've always been very drawn towards it – the music, the clothes, everything. I love the kitsch appeal of Americana and it was very much part of my look when I got signed.' Her music and videos definitely connect with the high-gloss dreamworld of a fantasy America. But does she actually like to eat their carbo-tastic delicacies?

'Yeah!' she replies. 'I'll eat at a diner three times a week when I'm in LA, particularly Mel's Diner. It's so trashy but I love it.' She has a soft spot for Mel's 'heart attack breakfast' of scrambled eggs, bacon and French toast, and, of course, pancakes with bacon. 'The Maple syrup makes it,' she says. 'We don't have it here, but we should.'

If there's a meeting point for Welsh and Greek food, it should probably be lamb, but Marina's less than keen on a meaty diet. 'My gran cooked a lot for us when we were in Athens and there were a lot of lentil soups and broad bean stews,' she says. 'And my mum, even though she's Welsh, introduced a lot of Greek food like *spanakopita* into our diets that was pretty healthy. Traditional Greek food is quite vegetarian, actually. It's only the modern diet that's full of Greeky meats. I'm not much of a fan of it to be honest. Too heavy.'

MARINA of THE DIAMONDS *loves* AMERICAN PANCAKES

But she still enjoys making the dishes her gran taught her how to cook, like *spanakorizo* (spinach and rice which you have with feta), plus *fakes* (lentil soup) and the green bean stew *fasolada*. She likes to bake and though she loves American food, she finds the routine of eating out every night when she's working there can take away the excitement. You should cook at home sometimes. Today she's on her way out to get fresh peas, for a pea stew. 'It sounds gross,' she says, 'but actually it's lovely because – secret ingredient – you put dill in it.'

'Cheese and vegetables every day,' says Marina Diamandis. 'That's the Greeks!'

American Pancakes with Bacon & Maple Syrup

makes 12

1 medium egg
300ml milk or buttermilk
1 tbsp sunflower oil, plus extra for frying
175g plain flour
2 tsp baking powder
1 tsp caster sugar
12 slices thinly cut streaky bacon or pancetta
knob of butter
good-quality maple syrup, to serve

Preheat the oven to 100°C/Gas mark 1. In a mixing bowl, whisk together the egg, milk and oil until evenly combined. Mix in the flour, baking powder and sugar to make a smooth batter. Set aside.

Heat a little oil in a frying pan and fry the bacon over a high heat until crispy. Place in the oven to keep warm while cooking the pancakes.

Heat a large non-stick frying pan over a medium heat and add a little knob of butter. You will need to cook the pancakes in batches. Pour in small ladlefuls of batter (about 2 tbsp per pancake), placing them well apart, and cook until bubbles begin to form on the top of the surface. Flip over and fry for another 2 minutes. Stack the pancakes on a warm plate and keep warm in the oven while you cook the rest.

Top the pancakes with the crispy bacon and liberally pour the glorious maple syrup over both. Serve immediately.

'My dad was very traditionalist and is quite against pop culture – so I've always been very drawn towards it.'

'The phall curry is mostly bravado, isn't it? It's lads egging each other on: "Go on, have the hottest one!"'

TONY HADLEY of SPANDAU BALLET *loves* CURRY & POPPADOMS

Spandau Ballet were Islington boys, but not the gentrified Islington of New Labour, Granita, million-pound terraced houses and destination restaurants. The band would evolve from kilted and fashion-forward New Romantics into the slick pop soulsters who made *True* and *Gold* but when they were growing up, their home area of north London was anything but desirable. Singer Tony Hadley laughs at the very idea that he and his mates would go out and eat together – not even for a curry.

'For us, at the end of the 70s, it was the kebab shop and the pub,' he says. 'When we were growing up, people just didn't go out to eat, or think of having wine with their dinner. You ate at home, you went to the pub with your mates and if you'd ordered even a glass of Liebfraumilch they would have lynched you.'

But in their own way Spandau and their club-friendly hits were part of the revolution in the lives of ordinary people – a revolution driven by such disparate factors as the explosion in British pop, the new leisure culture, style magazines like *The Face*, and even Thatcherism. In clothes, music or restaurants, the good stuff would now be available to everyone.

Prior to Spandau Tony was very traditional with food. 'But from the age of 20 I started travelling the world,' he says, 'and you can either be one of those artists that just wants Burger King or KFC or you can investigate what you find. I've always liked to try things. I don't understand why British people go abroad and then want English food. When Spandau started to take off, we were in the middle of an economic and social change. It was an interesting time for this country because music, fashion and eating habits all changed at the same time.'

He first tried a curry when he was 18 or 19, 'Before then, British people wouldn't know what a chilli was,' and it began a lifelong love of powerfully spiced food. 'I'm a hot freak,' he confesses. 'When I started on curries I thought a chicken korma was hot but I've far surpassed that now. I love a chicken jalfrezi with green chillies in it.' He won't quite go for the incendiary phall curry, 'It's mostly bravado, isn't it? It's lads egging each other on: "Go on, have the hottest one!"' But we've included a recipe in case he ever fancies trying it. And he can do a vindaloo no problem. Indian, Chinese, Indonesian, Mexican… he's up for all of it and he's always got a bottle of West Indian Ancona chilli sauce in the fridge. The last time he made chilli prawns he made a bit of a mess of it – too many chillies. 'I've always been over the top with everything.' He's even grown his own chilli bushes. 'I'm a bit obsessed,' he admits.

Travelling the world with his own band and with Spandau Ballet, who reunited in 2009 for a sellout tour, Tony discovered all the exciting food he could wish for. Eating Hong Kong street food was fantastic, he says – a real eye-opener. When he played in Bari they gave him a choice of a high-end restaurant or a café where the locals go. He chose the latter. 'Whatever the mum and dad and the aunt and uncle cooked, that was what you had, and they'd made their own wine too,' he says. 'It was just stunning.'

But it's the hot stuff that keeps him coming back. A few years ago someone from the record company took him out for a curry in Birmingham, to a very unpromising place underneath an underpass. 'It was poky, it was off the beaten track, it had threadbare carpet and it looked appalling,' says Tony. 'But to this day it was one of the best curries I've ever had.'

Bangalore Lamb Phall

serves 4

2 tbsp ghee
1 onion, peeled and finely chopped
4 garlic cloves, peeled and chopped
2.5cm piece of fresh ginger, peeled and grated
500g lean stewing or braising lamb, diced
½ tsp fennel seeds
½ tbsp cayenne pepper
200ml water
4 habanero chillies, chopped
4 serrano chillies, chopped
200g tomatoes, chopped

for the curry powder

1 tsp ground cumin
1 tsp ground coriander
¼ tsp ground turmeric
¼ tsp fenugreek powder
¼ tsp ground ginger

for the garam masala

¼ tsp ground cinnamon
¼ tsp ground cloves
¼ tsp freshly ground black pepper
¼ tsp ground cardamom

to serve

handful of fresh coriander, roughly chopped
plain yoghurt

First prepare the curry powder and garam masala, simply by stirring the ingredients for each spice mix together.

Heat the ghee in a large heavy-based saucepan over a medium heat. Add the onion and fry until starting to brown, about 5 minutes. Add the garlic and ginger and fry for another minute. Add the lamb and fry, turning, to brown. Mix in the curry powder, garam masala, fennel seeds and cayenne pepper, and cook for another minute.

Pour in the water and cook until it has evaporated. Add the chillies and then the tomatoes. Turn the heat down and simmer gently for 30 minutes, stirring occasionally so that the sauce does not catch on the bottom of the pan. Top up with a little water if the curry gets too dry. The curry is ready to serve when the meat is tender.

Serve scattered with the coriander and with a big dollop of yoghurt on the side.

N.B. Beware, this is an extremely hot curry.

'Musicians are highly sensitised to things that have a lot of craftsmanship in them... and cooking is one of those things.'
—Brian 'BT' Transeau

Knowing me, knowing ewe: The Kooks eye lunch. Hugh Harris (left) and Luke Pritchard.

In the days before muscle cars and weapon dogs, the Great British gentleman would assert his status by commissioning a portrait of himself surrounded by scores of children, hounds, horses, a plump wife and the bountiful fruits of his land. It is this particular vibe that Luke Pritchard and Hugh Harris of Brighton-born indie band The Kooks seek to resurrect in their ***Love Music Love Food*** photograph. They relax in a Huguenot house in London's Shoreditch with two unruly sheep from Hackney City Farm ('we wanted lamb but it's not the season', says Luke) and exude the confidence of Men of Substance – Luke dressed in Bill Sykes ***moderne***, Hugh in a more foppish outfit perhaps suitable for a future ***Doctor Who***. The air is alive with the aroma of mint. Perhaps this is what's making the sheep nervous.

'Lamb's the only thing I can cook and is my favourite meat,' explains Luke, singer and guitarist. 'I love it with mint, and I love the way it pisses French people off. You ask for mint sauce in a French restaurant and they just stare at you.' He and lead guitarist Hugh laugh. Luke has his own secret mint sauce recipe, passed down from his grandfather, and the band went back to his family's place on the Isle of Wight after they played the island's rock festival for, says Hugh, 'the most amazing Sunday roast.'

'Local lamb, that's my nan,' says Luke. 'Whenever you eat there she says, "It's all Isle of Wight! Everything on the table's Isle of Wight!"'

The sheep baa, nuzzle and make to escape. It's common for rock bands to affect vegetarianism but The Kooks subscribe to the circle of life approach: raise an animal, give it the best life you can, then kill it humanely and tuck in. Luke's family are farmers on the Isle of Wight – they now run a garlic farm – and he has seen animal husbandry first-hand. 'Meat is not murder,' he declares. 'Obviously animal cruelty is wrong and it should be stamped on hard. But most farmers do respect their animals. The problem is cheap food and industrialised farming, not meat eating.'

Hugh's family have a food connection too. His second cousins run what Hugh describes as the first fully organic cattle ranch in Australia. 'We're quite proud of that,' he says. 'I visited and we went kangaroo-spotting, which is the foxhunting of Down Under. You have to keep

THE KOOKS *love* LAMB

the population down, and they do it with shotguns instead of a pack of bloodhounds…' They're a world away from the faux-working class, raised-on-Tizer-and-Monster-Munch image that rock bands tend to cultivate. 'We're not posh,' says Hugh. 'The working class hero thing is a staple of rock and roll. But you shouldn't pretend to be what you're not.'

Fittingly then, they might just be the foodiest band to feature in ***Love Music Love Food***. The Kooks really like to eat. 'We hate it when bands travel to Tokyo and all they want is a burger,' says Luke. 'You may never see this place again! At least try the bloody food!'

Luke and Hugh have done China Tangs and The Dorchester ('amazing') and Jamie Oliver invited them to his famous reality show restaurant 15, which they loved. Hugh praises Les Trois Garçons, the sybaritic Shoreditch fixture, and Luke says he's in Medcalf on Exmouth Market 'at least twice a week. I love that place, I love their bavette steak, I love the fact that they always play Dylan records, I love the staff…it's brilliant.' They're wondering whether they can justify the expense of a trip to Heston Blumenthal's fabled Fat Duck. 'I don't know if I can stand having my palate raised so highly,' Hugh admits. 'Afterwards, everything else might taste rubbish.'

The Kooks also love to eat adventurously. In Japan, on Luke's birthday, they had the notorious puffer fish. Luke: 'Only four or five people die each year.' In America, they ate crocodile. Luke: 'With weird meats, people always say "Oh it's like chicken," but it really was like chicken. A slightly tougher chicken. Lovely, not swampy at all. I think it was a freshwater alligator actually…' In Sydney, they had highly-spiced kangaroo steak and in Verona deep-fried lamb's brains. Hugh: 'It was disgusting.'. They use phrases like 'gastronomically speaking' and they really know what they're on about. Here's Hugh:

'I'm quite into weird food, food that scares you. As someone who grew up in the West, eating that stuff is a real buzz. We went to Hong Kong and had what is supposed to be the best part of a chicken, which is the brain – right out of the skull with chopsticks.' Luke blanches a little. 'And it was a kind of creamy, cheesy, smokey, buttery goo of loveliness, like melted foie gras.' He searches for the right words.

'It tasted like a delicious cloud.'

'We hate it when bands travel to Tokyo and all they want is a burger. You may never see this place again! At least try the bloody food!'—***Luke***

How to Kook: Luke Pritchard in 'Bill Sykes moderne'.

Arabian Lamb Skewers

serves 12

1kg lamb mince
1 large white onion, peeled and finely diced
5 garlic cloves, peeled and crushed
2 spring onions, trimmed and thinly sliced
225ml pomegranate juice
4 tbsp olive oil (not virgin)
100g white breadcrumbs (ideally one-day old)
4 tsp cumin seeds
½ tsp ground cloves
2 tsp ground cinnamon
2 tsp cayenne pepper
1½ tsp freshly grated nutmeg
pinch of sea salt
8 tbsp red wine
2 tbsp cream sherry
4 tbsp currants
4 tbsp flaked almonds, toasted and chopped

to serve

flat breads
plain yoghurt
diced cucumber
finely chopped mint

In a large bowl, combine the minced lamb, onion, garlic, spring onions, 1 tbsp pomegranate juice and 2 tbsp olive oil. Mix thoroughly, using your hands, then cover and refrigerate for 24 hours.

Add the breadcrumbs, spices, salt, wine and sherry to the lamb mixture and mix well.

In a small saucepan over a medium heat, boil the remaining pomegranate juice to reduce to about 4 tbsp. Set aside to cool.

Add the reduced pomegranate juice, currants and almonds to the lamb mixture, combine thoroughly and leave to rest for 30 minutes.

Preheat the grill to medium. Use your hands to shape the meat into sausages and carefully push a skewer through the middle of each one. Brush with the remaining oil and grill for 15 minutes, turning regularly.

Serve the lamb skewers with warm flat breads and plain yoghurt flavoured with diced cucumber and chopped mint.

Mani of the Stone Roses and Primal Scream with some 'English soul food'.

'Sausages? They're English soul food, aren't they? And I'm an English soul man, so I love 'em.' Thus speaks Gary 'Mani' Mounfield of the Stone Roses and Primal Scream, player of unmistakeable heavy-duty bass lines on classics like ***Fools Gold, I Am The Resurrection*** and ***Kowalski*** and – for many – the man who taught the lolloping indie kids of the 1980s how to dance.

Bass and drums are often dismissed as 'music's meat and potatoes' by those who don't understand that rock and roll is nothing if it's not meaty, beaty, big and bouncy. The bangin' dancefloor hit and the Great British Banger perhaps have more in common than we admit. Why else has a huge free-range sausage in a wholesome hoagy roll become the essential food of the modern rock festival, an era the Stone Roses inaugurated with their own extravaganza at Spike Island on the River Mersey in 1989?

Mani has loved sausages all his life, so much so that as a kid in Crumpsall, Manchester he was even nicknamed 'Sausage'. Now, as well as a fervent Man Utd fan he's an equally fervent supporter of the best local bangers, from favourite butchers Littlewoods and Charcuterie in Heaton Moor. Or he'll venture north to acclaimed sausage-centric gastropub The Eagle in Barrow near Accrington. 'They make their own sausages,' Mani enthuses. 'They look amazing and taste lovely.'

'I hate all these conglomerates that are trying to put the little shops out of business,' he continues. 'Support your local butcher! You can trust him, he's part of the community. Mind you,' he admits, 'I will try anything in a sausage casing… apart from the donkey sausage we saw in France. I didn't go there, man. Big fan of donkeys, me.'

As a teenager Mani worked in an abattoir and for a while it put him off the untrustworthy corporate banger with its uncertain provenance. But then times changed. The Great British Sausage Revival of the past 20 years has warmed his heart. The limp

MANI of PRIMAL SCREAM & THE STONE ROSES *loves* BANGERS & MASH

and pasty, mass-produced pink extrusions that filled the shelves in the 70s and 80s have faded from view. In their place are affordable gourmet bangers in dazzling varieties of apple, mustard, chilli, sun-dried tomato…

Mani has a theory about this. 'Sausages were rubbish when we had a Tory government, weren't they? Then Labour got in and they became great! The moral is, vote Labour if you want good sausages.'

Food meant more than sustenance in Mani's family. His dad was in the Army catering corps and learned his trade from a proper Michelin-standard Swiss chef, 'a right bastard' who taught Mani's dad well. As kids Mani and his brother would help out their father at weekends when he worked in restaurants – 'we'd help him do the starters' – and for a while Mani dreamed of being a chef himself. Now he restricts himself to a simple repertoire: a mean Thai, a proper Sunday roast and a good full English.

Who ate what in the Stone Roses? Guitarist and musical architect John Squire was a vegetarian, though Mani says he relaxed later and eats a bit of chicken now. Singer Ian Brown loved anything Chinese or Vietnamese, 'He turned me on to Thai, did Ian,' and Caribbean food too. Drummer Reni, on the other hand, was 'the fussiest bastard I've ever seen in me life,' Mani recalls, laughing. 'Everything was on his banned list.'

The Scream, on the other hand, eat in a surprisingly healthy fashion given their reputation for excess. 'Bobby (Gillespie, singer) is a real sushi fiend,' says Mani. 'Whenever we're in Scandinavia or Germany it's sausages all the way for me and Andrew Innes. (Keyboards player Martin) Duffy is a down-to-earth feller, he'll eat anything, and little Barry (Cadogan, guitars) is a Vulcan… I mean ***vegan***…so he can't eat anything. Just a handful of hot gravel in the morning.'

As for Mani, 'It's not just sausages. I like everything. I'm the human dustbin, me, 'cos growing up I got used to having to clear me plate or get a clout. We don't do the nouvelle cuisine thing up North, you know…'

'Sausages were rubbish when we had a Tory government, weren't they? Vote Labour if you want good sausages.'

Sausages, Mash & Onion Gravy

serves 4

900g white potatoes, peeled and quartered
good pinch of sea salt
1 tbsp vegetable oil
8 good-quality pork sausages
50ml double cream
50g unsalted butter, melted
freshly ground white pepper
4 fresh thyme sprigs

for the red onion gravy

15g butter
1 red onion, peeled and thinly sliced
1 garlic clove, peeled and crushed
100ml red wine
290ml beef stock
1 tsp balsamic vinegar
1 fresh thyme sprig, leaves stripped
sea salt and freshly ground black pepper

Preheat the oven to 150°C/Gas mark 2. Place the potatoes in a large saucepan and cover with cold water. Add a good pinch of salt, bring to the boil over a medium heat and simmer until soft, about 20 minutes.

Meanwhile, make the gravy. Melt the butter in a small saucepan over a medium heat. Stir in the onion and garlic and cook for about 10 minutes. Add the red wine and reduce by half, then add the beef stock and bring back to the boil. Reduce the heat to a simmer and add the balsamic vinegar and thyme. Simmer gently for a further 15 minutes. Remove the thyme sprig. Season the gravy with salt and pepper to taste.

Heat the oil in a frying pan over a medium-high heat. Add the sausages with the thyme leaves and fry until cooked and golden brown, about 10–15 minutes. Place in the oven to keep warm.

Drain the potatoes, return to the pan and place back on the heat to let any excess moisture gently evaporate, about 1 minute. Take off the heat, add the cream and butter and mash until smooth. Season with salt and pepper to taste.

Serve the sausages with the mash and gravy.

Hello, spice boy: electronic musician Brian 'BT' Transeau with his beloved cinnamon.

US DANCE MUSIC producer Brian 'BT' Transeau helped shape the music that's his namesake – trance – with widescreen releases on Paul Oakenfold's Perfecto label and collaborations with club fixtures, including Paul van Dyk, Deep Dish and Armin van Buuren. He's also worked with stars as diverse as Britney Spears, Tori Amos, NSync and David Bowie. But he doesn't consider himself a DJ. With a classical background (he studied at the Washington Conservatory), he's more interested in taking electronic music into new realms of complexity.

His choice of favourite food, though, springs from an instinctive reaction and a surge of memory. 'Cinnamon's more than a food, it's my favourite smell,' he says. 'It reminds me of my mom cooking when I was a kid, of us baking together, of a time with my grandma… And the holidays too: the smell of Christmas and cinnamon brooms, Christmas cookies, a lot of really good childhood stuff. It's gone through my entire life with me.' A couple of years ago he and his daughter went to Vietnam and visited the Night Market where they bought an entire bag of rolled-up cinnamon bark. They slowly worked their way through it, and it's a lot better than the cinnamon you get in shops, a sweet bark that you can literally chew.

BT grew up in Maryland and had 'a pretty broad palate as a kid'. He was raised in a largely matriarchal household, with his mother, grandmother and aunt. Cooking was a big part of life. 'It's still important to me to have family mealtimes,' he says. 'Food is something to be enjoyed together, to talk about the day with the people you love.' And he does think there's an affinity between music making and cooking – that one kind of mixing lends itself to another. 'Things like compression or EQ are very much akin to seasoning, and choosing instruments or sounds is a lot like choosing your ingredients,' he says. 'Musicians are often highly sensitised to things that have a lot of craftsmanship in them, like fine woodwork or painting, and cooking is one of those things. If you're drawn to auditory balance you may be drawn to balance in other senses.'

Unsurprisingly, the sensually oriented Mr Transeau waxes very lyrical on the subject of his favourite restaurants. One is the unassuming Sushi Nozawa in the Valley in Los Angeles, also a favourite of *Love Music Love Food* participant and record producer Flood. Nozawa is ordinary looking and inexpensive, but there's frequently a queue out of the door for lunch. There's no menu and the sign on the wall says: 'Special Of The Day: Trust Me.'

'It's kind of notorious,' says BT, 'because celebrities get thrown out for talking on their cellphones. Chef Nozawa will take your plate away, tell you, 'Thank you for coming,' his wife will escort you out and you're never allowed in again. I literally have had nightmares about being banned from Nozawa because it is Japanese food that will make you weep.' And he tells an almost certainly libellous story about how he saw an A-list Hollywood actor being ejected exactly like that.

Then there's Sotto Sotto in Toronto, which is 'better than the best Italian food I've had anywhere. They have Canadian delicacies like ice wine there but the gnocchi and the pastas are absolutely exceptional.' And there's an Argentinian restaurant in Amsterdam called Bastille where the food is very simple, just baked potato and chicken, 'but it's second only to Nozawa as the best-prepared food I've ever had.'

But the overall best meal he ever had was in India, in a 'nondescript' restaurant in Mumbai. The place didn't look like much and something about the menu told him that these were somebody's grandmother's recipes. They had dhal, saag paneer, rice and butter chicken with cardamom and cashews… 'And literally every bite we took it was like, my God, how did they make this?' It was, as the best stuff often is, somebody's mother's cooking.

BT *loves* CINNAMON

Quince & Cinnamon Raita

serves 4

500ml plain yoghurt
2 quinces, peeled and grated
1 garlic clove, peeled and crushed
1 tsp ground cinnamon
6 fresh coriander sprigs, finely chopped
pinch of sea salt

Mix all the ingredients together in a small bowl and chill for 2 hours. Serve with your favourite curry.

'It's my favourite smell and it summons up a lot of really good childhood stuff. Cinnamon has gone through my entire life with me.'

V V BROWN *loves* MARMITE

ADMIT IT, WE'VE all wondered. If Marmite will spread on toast, will it also spread on other things? For British soul-pop minx and self-confessed Marmite fiend Vanessa 'V V' Brown – who has been enjoying the vitamin-rich yeast-extract spread since she was five, when she used to dunk her Marmite toast in her breakfast egg – the *Love Music Love Food* picture is something of a dream come true.

'I thought it would be fun,' she says. 'It's a gorgeous gooey substance, it almost feels like a moisturiser or an exfoliant. I was quite turned on by it actually!' She starts laughing and explains how the Marmite sort of solidifies on your skin. You don't realise how heavy and hard it will get. 'Every couple should give it a try,' she smiles. 'Marmite will definitely spice up the bedroom. You either love it or hate it, don't you? There's no other food that polarises people like Marmite.'

Her second choice was spinach. She's not much of a vegetable fan but spinach works for her, and helps with her mild anaemia. V V's mother is Jamaican, her father Puerto Rican, and in the Caribbean kitchen the local spinach variant callaloo goes with bacon to accompany the classic ackee and saltfish. 'Very healthy and hearty,' says V V. 'We used to have it around Christmas.' Try as we might, we couldn't combine Marmite and spinach. But perhaps V V could.

'My boyfriend says I'm a bit of a jazz cook,' she admits, 'I tend to experiment and just chuck everything in. You don't know what you'll get 'til you try.' Her successes include chilli'd sweet potatoes, glazing a lamb joint with chilli sauce with wine ('really nice!') and putting cous cous in a pineapple, then refrigerating it overnight. 'In the morning you get pineapple-flavoured cous cous in its own little bowl.' Among her disasters: salad cream on mince. 'It went hard in the fridge and looked disgusting,' she says glumly. Oh well. Nothing ventured.

Vanessa's mum and dad ran a school in Northampton, and the dinner lady was her Auntie Corinne who would cook fish and chips but also Caribbean food and the occasional Chinese. 'Much better than ordinary school dinners,' says V V proudly. Something of a musical prodigy, V V was courted by music managers and labels when she was as young as 15. At 19 she signed a deal that led to frustrating years trying to make it in the Los Angeles music world.

Marmite & Red Onion Scones

makes 8

75g butter
1 red onion, peeled and finely diced
180g self-raising flour, plus extra for dusting
100g wholemeal flour
1 tsp baking powder
1 tbsp Marmite
1 medium egg
2 tbsp plain yoghurt
3 tbsp milk, plus extra for brushing

Preheat the oven to 190°C/Gas mark 5. Melt 50g of the butter in a frying pan over a medium heat and gently fry the onion until soft. Set aside to cool.

Mix the flours and baking powder together in a large bowl, then rub in the remaining 25g butter using your fingertips until the mixture resembles breadcrumbs. Make a well in the centre.

In a separate bowl, whisk together the remaining ingredients, making sure that the Marmite and egg are well mixed into the milk and yoghurt. Pour into the well in the flour, add the cooled onion and mix together just until evenly combined, adding a little more milk if the mixture is too dry.

Turn out onto a floured surface and gently roll out until the dough is about 3cm thick. Using a scone cutter, cut out 8 rounds and place on a floured baking sheet. Score the tops with a sharp knife and brush with milk. Bake for 15–20 minutes until golden.

Cool on a wire rack. Best eaten warm.

'When I lived in America I truly, truly missed British food,' she says 'The portions are just too big, the chemicals... I became a bit afraid of food, to be honest. And you can't get tea! I used to carry PG Tips in my handbag wherever I went.'

After she returned to the UK, good honest from-the-ground-up gigging and songwriting finally kickstarted her career. She's modelled for M&S and, ironically, her album *Travelling Like The Light* became a hit in America. Now she can enjoy 'good old fashioned American diner food' omelettes and scrambled eggs.

'But I'm a simple girl,' she says. 'I don't like flashy restaurants and the people I work with know I'm not the Nobu girl.' She prefers quiet Thai or Japanese places, or a 'gorgeous' little place in Greenwich Village, New York, where her dinner is still lodged in her memory: fried mushroom starter, scallops with cauliflower, gorgeous bread with sun-dried tomatoes and a crème brûlée. 'There was maybe fifteen people in the restaurant and it was like home cooking, really cute and cosy,' she says. 'Just what I like.' And the best thing she's ever eaten? She's not joking, she says: it was her boyfriend's omelette just yesterday. It had salmon and onions in it and V V doesn't know what he did but 'it tasted like space food or something, *loads* better than it should have.'

You travel all over the world, and you go to all these fancy restaurants, and it's exciting and amazing. 'But you really, really miss home,' she says, 'and home cooking most of all.'

'Every couple should give it a try. Marmite will definitely spice up the bedroom!'

London-born DJ Paul Oakenfold has a strong claim to being the most pioneering figure in dance music. A funk and soul addict who helped hip hop to invade Britain as agent for Run DMC and the Beastie Boys in the mid-80s, he was also instrumental in triggering the acid house explosion at his London rave club Spectrum in the late 80s. As dance music grew to a worldwide phenomenon, 'Oakey' became producer-remixer to U2, Happy Mondays, Massive Attack and many more – and the first and biggest of the 'superstar DJs', playing in Europe, the Far East and the USA to audiences of thousands.

Now Paul lives in Los Angeles and he's cut down on his DJ-ing in favour of working on music for movies. Does this Chelsea FC fan miss home at all? 'Nah, I probably watch more Premiership games live than you do in England,' he says. 'We get 'em all here. And there are plenty of English restaurants and pubs. It's easy to get a good roast dinner in LA.'

Yes, the English roast – touchstone for the British expatriate and time-capsule of memory. 'For most of us who grew up in England it's arguably our favourite dinner,' says Paul. 'It's all about the ritual of it, the great food, the family being together on a Sunday. Life has got busier as the years have gone by but it's important to sit down and talk.'

The world-travelling elite DJ lifestyle kept his taste for good food alive, particularly Brazilian and Argentinian meat. In London his favourite restaurants are The Ivy and Simpson's on the Strand ('the perfect place for a roast dinner') and further afield he tries to visit Little India in Singapore if he's ever playing there. 'It's the district where all the Indians settled and it's been there hundreds of years,' he says. 'It's an institution – arguably the best curry in the world.' He's also interested in food politics and recommends the movie *Food Inc.* for an insight into what gets on your plate, and how it gets there. But the best meal he's ever had?

'It's got to be my mum's roast dinner,' he says. 'Otherwise I'll get a slap round the head.'

PAUL OAKENFOLD *loves*
A TRADITIONAL ENGLISH ROAST & A BOTTLE OF PERRIER JOUET

He grew up in a working class family. Dad delivered London's now-vanished daily paper the *Evening News* and mum worked for British Telecom. ('She was behind the scenes. She did everything but answer the phones.') When he was 15 Paul played in the traditional 'dodgy band' that every teenager dreams will make him famous, but his mum insisted he got a trade. Paul's gran was a cook so he gave that a go.

'I'm a qualified chef, I studied at Westminster Tech,' he says proudly. Meat and fish, main courses, pastry, practical and theory, he did the lot. Then he got a job with caterers J Lyons, working at establishment restaurants like the Army and Navy Club on Pall Mall. 'I really enjoyed the outside catering day trips,' he says. 'I did Wimbledon, Formula One… it was really enjoyable.' He laughs at the suggestion that it has any bearing on DJ-ing. 'What are you actually mixing apart from a cake mix, eh?'

A lot of what he learned in catering has stayed with him. He'll cook a chicken upside down so the juices run into the breast, and monitor everything closely. 'Overcooking is the worst thing you can do,' he says. 'Nice, fluffy overcooked potatoes are OK, they're part of a roast, but your meat can't be tough. If anything, undercook it and let it rest for a bit.'

Traditional Roasted Rib of Beef & Gravy

serves 8–10

2.5-3.5kg well-aged prime rib of beef on the bone
sea salt and freshly ground black pepper

for the gravy

570ml beef stock
55g butter
40g plain flour

Preheat the oven to 250°C/Gas mark 9. Score the fat of the rib and generously season with salt and pepper. Place fat side up in a roasting tray and roast for 15 minutes, then turn the heat down to 180°C/Gas mark 4. During roasting the fat will render and baste the meat. Cook according to your preference: for every 450g, allow 10–12 minutes for rare, 12–15 minutes for medium, or 18–20 minutes for well-done meat. Check the juices: pink indicates the meat is rare, clear indicates it is medium to well done. When cooked to your taste, transfer the meat to a plate and leave to rest in a warm place for 20–30 minutes.

Meanwhile, spoon off the fat from the roasting tray, then add the stock and mix with the meat juices. In a small saucepan over a medium heat, melt the butter, stir in the flour and cook, stirring, for 1–2 minutes to make a roux. Over a high heat bring the stock and meat juices to the boil, stirring and scraping the pan to dissolve any caramelised juices. Then whisk in the roux, a little at a time, until the juices have thickened to your liking. Season to taste.

Carve the beef into slices and serve with the gravy and horseradish sauce.

'It's all about the ritual of it, the great food, the family being together on a Sunday.'

HOLLYWOOD
1
14
80
6
2

Welcome to the Beggars Banquet. Kasabian and friends pay homage to the Rolling Stones' classic picture. Clockwise: Noel Fielding, Serge Pizzorno, a nymph with an owl, Tom Meighan, Chris 'Dibs' Edwards.

KASABIAN & NOEL FIELDING *love* A BEGGARS BANQUET FEAST

'Who wouldn't want to do the Beggars Banquet cover?' says Serge Pizzorno of hirsute rock-dance ne'er-do-wells Kasabian. 'It is one of the great rock and roll pictures. The Stones at their peak, eating this massive, decadent medieval feast... ***That's*** what rock and roll is supposed to look like.'

Kasabian, standard bearers for the communal euphoria of true mass rock and roll, jumped at the chance to recreate this classic image from the dawn of rock's aristocratic years. In June 1968 photographer Michael Joseph rented Sarum Chase, a house in Hampstead, and covered its huge banquet table with vast quantities of food, including a suckling pig. He brought in cats, dogs, a goat and a mandolin to cement the image of the Stones as opulent lords of the rock and roll manor, far removed from the rat race of the 1960s.

'It was summing up the decadence of the era, and the darkness,' Joseph said later. 'We wanted to put across the Stones as these very powerful young men.' The picture became the inner sleeve of the ***Beggars Banquet*** album, and its decadent aspect turned out to be prophetic. The Stones' dissolute guitarist and one-time leader Brian Jones would be dead a year later.

In this homage to ***Beggars Banquet*** Kasabian take the same positions as the Stones. Singer Tom Meighan is an imperious Mick Jagger, guitarist Serge is Keith Richard (complete with mandolin) and bassist Chris 'Dibs' Edwards is Bill Wyman. Stepping spookily into Brian's shoes is their good friend Noel Fielding of ***The Mighty Boosh*** who – equally spookily – met Kasabian when they played on the same bill as the actual, real Rolling Stones at the Isle of Wight Festival.

Noel had arrived by helicopter ('the best thing I've ever done,' he says), landing on the lawn of Kasabian's hotel as the band were drinking Pimm's. After bonding over a round of croquet they went to see the Stones, came back, stayed up all night and played croquet again the next day. 'We weren't quite as good at it the second time,' Noel admits.

After the festival the Stones had chartered a private ferry – apparently you can do that if you're the Rolling Stones – and Noel stowed away in a car belonging to Jimmy Jagger, Mick's son, under a load of camping equipment. 'I got out and sat next to Ronnie Wood for the short voyage,' he says. 'That was the best weekend I've ever had.'

Since then he and Serge have become good friends, with the comedian appearing in Kasabian's ***Vlad the Impaler*** both on video and live, and the guitarist co-writing songs for Noel's next Channel 4 show. 'You do meet a lot of people when you're on telly or in a band,' says the comic, 'but some people you really click with. Serge is like that.' It's a heart-warming story! 'Our girlfriends are always saying "You're in love, you two..."'

Both parties admit they're not exactly foodies. Shepherd's pie is about it for Kasabian, says Serge – no sushi or fancy dinners, just plenty of crisps and beans on toast. They are more choosy with their drinks. Tom likes a White Russian ('cos it goes down like a chocolate milkshake,' says Serge. 'He likes his Nesquik too'). Serge has been going through an Amaretto Sour phase and Dibs is a beer man, with a fondness for skunky ciders and old ales with bits of twigs in them.

'But we're terrible with food,' Serge says sadly. 'We'll go to Japan and we end up eating spare ribs every night. We just want good hearty food.' Then again he fell in love with the carne asada tacos at La Taqueria in the Mission District when Kasabian recorded their fourth album in San Francisco. 'I'd go every day if I could,' he says. 'I was brought up on Italian food, that's my benchmark and I can eat that all day. But the Mexican food in San Francisco...' He struggles with his conscience. A good Leicester lad of proud Italian descent, he can't bring himself to say it. 'It's nearly as good as Italian. Nearly.'

As for Noel Fielding, he says his favourite food is butterscotch Angel Delight. Or cereal. Or chilli. Go on then, Thai green curry. Oh, all right, lychees ('they're like perfumed eyeballs'). Or that cup of tea he used to get at half-time on the coldest, rainiest November afternoon when he played semi-professional football years ago: 'That cup of tea has magical powers.'

It has to be admitted that being supernaturally thin is a big part of Noel's job description. But his dad is French. Surely that's a temptation into the world of fine eating?

'I do like French food,' Noel admits, 'but I can't be eating cheese, can I? I have to get into glitterball jumpsuits for a living...'

Waiter? One large order of goat's head soup, please. This lot need feeding up.

'A massive, decadent medieval feast... ***That's*** *what rock and roll is supposed to look like.'*—***Serge***

Pheasant & Oyster Sauce Gyoza with Ponzu Sauce

makes 12–16

2 pheasant breasts, cut into small cubes
4 shiitake mushrooms, cleaned and quartered
1 garlic clove, peeled and roughly chopped
2cm piece of fresh ginger, peeled and roughly chopped
1 tbsp oyster sauce
1 tsp sesame oil
1 packet gyoza wrappers
2 tbsp vegetable oil

for the ponzu sauce

200ml good-quality soy sauce
juice of 2 limes

For the sauce, in a small bowl, mix together the soy sauce and lime juice and chill in the fridge.

Place the pheasant, mushrooms, garlic, ginger, oyster sauce and sesame oil in a food processor and pulse until smooth.

Lay out two gyoza wrappers at a time and brush lightly with water. Spoon 1 tsp of the pheasant mixture into the centre of each, being careful not to overfill. Fold the wrapper over into a half-moon shape and press the edges together to seal.

Heat the vegetable oil in a large frying pan. Gently fry the gyoza parcels in batches for about 3 minutes on each side; they should be golden brown and starting to crisp. Remove with a slotted spoon and drain on kitchen paper. Serve immediately, with the ponzu dipping sauce.

Jacobean Game Soup

makes 4 pints

25g butter
2 rashers streaky bacon, chopped
900g game carcasses and bones
2 celery sticks, chopped
2 carrots, peeled and chopped
2 leeks, washed and chopped
1 onion, peeled and chopped
2 litres chicken stock
1 thyme sprig
1 bay leaf
2 parsley stalks
8 black peppercorns
3 cloves
sea salt and freshly ground black pepper
100ml port

Melt the butter in a large saucepan and fry the bacon for a couple of minutes. Add the game bones and fry gently for 2 minutes. Stir in the celery, carrots, leeks and onion and cook until all the bones and vegetables are well browned.

Stir in the stock, thyme, bay leaf, parsley stalks, peppercorns, cloves and some seasoning. Simmer for 2 hours, skimming regularly to avoid the soup turning cloudy.

Strain the soup into a pan. Strip any meat from the bones before discarding them and add the meat to the soup. Simmer for another 30 minutes.

Stir in the port and serve immediately.

Black Pudding & Fig Stuffed Belly of Pork

serves 6

1.5kg pork belly, trimmed and scored
25g butter
3 tbsp brown sugar
2 small red onions, peeled and finely sliced
6 figs, quartered
300g good-quality black pudding, diced
1–2 tbsp vegetable oil, plus extra for brushing
sea salt
300ml good-quality cider

Preheat the oven to 200°C/Gas mark 6. Lay the pork belly on a board. Using a very sharp knife, slice the belly almost in half horizontally; do not cut the whole way through.

Place the pork belly on a draining rack. Boil a kettle of water and carefully pour over the pork skin to scald it. Dry the pork with kitchen paper and place back on the board.

Melt the butter in a small saucepan. Add the brown sugar and stir until dissolved, then add the onions. Cook gently until soft, about 5 minutes, then add the figs and black pudding. Cook until the mixture is soft and sticky, almost the consistency of marmalade. Remove from the heat and leave to cool.

Heat the oil in a frying pan. When hot, sear the pork on all sides. Remove from the pan and place in a roasting tin. Open the pork along the slice made earlier and spoon the black pudding and fig stuffing evenly over the bottom half. Close together and secure with cocktail sticks.

Brush the meat with some more oil and rub liberally with salt. Pour the cider into the bottom of the roasting dish. Roast on the middle shelf of the oven until the juices run clear, about 1 hour, basting the meat with the cooking juices.

To crisp the skin, turn the oven up to 230°C/Gas mark 8 and cook for about 15 minutes until the pork skin is puffed and crisp.

Cut the meat into chunks rather then slices to serve.

'Food tastes better when it's just been hauled out of the soil'
—Alex Kapranos of Franz Ferdinand

Block rockin' beets: the cultivated Alex Kapranos of Franz Ferdinand.

ALEX KAPRANOS of FRANZ FERDINAND *loves* BEETROOT

Rock stars are fond of getting back to their roots, but it's a fair bet that few of them have ever felt the loam trickling between their fingers as they coax a nutritious root out of the good earth. Not so Alex Kapranos, singer-lyricist with constructivist Scots rock band Franz Ferdinand, whose picture for ***Love Music Love Food*** stars the humble beetroot. It is a tribute of sorts to his self-sufficient parents ('they were very Tom and Barbara from ***The Good Life***'), to newly returned ideas of thrift and good husbandry, and to rebellion against characterless and uniform supermarket veg.

Though the young Alex 'hated' helping his dad in the garden, he now grows his own vegetables in his back garden in Glasgow and beetroot best suits the lifestyle of the touring musician. 'You just chuck it in the ground and it pretty much takes care of itself,' he says. 'Food tastes better when it's just been hauled out of the soil.'

Like the hardy beetroot, Franz Ferdinand's music draws its nourishment from complex soil (and as is the case with the noble ***Beta vulgaris***, no two songs are alike). Formed in Glasgow in 2002, Franz Ferdinand grew up on the sharp and angular Caledonian indie pop of Orange Juice and Josef K and the thrilling rush of dance and rave music. They also reconnected to rock and roll's intellectual tradition, taking their name from the assassinated Austrian Archduke whose death precipitated the First World War and the look of their record covers from Russian avant-garde artists.

As the thinking fan's rock and roll band it is fitting that Franz Ferdinand steer clear of the average band's diet of McDonalds and Haribo. In 2005 Alex began a weekly diary for ***The Guardian*** in which he detailed what he ate in all the places Franz Ferdinand visited. Not that life as a globetrotting rock and roll food detective is perfect. On arriving in a new city Alex will head into town to visit the markets, drink in the local food culture, marvel at the artisan meats and cheeses… 'And then you can't buy anything!' he says sadly. 'You haven't got a fridge on the tour bus...'

The son of an English mother and a Greek father, Alex Kapranos grew up on a standard British diet enlivened by his father's favourites: 'We'd have a very ordinary British diet of fish fingers and lasagne but then my dad would come back from Greece with an enormous tub of really stinky feta.' He was famous among his school friends for delighting in unheard-of alien delicacies such as – of all things – olives. The family would visit Greece every summer. 'I used to love going over because of the way people ate,' he remembers. 'In Britain eating is very personal, but in Greece it's communal. You have huge meals with the extended family round a table full of food. I loved that as a kid, it had a completely different atmosphere and I loved all the flavours, all that garlic and oregano and olive oil, the feta and the tzatziki.'

The Greek talent for rich, complex, slow-cooked food goes back, he says, to the fact that many years ago the average Greek person would not own an oven. Instead they would take larger dishes down to the bakery, the ***fourno***, where the ovens would be cooling after the morning's baking. 'You'd take your chicken or pastitsio or moussaka,' he says, 'and it cooks in this slowly-cooling oven for four or five hours, and you get these lovely rich flavours of cinnamon and garlic all coming together.'

Alex misses cooking when he's on tour. Everyone needs some physical activity in their life, he says – something that you can lose yourself in, let your mind wander off to deal with its troubles. If you don't have those moments, frustration and anxiety ensue. 'I feel like that on tour,' he says. 'Coming home and pottering round the kitchen is how I deal with it. I like cooking but I don't show off. It's just good for you to cook for your friends. I don't like recipe books, partly because I'm not very good at taking instructions. I tend to find some ingredients, probably some fresh vegetables, and see where it takes me.' He was briefly a vegetarian, but not now. 'The arguments for vegetarianism are very powerful,' he says, smiling, 'but my love of meat is very powerful too.'

So tell us, Alex Kapranos: what should we do with our home-grown, hand-picked, cherished and loved beetroot?

'OK, these two are the best ways,' he says in businesslike fashion. 'One: apples and beetroot go really well. Just grate them together. Tastiest salad ever. And two: a simple beetroot soup. If I have a bowl of beetroot soup…' and suddenly he's a little rapturous, 'all is well with the world.' New wave, slow food.

'If I have a bowl of beetroot soup, all is well with the world.'

Daube of Venison with Spiced-Infused Beetroot

serves 4

1kg lean rump of venison, cut into 5cm cubes
100g streaky bacon, derinded and finely chopped
2 onions, peeled and finely diced
2 celery sticks, diced
1 carrot, peeled and diced
3 garlic cloves, peeled and crushed
1 tsp chopped fresh thyme
1 bay leaf
finely pared zest of 1 orange
350ml full-bodied red wine or port
2 tbsp vegetable oil
1 tbsp plain flour
250ml beef stock
sea salt and freshly ground black pepper

for the spiced-infused beetroot

500ml red wine
200ml red wine vinegar
140g dark muscovado sugar
½ tsp ground fennel seeds
2.5cm piece of fresh ginger, peeled and grated
1 red chilli, deseeded and finely chopped
500g beetroot, cooked and peeled

You will need to start a day ahead as both the venison and beetroot are marinated overnight.

Put the venison into a large bowl and add the bacon, vegetables, garlic, thyme, bay leaf, orange zest and wine or port. Cover and leave to marinate in the fridge overnight.

For the beetroot, put the wine, wine vinegar, sugar, fennel seeds, ginger and chilli into a large saucepan over a medium heat and bring to the boil, stirring occasionally. Lower the heat and simmer for 20 minutes. Meanwhile, cut the beetroot into wedges and put into a large bowl. Pour the wine reduction over the beetroot, cover and leave overnight.

Remove the venison from the marinade with a slotted spoon and drain, reserving the marinade. Heat 1½ tbsp oil in a frying pan over a medium-high heat and quickly brown the venison in batches, turning to colour evenly; set aside on a plate.

Heat the remaining oil in a large flameproof casserole. Remove the vegetables from the marinade with a slotted spoon and place in the casserole dish, reserving the liquor. Cook for 3 minutes, then add the flour and cook for another minute, stirring. Slowly add the reserved liquor, the stock and some salt and pepper. Add the venison to the casserole, stir to mix with the vegetables, then cover and simmer very gently until the meat is tender, about 1½ hours.

Transfer the venison and vegetables from the casserole to a dish, cover and set aside. Drain the beetroot, adding its marinade to the casserole. Bring to the boil and let bubble to reduce for about 6 minutes until slightly thickened. Return the meat and vegetables to the casserole and add the beetroot. Heat through and serve immediately.

ROLF HARRIS *loves* CURRY

'IT'S JUST MY ABSOLUTE favourite food,' says Rolf Harris – avuncular painter and art educator, musician, creator of the Wobble-Board, late-flowering patron saint of Glastonbury and international treasure in both hemispheres. 'My wife and I have withdrawal symptoms if we don't have a curry every few days.'

Indian food has become central to the lives of Rolf and his wife Arwen, who he married in 1958. They first started going to London's new wave of Indian restaurants in the late 50s, when curry was far from widespread, and they've stuck with it ever since. Rolf has now developed a connoisseur's knowledge of curry houses in their local Bucks-Berkshire area. They don't like it fiercely hot, they're in it for the endlessly fascinating mix of spices, and for Rolf a chicken tikka masala is about right. 'One of the many great things about curry is that you can find your own personal optimum level of heat,' he says.

health reasons, and Rolf remembers the first time he had even a slightly rare steak. 'I must have been 18 or 19,' he says, 'and I couldn't believe how good it was.'

'Australian food is world-famous now and rightly so,' he continues, 'but when I was a kid it was overcooked British food, tomato ketchup with everything, very, very boring and every day your dinner was exactly the same. No wonder I love curry now.'

It's a great irony then that Rolf seldom gets to enjoy perhaps the greatest Indian food available in the music world, at the food stalls of the Glastonbury festival. He first played there in 1994 and the crowd instantly took him to heart. His show on the Jazz World stage in 2009 produced a roadblock in the surrounding lanes. But his reborn popularity with festival-goers means that he can't take more than a few steps outside the backstage compound.

'Everyone wants to take a picture or say hello or get you to sign their programme,' he says, 'which is lovely and I do like it – but you'd never get anywhere near your curry,' he says, laughing at a fate worse than death.

When he's touring he's made it a tradition to take the band out for a curry after every date. 'We get the promoters to scout ahead and we're rarely disappointed because England is the world curry capital.' He admits he's no great shakes in the kitchen, 'scrambled egg is about as good as it gets,' but why bother when every street in the land offers the finest dishes on earth? 'My wife's addicted to curry,' says Rolf, although you suspect she's not the only one.

His love of bright, assertive flavours surely comes from his childhood in Perth, Australia, where – with the best will in the world – his diet did not exactly sparkle on the plate. Rolf grew up on the 'very traditional' English food of the years before the Australian culinary explosion. His mother and father were from Wales, and his mum's approach in the kitchen was 'to cook anything – meat, vegetables, whatever – until it was almost incinerated.' His parents were from an era when you had to cook everything to death, for

Murg Kali Mirch Poori

serves 4

200g strong white flour, plus extra for dusting
50g chapatti flour
1 tsp curry powder
1 tsp ground turmeric
½ tsp sea salt
warm water, to mix
vegetable oil, for frying

Put the flours, curry powder, turmeric and salt into a large bowl and mix well. Slowly mix in enough warm water to mix to a dough. Turn out onto a floured surface and work with your hands until smooth and elastic. Place back in the bowl, cover and leave to rest for 30 minutes.

Knead the dough on a floured surface until light and springy. Divide into about 12 equal-sized pieces and roll into balls. Keep covered with a damp cloth. Take one ball of dough and roll out into a 10–12cm round; repeat with the rest.

Pour a layer of oil into a heavy-based frying pan to one-quarter fill it and place over a high heat. When very hot, carefully lower a dough round into the oil. Use a fish slice to baste and turn it so that the poori swells up. It will be cooked in a few minutes. When golden brown, remove from the oil with a slotted spoon and drain on kitchen paper. Keep warm while you cook the rest of the poori.

'When I was a kid, I ate very, very boring overcooked British food. No wonder I love curry now.'

'Sitting down to eat with the people close to you is one of those very few completely guilt-free pleasures.'

—Brian May of Queen

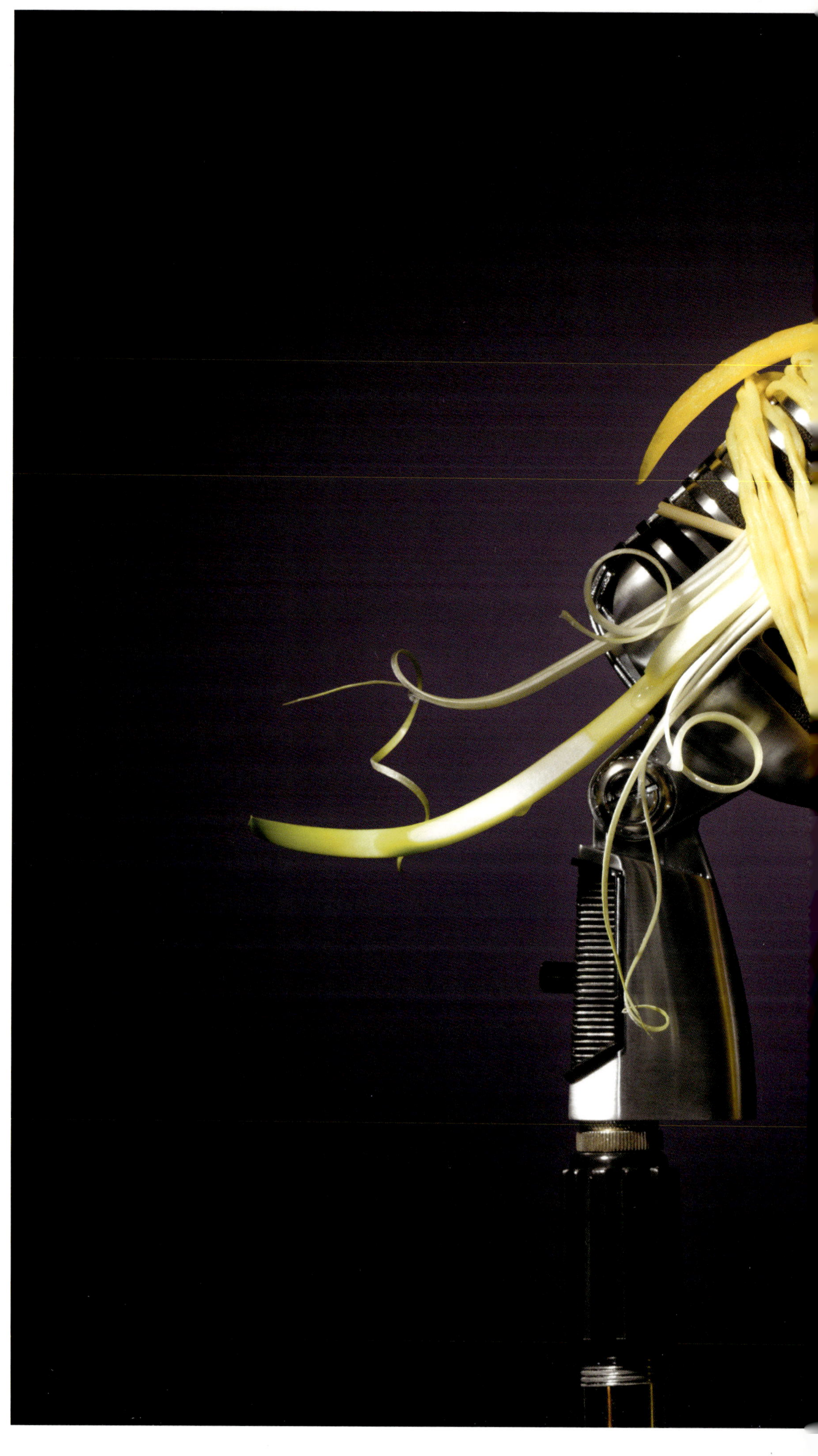

'Fondue is very 70s chic, but my parents were very 70s chic! We'd have Fondue Night with melted cheese everywhere. It was lovely, messy fun.'

The Soft, Silken, seventies texture of an unashamed, unadulterated *Abigail's Party*-style fondue is not, perhaps, the dish we most associate with chart pop. But if we've made our peace with musical guilty pleasures – a little Captain & Tennille here, a little Leo Sayer or Judie Tzuke there – then why not show the same open-mindedness towards their neglected culinary equivalents? Everything goes better with cheese. Just ask All Saints singer turned television presenter and fondue fan, Mel Blatt.

'Fondue is very 70s chic,' she concedes, laughing, 'But then my parents were very 70s chic themselves. I grew up eating fondue and I still remember the excitement when I was little and we'd have Fondue Night. It was our treat. My mum would make it, we'd have the long forks, lots of bread – we'd do it properly. It was really informal and there was melted cheese everywhere. It was lovely, messy fun.'

Mel continued her dedication to Switzerland's signature confection of melted cheese through her All Saints years, occasionally persuading her bandmates to give it a go. 'We were working in Switzerland once and I thought, 'I'm not coming here without having some proper fondue'. But then the schedule was so tight that we didn't have time,' she recollects sadly. 'The other girls weren't really into it. But I could understand that because, you know, it's an awful lot of cheese…'

With a French mother and a Jewish father of Polish-Russian extraction, Mel had her pick of two of the world's great food cultures. But she admits she only started to investigate her food heritage as she grew up. 'I was never into the fish balls and traditional Jewish food but I've been getting into things like chopped liver lately and thinking, "Why did I not love this years ago?" My mum used to cook with a lot of flair but she cooks simpler food now and it's fantastic – a beautiful soup, or some really good seafood.'

MELANIE BLATT *loves* FONDUE

At home Mel's speciality is cooking meticulous, big mum-sized roasts but she occasionally gets the old fondue pot (or caquelon) out – especially for birthdays. Daughter Lilyella too loves the fondue, as well as having a secret fondness for yellowtail sushi with jalapeño. 'She's a sophisticated girl,' mum notes proudly.

And the secret of La Fondue de Blatt? English Cheddar. 'I usually think you should do fondue properly, the Swiss way,' she says, 'But this tastes so good. And why shouldn't England have its own fondue? We've got the cheese.' Her proudest moment, she says, was when her sister tasted Mel's own recipe and said: 'You make it better than mum.'

Traditional Swiss Cheese Fondue

serves 6

1 garlic clove, halved lengthways
1 tbsp cornflour
2 tsp kirsch
330ml good-quality dry white wine or beer
1 tbsp lemon juice
225g Emmental cheese, coarsely grated
225g Gruyère cheese, coarsely grated
1 baguette, pain de campagne or sourdough loaf, cut into bite-sized pieces

Rub the inside of a heavy-based medium saucepan with the halved garlic and then discard.

In a small bowl, stir together the cornflour and kirsch until smooth. Put the saucepan over a moderate heat and add the wine and lemon juice. When simmering, gradually add the cheese to the pot, stirring constantly in a zigzag motion, to prevent the cheese from balling up; do not let it come to the boil.

When the cheese has melted and is creamy, stir in the cornflour mixture. Simmer gently for 6–8 minutes, until the mixture has thickened.

Transfer to a fondue pot and set over a burner at the table. Serve immediately, with the pieces of bread for dipping.

'You need subtlety, pepperiness and really fresh bean sprouts and peppers – and plenty of prawns.'

IN THE BOOK *McCarthy's Bar* the late travel writer and humorist Pete McCarthy wrote that you can judge the quality of any restaurant by its Singapore noodles. They're a bellwether – if a place can't be bothered to get Singapore noodles right, it won't get anything else right either. 'He was bang on, there,' says Tony Christie, mighty-lunged Sheffield soul vocalist, freeman of the City of Amarillo in Texas, and runner-up in *Come Dine With Me* (he came joint second behind Janet Ellis from *Blue Peter*).

'A bowl of Singapore noodles will show you whether they're taking care with the ingredients, the cooking, the attention to detail. I've had some terrible ones where they just throw a bit of curry powder in. That's not Singapore noodles! You need subtlety, pepperiness and really fresh bean sprouts and peppers – and plenty of prawns.'

Singapore noodles are what Tony relies on when touring around the world. 'The best are in Indonesia and all the many Chinatowns around Australia,' he says. 'Done right, it's the perfect touring musician's food.' After a lost couple of decades in cabaret, Tony's career is now on its third and possibly strongest wind. Big in the 60s and 70s, his fortunes were restored in the 2000s, first by the Peter Kaye-assisted re-release of *Is This The Way To Amarillo?* And then by a couple of copper-bottomed albums – one produced by fellow Sheffielder and *Love Music Love Food* participant Richard Hawley – that reminded British listeners of what a powerhouse vocalist Christie has always been.

His four decades in show business are a far cry from his childhood in a mining community near Doncaster. With his father away in the RAF, his mother had to raise not just Tony, his brother and her own brothers but look after her own father too. She did it with the classic Yorkshire diet – a roast with Yorkshire pud – but also with the fruits of their own allotment and pig-sty. (It was kept from the kids whenever one of the pigs had to 'go away'). Now he loves seafood, hot curries (madras-strength), tom yum soup and a good rib-eye steak. When he starred in the West End Show *Dreamboats And Petticoats* he and his wife lived for almost four months in Soho's infamous Groucho club. 'They make some of the best chips you've ever had in your life,' he says. 'Proper *fat* chips, with a chilli mayo.'

And he's been in the game long enough to be suspicious of the music business's fondness for wining and dining. They'll take you to some multi-starred restaurant, 'and then you'll get a great big plate with a little dollop of nothing in the middle.' Like anyone else who's had to work his way to the top – twice, or even three times – Tony wants to enjoy it while he's there.

TONY CHRISTIE *loves* SINGAPORE NOODLES

Singapore Noodles with Prawns

serves 2

200g raw tiger prawns, peeled and deveined
225g dried rice vermicelli
4 tbsp grapeseed or groundnut oil
1 medium onion, peeled and thinly sliced
1 red pepper, cored, deseeded and thinly sliced
1 green pepper, thinly sliced
1 tbsp curry powder
1 tsp ground turmeric
1 tsp sea salt
1 large egg, beaten
55g bean sprouts
1 tbsp sesame seeds, toasted in a dry pan

Keep 4 prawns whole and cut the rest into 1cm pieces.

Bring a medium saucepan of water to the boil. Add the vermicelli and cook until just softened, about a minute. Drain immediately and set aside.

Meanwhile, heat half the oil in a wok over a medium heat and add both the chopped and whole prawns. Cook for about a minute, stirring occasionally. Remove from the heat and set aside.

Heat the remaining oil in the wok over a medium heat, add the onion and cook until softened and lightly browned. Stir in the peppers and cook until starting to soften. Then add the noodles, curry powder, turmeric and salt and toss to mix, adding a little more oil if necessary.

Push the noodle mix to one side of the wok, and drop the beaten egg into the other. When the egg is firm, break it into smaller pieces, then toss in the bean sprouts and chopped prawns. Mix everything together and taste, adjusting the curry powder and salt if necessary.

Serve garnished with the toasted sesame seeds and cooked whole prawns.

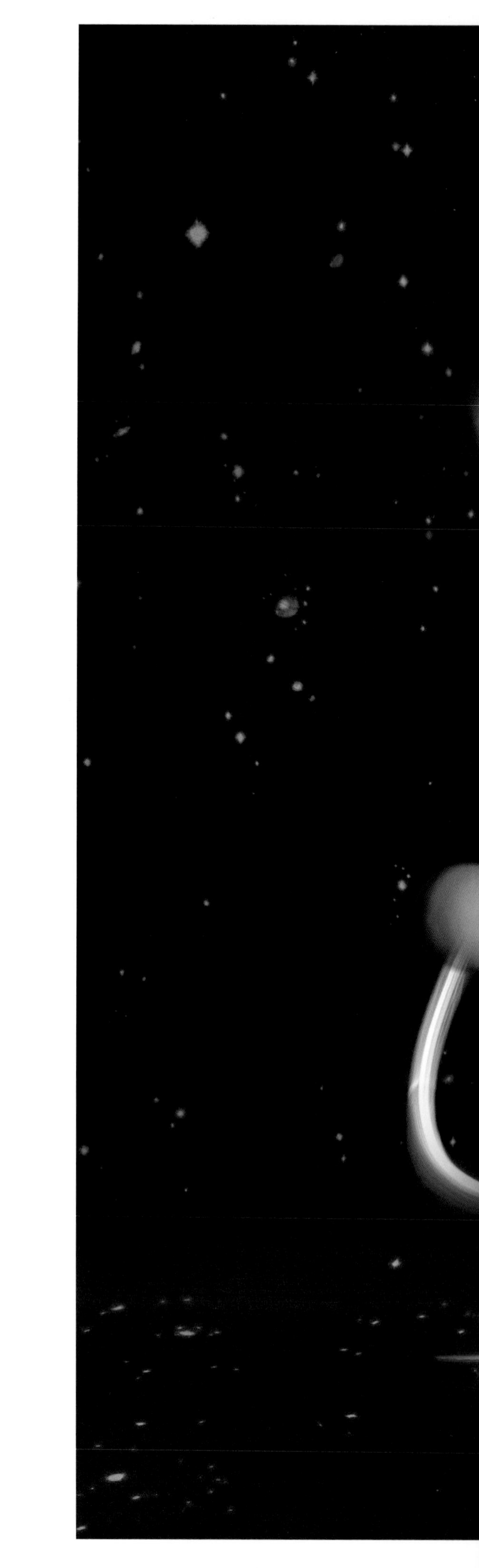

Hot space: Brian May of Queen orbited by his beloved grapefruit.

Pink Grapefruit & Mint Granita with Black Raspberry Sauce

serves 4

for the granita

6 ripe pink grapefruit
225g caster sugar
225ml water
10 small fresh mint leaves

for the raspberry sauce

300g ripe raspberries
2 tbsp icing sugar
3 tbsp black raspberry liqueur

Finely grate the zest from the grapefruit and squeeze the juice. In a small saucepan, dissolve the sugar in the water over a medium heat. Add the grapefruit zest and reduce the heat to a simmer. Cook until the zest is tender, about 20 minutes. Pour into a bowl and let cool. Meanwhile, strip the midrib from the mint leaves and shred them finely. Add to the sugar syrup with the grapefruit juice.

Pour the mixture into a shallow freezerproof tray, cover with cling film and place in the freezer. Stir and scrape the mixture with a fork every 30 minutes to make it light and fluffy. Keep frozen until ready to serve.

For the sauce, mix all the ingredients together in a bowl and leave to stand for 10 minutes, then blitz to a purée using a hand-held stick blender. Pass the raspberry sauce through a sieve into a clean bowl, pressing the fruit in the sieve with a wooden spoon, until only the seeds remain. If the sauce is a bit thick, add a little more raspberry liqueur. Chill until ready to serve.

Serve the granita in shot glasses with the sauce poured liberally over the top.

'The sun and the grapefruit have a lot in common, don't they? The great yellow orb... there may be some cosmic resonance there.'

Our universe is defined not just by the rocks that spin through the darkness of space, but by the rock that fills the airwaves. How do we relate that cold and unknowable blackness to the values of light, love and life-affirming major chords that spring from a big red guitar? Dr Brian May, PhD – Queen guitarist and songwriter, and qualified astrophysicist – pulls it off in his *Love Music Love Food* photograph, wherein his favourite food, the nutritious grapefruit, takes the place of the sun at the centre of our solar system.

'I've loved grapefruit ever since I was a kid,' he says, 'and I'll often have one for breakfast.' When he was about ten he was asked to write an essay about a favourite fruit. Brian wrote 'My favourite food is the grapefruit – I think it should be called a great-fruit!' His opinion hasn't changed much since.

'The sun and the grapefruit have a lot in common, don't they?' he muses, not entirely seriously. 'The great yellow orb… there may be some cosmic resonance there. Perhaps the grapefruit is mimicking the shape of the sun which gave it life? There is so much we don't understand…'

He also wanted to choose something that represents his changing beliefs about food over the years. For the past decade he and his wife, the actress Anita Dobson, have gradually moved away from eating any animal products at all, and if possible anything that causes suffering to a living creature or the surrounding environment either. Grapefruit is very much at the good end of the scale – it's not just vegetarian, it's vegan – and the damage caused in its cultivation is minimal.

'Put simply, I don't feel bad when I'm eating it,' he says. He and Anita haven't been strict vegetarians for very long, but the non-meat diet agrees with him. He's even lost weight. The myths you hear when you're growing up – like 'vegetarians don't get enough protein' – have all now been proved to be false, he says. 'And after all the work I've been doing on animal welfare lately' – Brian has campaigned against the culling of badgers and to keep the hunting ban in place – 'it made less sense to eat animals at all. It seemed like hypocrisy.'

BRIAN MAY *loves* GRAPEFRUIT

Brian doesn't cook himself, 'I'm not allowed near the kitchen,' but Anita produces vegetable-based dishes in endless variations. They're not into nut cutlets or imitation steaks. 'Good organically grown vegetables are delicious and nutritious in themselves,' he says. 'They don't need to be messed about with to make them nicer.'

It's a settled and simple diet – very different from the opulence of Queen's heyday when the band's parties were the stuff of legend. But, privately, says Brian, the four band members were not quite so over-the-top. When they were just beginning to be successful, around *Bohemian Rhapsody* in 1975, Freddie Mercury used to invite his bandmates to a particular Indian restaurant in Knightsbridge. 'I wasn't that keen on Indian food then,' says Brian, 'but what you got there was absolutely incredible and Freddie was in his element – he loved it. And the dessert was topped with real gold leaf, which was a real eye-opener for me, to Freddie's amusement…' But they were projecting an image of being rich successful rock stars rather than living it, he says. Until then they had only occasionally been able to afford to eat out at all. 'Before *Bohemian Rhapsody* it was home cooking and fast food for us. It's amazing how different it was from the way it looked.'

It didn't stay that way for long. Queen had hits around the world and became indisputably the biggest British rock band of the 70s and 80s. With it came the attendant lifestyle. Brian remembers going to a 'very very famous' five-star restaurant in Switzerland in celebration of another number one album, and being faced with baffling nouvelle cuisine. 'I couldn't deal with it. They were giving you one pea at a time and I just ended up laughing.' Drummer Roger Taylor, who had been the most enthusiastic about visiting this place, had to leave because the food suddenly made him violently ill. 'I've never really got on with haute cuisine,' says Brian. 'I like really, really simple food. Always have, really.'

Eating out together kept Queen close in the early days. 'A meal out is often the best place to sit down and discuss and plan stuff,' says Brian. 'It was slightly less so in the middle of our career maybe; when we were touring a lot we sort of split into factions. But towards the end, when we knew we were losing Freddie, I can remember a lot of really warm, close and communicative meals together in Montreux.' The Swiss town at the foot of the Alps was one of the few places where Freddie wasn't hounded by journalists eager to confirm rumours that he had contracted AIDS. 'He was able to live almost a normal life there,' says Brian. 'The band sort of congregated there, and going out to eat together was one of the great pleasures of that really difficult time.'

Freddie died in 1991 and Brian clearly still misses his old friend. The Queen story contrasts the extremes of outrageous achievement and great personal loss, which Brian still feels. 'I can certainly remember times when life had gone so terribly wrong that I felt guilty about just about everything,' he says. 'But sitting down to eat with your friends or your family, the people close to you, is one of those very few completely guilt-free pleasures.'

Asked about his favourite food memories, Brian finds that it's the small things that stand out. 'There was a hotel – Atlantis? – up on a grassy hill outside Zurich, right in the countryside – you could hear the cowbells clinking at night.' He remembers asking room service for an omelette with onions and vegetables, expecting nothing special, but what turned up was delicious beyond description.

'It was all subtle and melting with just the right amount of herbs… That was years and years ago and I still remember it,' he reminisces. 'Maybe there were other things going on in my life at the time that made that stick in my mind. But in that moment, that one thing on my plate was absolute perfection. Just like a grapefruit!'

Largo
40-60
Adagio
66-76
Moderato
108-120
Presto
168-200
Allegro
120-168
Prestissimo
200-208
Wittner
MAELZEL
METRONOM

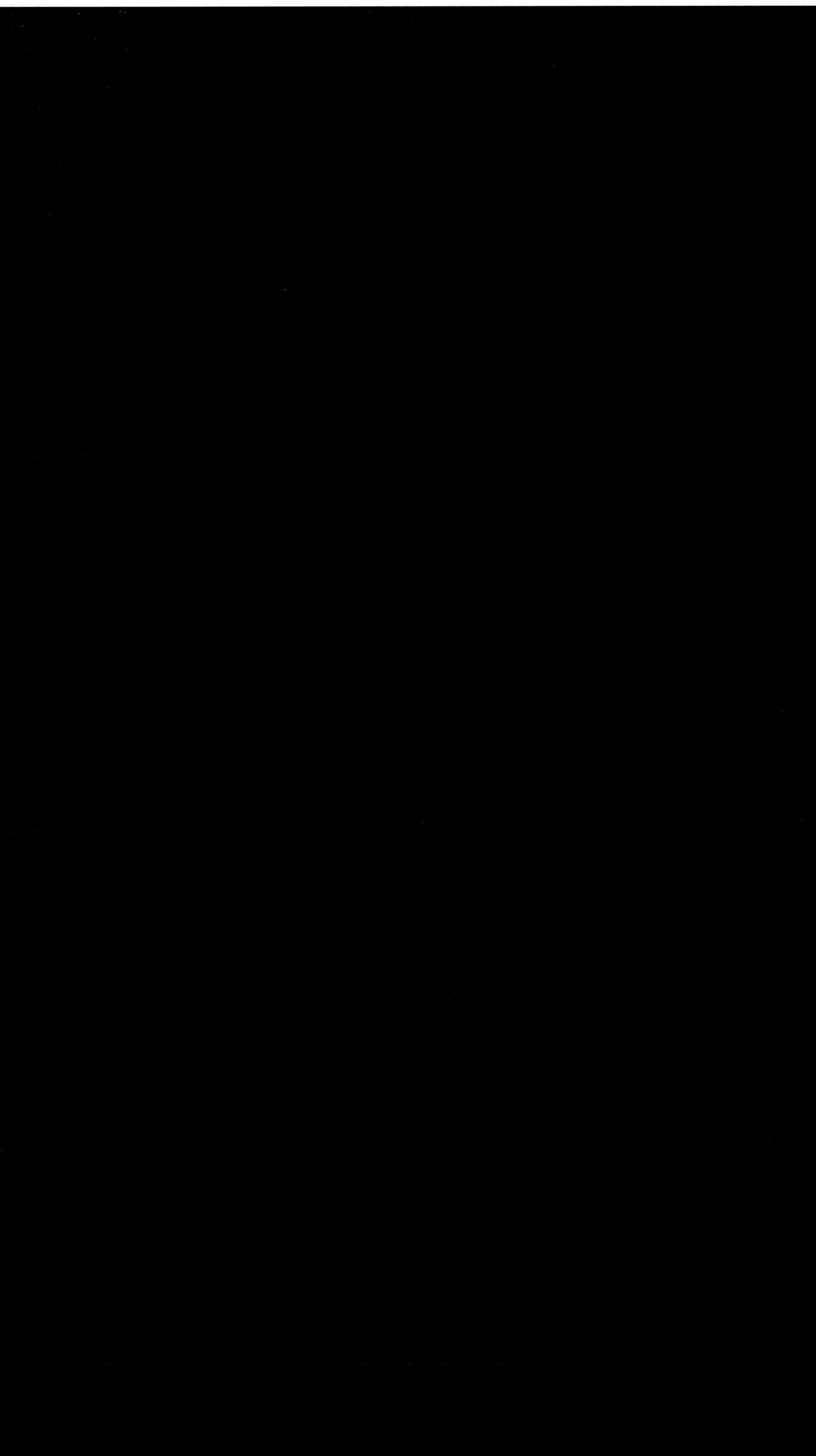

'If you're hungry enough, any meal is going to taste like manna from heaven.'

—Kelly Jones of Stereophonics

No sleep 'til Bangkok for Thai food lovers Papa Roach. From left: Tony Palermo, Tobin Esperance, Jacoby Shaddix, Jerry Horton.

Thai Fish Balls with Sweet Pickled Fruit Salsa
makes 8

for the sweet pickled fruit salsa

1 dragon fruit, peeled and grated
100g pickled ginger, finely diced
¼ hard unripe cantaloupe melon, peeled and grated
1 hard unripe mango, peeled and grated
4 lychees, peeled, stoned and finely sliced
6 spring onions, trimmed and finely sliced on the diagonal
1 garlic clove, peeled and finely chopped
2 tbsp rice wine vinegar
3 tbsp mirin (Japanese cooking wine)
1 tbsp fresh coriander leaves, chopped

for the Thai fish balls

500g skinned white fish fillet, roughly chopped
1 tbsp Thai fish sauce
1 lemongrass stalk, tough outer layer removed and thinly sliced
2 tsp red Thai curry paste
1 tbsp fresh coriander leaves, chopped
oil, for deep-frying
sea salt and freshly ground black pepper

Put all the prepared fruit salsa ingredients in a medium bowl and stir to combine evenly, then cover with cling film and chill for 2 hours.

To make the Thai fish balls, put the fish, fish sauce, lemongrass and curry paste into a food processor and pulse until just smooth. Turn into a bowl and mix in the chopped coriander.

With wet hands, divide the fish mixture into 8 portions and roll into balls, then place on a plate and chill for at least 1 hour to firm up.

Heat a 4–5cm depth of oil in a medium, deep, heavy-based saucepan. Once hot, very carefully lower the fish balls in, one at a time, using a slotted spoon. Fry for 4–6 minutes until golden brown. Lift out with the spoon and drain on kitchen paper.

Season the fish balls with salt and pepper and serve at once, with the pickled fruit salsa – adding a little more mirin if it is a little tart for your taste.

Sour Thai Curry Soup
serves 4

7 dried red chillies, soaked in water until soft
3 red onions, peeled and roughly chopped
5 garlic cloves, peeled and roughly chopped
2.5cm piece of fresh ginger, peeled and roughly chopped
½ tsp Thai shrimp paste
3 medium eggs
2 tbsp Thai fish sauce
2 tbsp oil, for frying
700ml water
1 tbsp tamarind juice or lime juice
4 spring onions, trimmed and thinly sliced
palm sugar, to taste
sea salt and freshly ground black pepper
fresh coriander leaves, chopped, and sprigs, to garnish

Put the chillies, onions, garlic, ginger and shrimp paste in a food processor and pulse until smooth. Set aside.

In a bowl, lightly whisk the eggs together with 1 tbsp fish sauce. Heat the oil in a frying pan and pour in the egg. Fry on both sides until just firm. Turn onto a board and leave to cool. Roll into a cigar shape and finely slice on the diagonal; set aside.

In a medium saucepan, bring the water to the boil. Stir in the chilli and garlic paste and heat gently until dissolved. Add the remaining 1 tbsp fish sauce, the tamarind or lemon juice, spring onions and palm sugar to taste. Season well with salt and pepper.

When ready to serve, divide the strips of egg between 4 bowls. Ladle the soup on top and stir in some chopped coriander. Garnish with coriander sprigs.

'Your fingers are burning, your mouth is burning... it's wonderful.' —***Jacoby***

JACOBY SHADDIX of PAPA ROACH *loves* THAI FOOD

IT'S HARD WHEN you're an American band touring Europe – especially if you're from northern California, the cornucopia of the United States where eating fabulously well is considered a basic human right. The food in Europe is just *weird*: heavy meats, strange cheeses, unfamiliar flavours, the coffee isn't right... and in England they just boil everything.

'It's always *interesting* for American bands,' says Jacoby Shaddix, irrepressible frontman for Californian alt. metal band Papa Roach, diplomatically. He relates how they felt very far from home on their first European tour until they found their oasis, the Thai House restaurant in Cologne, Germany, a place they loved so much that they still go back. At the Thai House, Papa Roach binged on 'flaming hot' red beef curry, Pad Thai, basil chicken, and an 'awesome, super-spicy' crab pot containing whole crustaceans that you had to break open by hand. 'If you've got any cuts on your fingers they're burning, your mouth is burning... it's wonderful.'

As the conversation flowed, Jacoby mentioned a friend back home called Ty. A waitress overheard, misheard and produced a giant Mai Tai. 'It was like a bowl with dry ice frothing up, smoke everywhere, and four straws,' says Jacoby wistfully. 'We pounded four or five of them and got good and schnockered by the end of the night. Now it's become a P Roach tradition to hit the Mai Tais at Thai House. We know the family who own it really well, and they always take care of us.'

Jacoby first fell in love with Thai food in his early 20s when he worked at Travis Air Force Base hospital, north east of San Francisco, just as Papa Roach were taking shape. There were a lot of Asian people on staff. Among them was a Thai lady who would bring in food and ask Jacoby if he wanted to try it. He got so into it that she would bring in Thai stuff especially for him. 'I always loved Chinese, but Thai is the real deal,' he says. 'I like the burn but it's lighter, it tastes fresher, it's healthy but it sure isn't dull. The soups are killer, the salads are great, and you don't feel bogged down with grease. There ain't no gut-bomb in Thai.'

His parents were hippies, which meant a lot of wholegrain healthfood on the menu in the Shaddix household. His mother also used to cook tuna casserole, which is less of a fond memory for Jacoby. 'To this day I can't stand it,' he admits. 'I gag if I smell it. I don't know why. I love tuna.' No wonder he went for the bright flavours of Thai when he grew up.

Food is almost an obsession for Papa Roach. Their guitarist Jerry Horton will make a note on his phone of interesting restaurants for future visits. If they're in a particular city, he can just pull a name off the list. 'That's one of our favourite things to do on a day off,' says Jacoby. 'The band and the crew posses up. If you've had two or three days of bad catering you really want a good meal.' Currently top of the list is a place in Connecticut that purports to be the birthplace of the American hamburger. 'The older I get, the more food matters to me,' Jacoby says. Before the band got started, he'd wanted to be a chef. 'Maybe that's going to be my second life.'

He's a big fan of the Red Fort, London's esteemed Indian restaurant, 'It fuckin' rocks, dude!' And the venerable Carnegie Deli in New York – inspired by the Woody Allen sandwich on the menu, he freestyles a recipe for the Jacoby Shaddix sandwich, 'Bang, boogie, let's talk about it: toasted garlic sourdough, chopped pastrami with a little onion. Swiss cheese on top with garlic mayo and you're done. Bang!'

Then he gives us another recipe – for his favourite snack. Take a Triscuit cracker, add pepper-Jack cheese, a little Tapatío hot sauce and put in the microwave for 25 seconds.' 'Hey presto,' he says. 'Ghetto nachos!'

There are many reasons for bands to stick together – dogged determination, a shared mission to live or die in the service of rock and roll, fear of finding other gainful employment – but Bridgend metalcore quartet Bullet For My Valentine may have found the best one. The band that eats together rocks together.

When *Kerrang!* and *Metal Hammer* magazine award-winners BFMV were recording their third album *Fever* in Malibu, singer-lyricist Matt Tuck would cook for the whole band pretty much every day. So much for the myth of the rock frontman as an isolated figure: after an exhausting day working and reworking the songs over and over again, Matt would go down the hill to the local store, collect a load of fresh meat and vegetables, and barbecue it for his bandmates. They'd eat together on the patio, enjoying the California sun, and unwind from the day's exertions. 'It was beautiful,' says Matt.

Bullet For My Valentine are mates, a band who worked their way up from modest beginnings in South Wales and weathered the fads of the metal world until they secured a reputation as one of the best hard rock bands in the British Isles. They know each other inside out.

'We're similar people and we all have similar tastes,' says Matt. 'We're fairly healthy, but we binge on British junk food every now and again. Our little treat on tour is fish fingers, beans and chips, which we always ask the caterers to cook, but there's also salads, curry and so on. It's British-style food.'

Hence their choice of Indian kebabs for *Love Music Love Food*. 'Indian food is comfort food for us. It's what we most miss when we're away, especially kebabs. A really good curry or a bit of tandoori is a British staple now. Every time we go on tour outside the UK we can never find a good Indian.'

The band are, he admits, curry maniacs and have become quite educated about it. They can go through a menu and translate the subtleties of the ingredients and styles of cooking. And how hot do they go? 'Personally I *can* go superhot,' says Matt with a cagey laugh, 'but I'll usually go medium, like a madras, rather than a vindaloo or a phall. You're just torturing yourself there. What's hotter than a phall? A bowl of fire. With extra chilli.'

He's a 'huge' cook at home and he tries to make something fresh every night. A mean steak, Thai curry, seared tuna salad, pasta sauce… nothing too elaborate, but he takes a lot of care. 'I've had no complaints from the band or my girlfriend,' he says. 'Not yet.' Interestingly, he's a meat-eater but a supporter of People for the Ethical Treatment of Animals too.

BULLET FOR MY VALENTINE *love* INDIAN KEBABS

Lamb & Okra Shish Kebab

serves 4

1kg lean leg or shoulder of lamb, cut into 4cm cubes
2 green peppers, cored, deseeded and cut into 2cm pieces
200ml olive oil
½ tsp finely chopped fresh oregano
1 tbsp finely chopped fresh mint
2 garlic cloves, peeled and crushed
1 tbsp light soy sauce
1 tsp pomegranate syrup
1 tsp brown sugar
2 large red onions, peeled and cut into eighths
500g okra

Put the lamb, peppers, olive oil, oregano, mint, garlic, soy sauce, pomegranate syrup and brown sugar in a large bowl. Roughly break up the layers of onion and add to the bowl. Mix well, then cover and leave to marinate in the fridge for 4 hours.

Skewer the marinated lamb and all the vegetables onto 4 long kebab skewers in the following order: onion, meat, okra, meat, pepper, meat, onion; save the marinade liquor.

Heat up a griddle pan, the grill or barbecue. Baste the kebabs with the reserved marinade. Griddle, grill or barbecue for about 10 minutes, turning and basting the skewers after 5 minutes.

Serve the lamb skewers with warm flat breads and baba ganoush.

N.B. If using bamboo skewers, pre-soak them in cold water for 30 minutes to prevent them scorching with the heat.

'I do eat meat,' Matt says. 'It's fur that bugs me because the way it's farmed is horrendous, it's indefensible. If we can persuade some Bullet fans to give fur a miss, then we want to do it. But it is possible to find meat that's reared and slaughtered humanely. I try to buy only meat that's been well reared, as far as it's possible to know that. I am a meat-eater, but you can be an ethical meat-eater.'

BFMV now have a worldwide following. Where are the best places they've eaten? Whenever they go to Japan they always visit the same restaurant near the Shibuya Excel Hotel. The name being written in Japanese, Matt can never remember what it's called. 'They do sushi, crazy chilli-prawn croquettes, meat skewers, crazy soups and broths… It's literally outstanding.' But the best of the lot is Katana in LA on Sunset opposite the Grafton Hotel. 'It's absolutely incredible. I'll eat there every day if I can.' Matt goes into raptures about the diced hamachi or yellowtail tuna with jalapeños, and the spicy tuna rice cakes. 'I could go on. That restaurant is insane.'

Tell us, Matt. Which curry, in your opinion, is the most metal? He thinks for a bit. 'Chicken Pantera!'

'A really good curry or a bit of tandoori is a British staple. It's what we most miss when we're on tour.'

Abra-kebabra! (from left) Bullet For My Valentine's singer/guitarist Matt Tuck, a friend and guitarist Michael Padget.

Ace of cakes – Howling Bells (from left): Joel Stein, Juanita Stein, Glenn Moule, Brendan Picchio.

'I like a corner shop cupcake. There's probably something in there that's bad for you – but whatever it is, I love it.'—***Joel***

HOWLING BELLS *love* CUPCAKES

'I DON'T THINK any of us realised how permanent the dye was,' says Juanita Stein of Howling Bells of their cupcake-fuelled food fight for *Love Music Love Food*. 'I had blue on my face for a week.' It is all the fault of her brother Joel, guitar and keyboards player with the acclaimed Australian band who mix sunny and blissed-out alternative pop with impulses of a darker nature (you could almost call them The Velvet Downunderground). Joel is the real cupcake fiend in Howling Bells.

'I love cupcakes!' he says. 'Can't get enough of the little bastards. And I like the really cheap ones, not the fancy £3 cakes from the cute little speciality shops. I like a corner shop cupcake. There's probably some ingredient in there that is terribly, terribly bad for you but whatever it is, I love it.'

Juanita and Joel grew up in Sydney with a musician father and an actress mother. In contrast to all the steak-on-the-barbie clichés of Australia theirs was, says Juanita, a 'very healthy household, not a lot of meat or junk food, just lots of good vegetarian stuff. Although,' she admits, 'Dad would sneak out for KFC every now and again…' Things were a little less healthy when they and their bandmates moved to the UK in 2004 at the invitation of Coldplay's producer. They lived four in one freezing room and ate badly. Joel got a job on a farm where he collected geese eggs and dug the gardens. 'The only song that was going through my head then was Bob Dylan's *Maggie's Farm*,' he says. But hard work paid off and they got to make their second album in Los Angeles.

They travel back to Sydney often and are proud of its food culture, with its unrivalled vegetables and seafood, and its Asian, Middle Eastern, European and especially Greek influences. Apart from the fantastic restaurants on Crown Street there's Il Baretto, the Italian place run by the mother of Howling Bells' bass player Brendan Picchio – in the past Brendan was known to wait tables there. 'We are a multi-talented band,' Juanita jokes, but then she adds that it really *is* a brilliant restaurant. Her own favourite dish is 'Super, super, super fresh sushi, served super cold.'

The best thing Joel ever ate, he thinks, was a common or garden burger after a night out a few months ago – he had a terrible hangover and it felt like manna from heaven. For Juanita it was at 'a little shack of a restaurant in Provence. We'd hiked up the hill and it was all about the experience of watching the sunset on the lavender fields. It was one of those places where they just serve what they have, you don't choose, and we had fish. The whole thing was amazing, it couldn't have been better. I wonder if I'd had the same dinner on Tottenham Court Road, would it be the same?'

Meanwhile, as he prepares to come back from Sydney to start work on a new album, Joel's got a new discovery. 'I'm getting into my fried peanut butter,' he says. He visited a friend in Nashville, a friend made it for him and now he's hooked. 'I'm getting into a whole Elvis thing. I'll probably put on about 45 kilos. It's very, very bad,' he admits. 'But it's also very, very good.'

Cup Cakes

makes about 18

100g margarine, softened
100g caster sugar
2 medium eggs
100g self-raising flour
1 tsp baking powder

for the glacé icing

225g icing sugar
3 tbsp warm water
few drops of food colouring

OR

for chocolate butter icing

175g butter, softened
350g icing sugar, sifted
50g cocoa powder
3 tbsp hot water

Preheat the oven to 200°C/Gas mark 6. Line 18 holes of two cupcake trays with paper cake cases. Put all the ingredients into a large bowl, and beat using an electric whisk until the mixture is smooth, about 2–3 minutes. Spoon the mixture into the paper cases to half-fill them.

Bake for 15–20 minutes until the cakes are well risen and golden brown. Lift out of the tins and place on a wire rack to cool. Meanwhile, make the icing of your choice.

For glacé icing, sift the icing sugar into a large bowl. Using an electric whisk, gradually blend in the water until the mixture is fairly stiff, adding tiny drops of food colouring until you get the desired shade. Spread on top of the cooled cakes.

For chocolate butter icing, beat the butter and icing sugar together in a large bowl, using an electric whisk, until pale and fluffy. In a small bowl, mix the cocoa and hot water together until smooth, allow to cool, then add to the butter icing. Whisk together, and pipe or swirl on top of the cooled cakes.

N.B. For chocolate cupcakes replace 25g of the flour with cocoa powder.

KELLY JONES of STEREOPHONICS

loves

WINE GUMS

SOMETIMES FOOD IS MORE than what's on your plate at the end of the day. Sometimes it's a time machine. When Kelly Jones – whisky-voiced singer-guitarist with Cardiff's gargantuan stadium rock band Stereophonics – was a kid, Christmas meant eight-pound boxes of Lyons' wine gums and Midget Gems in the house. His mother used to put ten bob a week in to the shop over the year to buy them – proper retail boxes, the ones you'd see in shops – and they would last Kelly, his brother and his dad to the end of January. It was heaven. Does the thought of them give him pangs?

'Yeah, it does actually!' he says with a smile, 'especially now that I've got kids myself. You think of your own dad coming home with a quarter of wine gums, and how you pestered him. I was always a kid for chewy sweets, we used to buy Cola Bottles and all that stuff, and now there's always sweets on the tour bus. You never grow out of them, do you?

'And no, we don't do the rider thing and chuck any of the colours out.' He pauses and considers. 'Except maybe the black liquorice ones. They can go straight in the bin.'

Kelly grew up in the former pit village of Cwmaman. Everyone in the family was a factory worker – dad in the steelworks, mam making tellies for Hitachi or JVC – so the dinner had to be on the table every day at quarter to five. His mother cooked traditional fuel for a hungry workforce: bangers and mash, corned beef pie, fish, roasts. 'It sounds daft now,' Kelly says, 'but when I was growing up pasta and broccoli were only just coming in. They were new, they were almost a treat. I went on my first foreign holiday when I was 14 and after that it was all garlic bread and spaghetti in the house...'

But Kelly didn't fancy the factory life. He went to work on a fruit and veg stall and then to art college, 'while I worked out what the fuck I was going to do. If you go into the factory,' he says, 'you never get out.'

Stereophonics formed in 1992 and through dogged hard work took their democratic, user-friendly rock and roll – half indie, half Led Zep – into the top ten and the stadiums. When they started out they survived on Ginster's buffet bars and lager. They eat better now but nothing flash. If they get a day off in the middle of a tour they'll just find the best Indian restaurant in the city, book it from seven and then just eat all night. Kelly looks forward to a proper Indian dessert and the traditional yoghurt drink Lhassi.

Red Wine Gum Vodka

serves 2

1 bottle good-quality vodka
15 red wine gums
15 cherries, washed and frozen

Open the bottle of vodka, pour a generous double shot into a glass and set aside. Drop the wine gums into the bottle; if the vodka starts to rise past the bottleneck decant some more into a glass.

Replace the lid and wrap the bottle in cling film. Lay on a shelf in the dishwasher and set to a regular cycle. Once finished, leave the bottle to cool. The wine gums should have melted and coloured the vodka; if some of the wine gums are still intact put through the dishwasher cycle again. Unwrap and shake really well. Place in the freezer until ready to serve.

Serve in shot glasses with the frozen cherries.

NB Any colour wine gums can be used, but if the colours are mixed the vodka will go a green-grey.

The band prefer to spend their money on quality booze: Kelly likes Czech Budvar, the red Peroni, decent ales like Sussex bitters or a good bottle of Bombay Sapphire gin. For all their success he's still bemused by the antics you see from the rock A-list. 'We did a tour with the Red Hot Chili Peppers and they had blood group diets,' he says – a menu tailored for your specific blood group. 'Never seen anything like it.'

Even London remains a little weird to Kelly, who's been a rock star since 1997 but is still quietly proud to be a Valley Boy – an outsider. In the Capital people go out drinking in the week and stay at home all weekend. In the rest of the country it's the other way round. Why is that? Probably because they're all sharing flats and they don't *want* to go home, he thinks. They just hide in the boozer.

Having grown up with their noses pressed against the window of rock and roll, Stereophonics seized opportunity with both hands when it arrived. Kelly remembers their first big rock and roll dinner, at Pied à Terre in Soho the very night they signed with Richard Branson's V2 Records. 'It was about as extreme as it gets,' Kelly remembers. 'To go from having your mam's corned beef pie to this place where there was more glasses on the table than we had in our house... it was so different from what we were used to.' When the waiter came round to ask if we wanted white wine, red wine, beer or water, Kelly told him 'all fucking four.'

There were hangovers the next day, but the label gave them fifteen hundred quid in £50 notes to go shopping on Oxford Street. They bought terrible jeans from all the tourist shops, so excited by the experience that they never stopped to check if the clothes looked any good. 'We never wore any of it,' Kelly admits. But it didn't matter. This, Stereophonics thought, was as good as it could possibly get.

'We were like starving men,' says Kelly. 'And you can only judge a meal by how hungry you are. If you're hungry enough, it'll taste like manna from heaven.'

'I was always a kid for chewy sweets, Cola Bottles and all that stuff. You never grow out of them, do you?'

CLARET

ROB ZOMBIE *loves* PUMPKIN

ROB ZOMBIE, HEAVY metal hero and director of gore-laden shlock-horror films, has a voice so astonishingly deep and mellow that you feel like you're speaking to a movie trailer – specifically a trailer for the sort of lurid and blood-spattered movies that Rob makes, like his own low-budget *House Of 1000 Corpses* or the hit remake of *Halloween*.

Pumpkins are, of course, the evil, grinning patron saint of Halloween but Rob enjoys eating them as well as using them to scare young children. 'A fine pumpkin pie can really hit the spot,' he says sagely. 'I'm from New England where there's pumpkins everywhere, and I never met a pumpkin pie I didn't like. I guess it's all in the crust…'

As is often the way in heavy rock, the more ghoulish and outrageous the image, the friendlier and more grounded the person. Rob made his name with the quasi-Satanic industrial-metal band White Zombie in the 90s and in his solo music career he's delved into the mythology of horror movies. But he's actually a cheerful and gentlemanly vegetarian with a driven work ethic. With his finger in so many pies – few of them pumpkin – he needs one.

Rob stopped eating meat after he saw the famous expose of the meat industry *The Animals Film*, narrated by Julie Christie, on TV, in about 1981, when he was in high school. 'It was just so disgusting that I never ate meat again,' he remembers. 'When you're a vegetarian, it's not about what you want to order in a restaurant, but what you *can* order. I scan the menu and go nope, nope, nope. You usually end up with the most boring thing on the menu.' He was pleasantly surprised on his last British tour when the veggie catering turned out to be great. He had vegetarian Beef Wellington: 'All Wellington, no beef. It was delicious.' He doesn't cook himself, although his wife Sheri does an 'amazing' butterbean stew.

A lot of vegetarians don't think veggie food should imitate the taste of meat but Rob doesn't really care. 'If it tastes good, I'll eat it. Veggie burgers have gotten really good and the fake bacon is good too. I've been vegetarian a really long time so I kind of forget what the real stuff tastes like.' He is a big fan of the 'tofurkey,' the tofu-based Thanksgiving choice for non-carnivores, which is perhaps a little too tasty for its own good. You'll have friends and family over, he says, and most of them will want real turkey. But then someone will taste the tofurkey and it's, hmm, that's pretty good, let me have a little more… 'And you're like, no, you got your own stuff. We cooked you a goddamn real turkey, get your hands off ours!'

Where is the best catering to be found, in the worlds of music or movies? It's hard to say, says Rob. They can both be pretty good. People eat more in the film world because there's a lot more waiting around and food is always there, in front of you. 'It's pretty easy to gain 20 pounds without even thinking about it.' But having started out in the DIY post-punk era, Rob's very conscious of cost on his movies. 'I hate waste, in catering or elsewhere,' he says. 'You want the money to go on screen, that's all that matters. Nobody watches a movie and thinks, oh, I hope they ate well and had nice trailers and hotels.'

It's the same with the minimal backstage rider for the Rob Zombie band. 'We have almost nothing,' he says. 'I can't stand the idea of it being thrown away.' They hardly eat on tour, he says, because you don't want food in your stomach during a show and afterwards you're too exhausted to eat anyway. 'We pretty much live on breakfast.'

Truthfully, he says, he could live off pizza for three meals a day, and has done so in the past. When he was really poor, living in New York City in the early 80s, pizza was 75¢ a slice and he ate little else. But he can't do without coffee.

'I will pretty much drink coffee all day and all night,' he admits. 'I've been drinking it since I was a little kid, and I've become so immune to caffeine that I can pretty much drink ten espressos and still pass out if I'm tired.' Rob gets super-intense headaches from caffeine withdrawal if he's ever deprived of his fix. But with music, movies and now comic books on his agenda, perhaps he needs it.

Rob, what's the best coffee? 'McDonalds,' he replies. 'I know, it's weird. You'd expect it to be bad but it's really great coffee. You know, I'm not that picky…'

Chilli & Pumpkin Seed Tapenade

serves 6

- *6 tbsp pumpkin seeds, shelled*
- *3 green peppers*
- *1 green chilli pepper*
- *small bunch of fresh coriander*
- *2 garlic cloves*
- *½ tsp sea salt*
- *freshly ground black pepper*
- *4 tbsp olive oil*
- *2 tbsp lemon juice*

Preheat the oven to 180°C/Gas mark 4. Scatter the pumpkin seeds on a baking tray and roast for 6 minutes. Tip onto a plate and set aside to cool.

Place the whole peppers and chilli on the baking tray and roast in the oven for 15–20 minutes, or until the skin blisters, then place them all in a bowl and cover with cling film; set aside until cool. Peel away the skin from the peppers and chilli, then halve, core and deseed, keeping only the flesh and juices.

Put the pumpkin seeds, coriander, garlic, peppers and chilli (with their juices) into a food processor and pulse until coarsely chopped. Season with the salt and black pepper. With the motor running, slowly add the olive oil and lemon juice through the feeder tube. The tapenade should be of a pâté-like consistency. Transfer to a bowl and chill for 1 hour before serving.

Serve on pizza or pitta bread.

'I'm from New England where there's pumpkins everywhere. I never met a pumpkin pie I didn't like.'

Marshall

'I'm like, "Yes! Lobster! Oysters!"
As much expensive stuff as I can get!'
—Paloma Faith

Peter Hook of New Order and Joy Division has a thing for tandoori crab claws.

Do you remember the first time? Peter Hook, the emblematic low-slung bass player with Joy Division and then New Order, certainly does – his first time with Indian food at least. He first tried it in the saddest circumstances imaginable, in the months after the suicide of Joy Division's troubled singer Ian Curtis in 1980. Hooky had lost a friend and, it seemed, a career and he was only 24.

Though the remaining members – Hooky, guitarist Bernard Sumner and drummer Stephen Morris – had decided to carry on as New Order, they had no frontman. Casting around for ideas they'd gone to Sheffield to the Western Works studio owned by their friends, Cabaret Voltaire, who had offered to sing on a track or two. At the end of the day, Richard and Mal of Cabaret Voltaire took them for a curry.

'It was the only place open,' Hooky remembers. 'I was a working class Manchester lad who'd been brought up to think that curry and Chinese were the work of the Devil. It was egg and chips all the way with us. We were on £1.50 a day so it was have a drink or eat – you couldn't have both. But I'd always loved the smell of Indian food and I thought, why not, I'll give it a go. And I was completely sold on curry. Never looked back.' It's a wonderful thing when your friends rally round at a grim time, he thinks. They even managed to record something they were quite proud of, though they never released it. It didn't matter. New Order were finding their feet.

Three decades later he's still in favour of the restorative powers of Indian food, in this case the succulent tandoori crab claws from his favourite Indian restaurant, the Jai Kathmandu in Northenden. People in Manchester will go down the Curry Mile but,

PETER HOOK of JOY DIVISION & NEW ORDER *loves* TANDOORI CRAB CLAWS

he says, it's rubbish, a trap for drunks. Hooky's been going to the Kathmandu for about eighteen years. 'It literally is the best curry house in Manchester,' he says. 'God, the hours I've spent in there. Not always eating.'

Joy Division were a hard-up band. 'It was never sullied by money, because we were as skint when it ended as when we began,' but things turned out differently for New Order. They discovered first hip hop and then house music, becoming influential in a very different way to Joy Division. Hits like *Blue Monday* and *True Faith* followed and they travelled the world. One of nature's storytellers, Hooky remembers record label staff taking them for what he claims was the then-most expensive Japanese meal in the history of New York City: '£680 in 1981 money! We used to get spoilt rotten. They used to take us to all these fancy places but funnily enough you'd always have to stop for a burger on the way home. Tiny little portions, they were…'

New Order also helped to trigger the superclub explosion of the late 80s with their investment in the Haçienda, the club that became England's key temple of acid house. Designed to compete with the luxury clubs of New York, it changed clubbing in Britain and provides the yellow-and-black colour scheme for our photographs. The Haçienda also proved financially ruinous, consuming so much of New Order's royalties that their label Factory went bust (Hooky wrote a book about it called *The Haçienda: How Not To Run A Club*). What few people remember is that, alongside the state-of-the-art sound system and the Ecstasy dealers who sneaked in, the 'Haç' also had a restaurant.

'I was about the only person to eat in the Haçienda,' says Hooky. 'When we first opened it, we had a proper chef and he was mega! His chicken pancakes were a delight. I used to eat there all the time, it saved me a few bob. But it's fair to say the Haçienda wasn't known as a place to eat… With our lot they'd party for three days and then they'd need a plate of chips or they'd collapse.' The restaurant didn't last. It turned out that chips were all the ravers needed.

Hook left New Order in 2007 and now DJs and plays with his own band, The Light, whose projects include touring Joy Division's classic album *Closer* in its entirety. And does Hook cook? 'When I was touring I was always too knackered to contemplate cooking,' he says, 'but now I actually enjoy it. I do spaghetti and meatballs, and I'm told my grilled salmon is quite good.'

And what would he like to eat right now?

'My mum's Sunday lunch,' he says wistfully. 'She's been gone 10 years and I'd give anything to be able to have that again.'

'I was about the only person to eat in the Haçienda restaurant. Our lot would just party for three days and then have a plate of chips.'

Tandoori Crab Claws, Saffron Pilaf & Dahl

serves 4

12 large crab claws

for the marinade

5 garlic cloves, peeled and roughly chopped
2.5cm piece of fresh ginger, peeled and roughly chopped
1 medium onion, peeled and roughly chopped
225ml plain yoghurt
3 tbsp lime juice
2 spring onions, trimmed and finely sliced
¼ tsp ground cardamom
¼ tsp freshly grated nutmeg
¼ tsp ground cloves
¼ tsp ground cinnamon
2 tsp cayenne pepper
1 tsp ground cumin
1 tsp ground turmeric
½ tsp sea salt
½ tsp freshly ground black pepper
handful of fresh coriander, chopped

to serve

lime wedges

For the marinade, in a food processor, purée the garlic, ginger, onion, yoghurt, lime juice, spring onions and spices. Season with salt and pepper and stir in the chopped coriander. Put the crab claws in a large bowl and spoon over the marinade. Turn the crab claws to coat well, then cover the bowl with cling film and refrigerate overnight.

Preheat the grill to medium. Remove the claws from the marinade and place on a grill rack. Grill the claws for about 4 minutes on each side until hot and a little charred. Serve with lime wedges for squeezing over.

for the saffron pilaf

45g butter
seeds from 6 cardamom pods
4 cloves
3 cinnamon sticks
1 onion, peeled and finely diced
280g long-grain rice, rinsed in cold water
750ml vegetable stock
1 tsp sea salt
¾ tsp saffron threads, soaked in 2 tbsp boiling water

to serve

small bunch of fresh coriander, chopped, or flaked almonds, toasted

Melt the butter in a large saucepan over a medium heat. Add the cardamom, cloves and cinnamon and fry for 2 minutes, stirring occasionally. Add the onion and sauté until golden brown. Tip in the rice, reduce the heat to low and fry gently for 5 minutes.

Add the stock, salt and infused saffron. Cover and cook until the rice is cooked and all the liquid is absorbed, about 40 minutes. The rice should be a beautiful deep yellow colour. Fluff it up with a fork and scatter over the coriander or almonds before serving.

for the dahl

400g toor dahl (or yellow split peas)
1½ tsp sea salt
about 500ml water
½ tsp grated fresh ginger
1 small hot chilli, deseeded and chopped
1 tomato, diced
3 tsp lemon juice
½ tsp ground turmeric
1 tbsp vegetable oil
1 tsp cumin seeds
pinch of chilli powder
pinch of asafoetida
2 garlic cloves, peeled and crushed
freshly ground black pepper
handful of fresh coriander, chopped

Rinse the toor dahl and soak in a bowl of cold water to cover for 30 minutes, then drain.

Tip the dahl into a large saucepan, add the salt and fresh cold water to cover the dahl by about 1cm, then bring to the boil. Reduce the heat to medium and cook for 15–20 minutes until the dahl is tender and thick, adding more water during cooking if it appears to be drying out. Add the ginger, chilli, tomato, lemon juice and turmeric and simmer for a few minutes.

Meanwhile, heat the oil in a frying pan over a medium heat and fry the cumin, chilli powder, asafoetida and garlic for 2 minutes. Stir into the dahl and season well.

Scatter over the chopped coriander and serve.

'I'm quite international. All the cultures I'm close to are really foodie cultures, so I'm really lucky.'

PALOMA FAITH, THE extrovert burlesque-pop princess who's also an actress, has a particular memory of something beautiful she ate when she was little. She was about nine years old and she'd gone to Spain to stay with her dad, who had split from her mum when Paloma was tiny. Her father took her out on a boat to a little island with his friends, where they built a fire, put a paella dish on it and brought fish straight out of the sea. They cooked a fresh paella and ate it right there. 'It was the most wonderful meal I think I've ever had,' says Paloma, and that's why she chose paella for her *Love Music Love Food* picture.

She's never tried to cook paella herself. She's got the proper dish and she is 'really good at Spanish food', making tortilla, tapas and paprika chicken, chopping the chorizo… but she's frightened that she'll be disappointed if she screws up a paella. 'My dad's an amazing cook,' she explains, 'and I feel like I've become quite a good cook later in life. It sounds so boastful to say I'm really good at cooking, but I know I am. But paella is the one thing I can't do, so it's become really special to me.'

In fact it was a toss-up between paella and dim sum for the photo because her stepfather is British Chinese. The family would go for dim sum at a 'real Chinese family place' in Greenwich instead of having an English Sunday lunch. 'It's still one of my favourite places,' she says. She's got family in Italy too, so she knows her way around pasta dishes as well.

'I'm quite international,' Paloma says proudly. 'All the cultures I'm close to are really foodie cultures, so I'm really lucky.' Food-friendliness can have its downside, though. She doesn't understand women who thank her for 'celebrating your femininity by being a curvy woman' – she just thinks she's got a healthy appetite. She's only a size 10. 'But I'm a bit like a Pac-Man with eating…' She's taken up exercise while she writes her second album, not so much to get fit as so that she can eat more of what she wants.

Paloma grew up in Stoke Newington, north London, which used to be full of 'horrible chicken shops' but has now gentrified with more than its fair share of decent restaurants. Paloma remembers when it was a squatters' neighbourhood. Now it's the grown-up sibling of youthful, hipster-friendly Dalston, where Paloma likes to go for Turkish food at the famous Mangal restaurant. The artists Gilbert and George eat there every day. She also likes the tapas place Café España on Old Compton Street ('I can never remember what it's called, we just say "let's go to the Spanish!"') and the Magic Wok on Queensway too. She's a London girl.

PALOMA FAITH *loves* PAELLA

Paloma misses cooking badly. The weekend before her live duet with Cee-Lo Green at the 2011 Brits she had her first day off in ages. Grabbing her chance, she went to the fishmonger for clams and made spaghetti alla vongole. 'It's really easy to make, and you can stand there watching all the little clams open up for you.'

But what's the point of being in the world of music if you're not going to enjoy it? Some people, particularly American artists, take comfort in food from home. They want a burger or a bucket of chicken. 'But I'm more like Shirley Bassey or Eartha Kitt,' she says. 'I'm like, 'Yes! Lobster! Oysters!' As much expensive stuff as I can get.' Her record label took newly-signed Paloma to the opulent fish restaurant J Sheekey's near Leicester Square. When she asked if she really *could* have anything she wanted, they told her that Victoria Beckham had had all the caviars when she signed her deal – so Paloma couldn't possibly do worse than that.

Oh really, thought Paloma, who went ahead and ordered a seafood platter for two people – beautiful whelks, snails, cockles, razor clams, crab – just for herself. Then she had lobster and chips. And she ate the lot.

Paella

serves 6–8

light olive oil, for cooking
1 chicken, about 1.6kg, jointed and portioned into small serving pieces (about 12)
1 large onion, peeled and finely diced
1 red pepper, cored, deseeded and diced
1 green pepper, diced
6 garlic cloves, peeled and thinly sliced
1.5 litres water
20 mussels, cleaned
250g clams, cleaned
250g small raw prawns, peeled (shells reserved)
good pinch of saffron threads
1 good-quality chicken stock cube
500g paella rice
250g squid rings, halved
100g freshly podded peas
200g jar roasted red peppers, drained and sliced into strips
lemon wedges, to serve

Heat a thin film of olive oil in a large saucepan over a medium heat. Add the chicken pieces and fry gently, turning frequently, until beginning to brown. Add the onion, peppers and garlic and fry, stirring often, until the vegetables are softened and the chicken is golden brown.

Bring the water to the boil in a large saucepan. Add the mussels and clams, cover and cook for 2–3 minutes until the shells open (discard any that remain closed). Strain the water into a medium saucepan. Set the mussels and clams aside.

Bring the water back to the boil. Add the reserved prawn shells and saffron, and crumble in the stock cube. Simmer for 10 minutes; the stock should be a deep yellow colour. Strain into a bowl, discarding the shells.

Heat up a large paella pan or deep frying pan. Add the chicken, onion, peppers, garlic and clams. Add the rice and mix well, then add the prawns and squid. Pour in three-quarters of the saffron stock and stir well. Add the mussels, prawns, peas and red pepper strips. Cook for 20 minutes, stirring occasionally to make sure the paella is cooking evenly and adding more stock if needed.

When the rice is tender, serve the paella straight from the pan with lemon wedges for squeezing over.

JO WOOD *loves* ROCK & ROLL STEW

WHEN KEITH RICHARDS TELLS you you're developing a bit of a habit, you should probably listen to him. Jo Wood, former model and then-wife of Rolling Stone Ronnie Wood, had experienced a food-related epiphany in the early 90s and began eating all-organic. Accompanying Ronnie on the Stones' numerous tours, she insisted that the on-tour chef provided organic dishes and converted Mick Jagger's then-wife Jerry Hall and Keith's wife Patti to the benefits of additive-free food. In the mid-2000s, even Charlie Watts took an interest after his bout with cancer.

'I was so manic for it,' she recalls. 'Eventually Keith turned round to me and said "The trouble with you, Jo, is you're *addicted* to that stuff." And when Keith Richards tells you you're addicted...'

Jo turned on to organics after a misdiagnosis with the digestive disorder Crohn's Disease in the late 80s. After a couple of years of extreme pain, in 1992 she was contacted by a herbalist who put her on a strict organic diet – no salt, nothing white or refined. Jo started to feel great almost immediately.

That's where the obsession began. She even had her own portable touring stove built. 'I could check in to the Ritz Carlton, have the stove brought up to the room in its flight case, and then just pop out to Whole Foods for ingredients.' She'd cook fish and rice for Ronnie in their hotel room. 'I set off more fire alarms with burning the toast than the Stones ever did,' she admits.

By 2005 Jo had investigated organics enough to launch her own skincare range, Jo Wood Organics, offering bath and body lotions and eau de toilette free from synthetic additives. Now divorced from Ronnie Wood, she's ventured into organic cooking with her own pop-up restaurant, Mrs Paisley's Lashings, serving food from her own garden, at first in her own home and latterly at festivals like Harvest At Jimmy's, run by TV farmer Jimmy Doherty.

'I made up the name Mrs Paisley,' she says, 'but I thought it didn't sound quite right. My son said "I've got a good word for you: Lashings" and it seemed to sum up organic food – great food, and lots of it.'

When the Stones travelled across America, everyone would be on the lookout for their own private diversions. For Jo, it was an organic supermarket called Mrs Goochie's. She couldn't imagine such a thing at home – it was like being in heaven, and she'd buy tons of stuff and bring it home with her.

'Imagine being in the Rolling Stones touring party,' she says, laughing, 'and being done for smuggling *food* in...'

Rock & Roll Stew

serves 4–6

2 tbsp olive oil
6 chicken thighs
1 butternut squash, peeled and deseeded
2 sweet potatoes, peeled
4 carrots, peeled
1 onion, peeled and chopped
4 garlic cloves, peeled and chopped
2cm piece of fresh ginger, peeled and chopped
400g tin chickpeas, drained and rinsed
125g orange lentils
sea salt and freshly ground black pepper
pinch of freshly grated nutmeg
750ml chicken stock

Preheat the oven to 150°C/Gas mark 2. Heat the olive oil in a large ovenproof pan, then add the chicken thighs and brown well. Remove with a slotted spoon and set aside.

Cut the butternut squash, sweet potatoes and carrots into equal sized chunks. Add the onion to the pan and cook until tender but not coloured. Add the garlic and ginger and continue to cook for 1 minute. Stir in the chickpeas, butternut squash, lentils, sweet potatoes and carrots, and season with salt, pepper and nutmeg.

Return the chicken to the pan and pour over the stock, making sure everything is covered by about 2cm. Put on the lid, bring to a simmer and place in the oven. Cook for about 1 hour until the vegetables are tender and the chicken is cooked through.

'Keith Richards said: "The trouble with you, Jo, is you're ***addicted*** *to that stuff."'*

Abena Ofei
Adam Corbett
Ady le Roux
Alex Macilwaine
Amanda Ashed
Amy King
Aya Nishimura
Becki Jenner
Brenda Spooner
Callum Winton
Carrie Farncombe
Cath Roddick
Charlie Inman
Chris Mosey
Cristine Leone
Christine Walsh
Clare Pentson
Claudia Burlotti
Dagmar Hewell
Dan Dennison
Damian Krubelski
Daria Danowska
David Vanderhook
David Wall
Dean Chalkley
Dorita Nissen
Eleni Xintaras
Ellie Jarvis
Emilie Bailey
Emma Dalzeil
Emma Osborne
Emma Pack
Evannia Paine
Fay Leith
Fiona Fletcher
Geordie Barrie
Greg Caruso
Greg Mendham
Gustavo Murillo
Hamish Doyne-Ditmas
Helen Buckley
Howard Greenhalgh
Ignacio Roman
Jack Sargeson
Jade Simpson
Jamie McCartney
James Frew
James Robotham
Jasmine Blatt
Jessica Meyer Jones
Jessica Price
Jessie Shane
Jim Agnew
Joe Short
Joe Strinati
Jorn Van Oostende
Karl Barnes-Dallas
Karl Slater
Kate Booker
Kathy Kordalis
Kati Haberstock
Libby Speakman
Lily Lam
Lorna Dixon
Louise Bryan
Lucia Cardenas
Lucienne Sencier
Lucy Harvey
Luis Carreola
Lulu Watson
Lynda Doyle
Maha Saade
Mark Brown
Max Sobol
Michael Piper
Mick Pantaleo

Minseok Kim
Mira Parmar
Nat Van Zee
Natascha Jones
Neal Kirke
Niaomi Parry
Nico Ghirlando
Nikki Ahmed
Nikki Seymour
Nikki Wolff
Paul Redmond
Paula Salischiker
Phil Dunlop
Polly Hibbert
Robbie Maynard
Robert Morales
Rosie Scott
Roxxi Dott
Sam Gilmore
Sam Hoffman
Sarah Brading
Sarah Tildesley
Saskia Hofman de Gama

crew

Simon Izzard
Sophie Hart Walsh
Sophie Jacobs
Stefano Menini
Steve Ritchie
Steven Jensen
Stuart Miller
Su Han
Tanya Collier
Toby Fisher
Tom Brill
Tom Fallon
Tom Mumford
Tom Weatherill
Tundun Sanusi
Vernon Francois
Yolande Wall
Yuka Hirata
Zara Lee
Zoe Taylor

management/pr/artist liaison

Adis Adamson
Alice Smedley
Alistair Norbury
Andrea Mills – Silentway mgmt
Andy Gould & Sarah Martin – Spectacle Group
Andy Shillito
Anna Bobkowska – Nettwerk mgmt
Bev Burton – KillerB Music
Brian Message & Arwen Hunt – ATC mgmt
Briana Dougherty – Darling PR
Briony Turner – Darkstar mgmt
Cassandra Gracey & Alan Jewell – CrownMusic mgmt
Caroline Cabral – Purple PR
Cerne Canning – Supervision mgmt
Charlotte Scott & Claire Horsemann – Sony music
Claire Bartlett – Duck productions
Clare Maxwell – Raw Power mgmt
Clare Moon – Paul Weller mgmt
Chris Hewlett PR & mgmt

Conrad Murray – SJM Concerts
Dan Rosenthal – Perfecto Records
David Burn
David Taylor – BSP mgmt
Debbie Gwyther
Dennis & Mrs. Desmond at Oxegen
Divinea Plummer
Doug Hart – Hydrogendukebox mgmt
Emily Harper
Emily Wheating & Debbie Gwyther – ATC mgmt
Flip Dewer – Lateral mgmt
Gareth Williams
Ged Malone
George Allan – Extreme
Georgia Broaders
Georgia Weyman – Empire mgmt
Gill Snow
Graham Welch & Tina Peacock – Electric Canyon mgmt
Hugh Gadsdon – Hannah mgmt/Barbera Music
Imelda Mounfield – AllStars mgmt
Jamie Johnston – The Shipping Forecast music company
Jamie Lilywhite – CrownMusic mgmt
Jamie Oborne – All on Red mgmt
Janet Choudry – EMI music mgmt
Jeremy Bates
Jess Barratt – Nostromo mgmt
John Coyne
Jools Broom & Cookie Brusa – Trinifold mgmt
Kat Garbutt – Wallace Productions
Larry Tull – Rebel Waltz mgmt
Liz Gould – HallorNothing mgmt
Lotte Faulkner
Mark Starwood – Starwood mgmt
Mark Sher
Matt Glover – Blueprint mgmt
MCD Productions & Oxegen Festival
Melvin Benn at Reading & Leeds
Michelle Kerr – Roadrunner Records
Missy Strasner
Mooney Baybuck – BL mgmt
Martha de Lacey
Natalie Hicks – Ignition mgmt
Natalie Seymour & Dan Garnett – Nettwerk mgmt
Nathan McGough & Vicky Saunders – McGough mgmt
Nikki Lissette
Nikki Seymour
Pat Lake-Smith – Lake Smith Griffin Associates
Patrick Bustin – PBJ mgmt
Paul Everett – Wonderland mgmt
Rachel Graham – Passepromo mgmt
Raf Edmonds
Rhys at GLC
Richie Clark – Black Book mgmt
Rick Mayston
Rob Ballantine, Chris Yorke & Andy Redhead at SJM Concerts
Robert Reynolds
Ronnie Tee – VisionArtists
Ros Earls – 140db
Roxanne Nejad
Sam Eldridge – Urok mgmt
Sarah Lowe – Fifth Avenue PR
Sean Cooney – Fleming associates
Sean Fitzgerald – Seraphina mgmt
Simon Burke-Kennedy – Pocket Rocket Music
Sony BMG
Sue Harris – Republic Media
Sulinna Ong
Tristan Lillingston – Raw Power mgmt
Universal Music
Vanessa Saunders – Quietus mgmt
Warren Kennedy
William Rice – Purple PR
Yaran & Matthew Page – Riot mgmt
Zoe Taylor

All About Animals
All Saints
Amy King & Marc Dautlich
Backstreet Merchandising
Bapty Prop Store
Bar Italia
Beat About The Bush Instrument Hire
Bibendum Oyster Bar & Restaurant
Bibendum
Big Sky Studios
Boxfly Media
British Airways
Cadburys
Castle Gibson
Chase 55 Prop Store
Chic Little Devils
Christiana Bagusat
City & Islington College
CityJet
Direct Lighting
Dominos Pizzas
DZD
E Frames
FastFrames
Festival Republic
Filmscape
Flint London
Forward PR
Frankie's at Selfridges
Frogtown Studios
FX Rentals
Gail Smith Flowers
Gavin Martin
Gibson Guitars
Glennfreight Shipping
Graham Wapling/Lakesdown
Granger Herzog Prop Hire
Greensets Fisheries
Hackney City Farm
HallorNothing
Harriet Slaughter
Harrods
HERS agency
Ignacio Roman
Ilford
Isolated Ground
Jai Katmandhu
Jaques London
Jasmine Studios
JedRoot
Jessie Shane
JJ Locations
K West Hotel
London Taxidermy
Lotus PR
LSW Props
Magpie Studio
Mandy Coakley Represents
Marks & Spencer
Matt Fisher
MCD/LiveNation
MiauHaus Studios
Mr Fish Restaurant
Naked Artists
Osushi restaurant
Paul Redmond Studio
Paula Salischiker
Peartree
Permajet
Phink TV
Plan 9
Polly Hibbert
Popcorn Tour Catering
Pro Centre
Purple PR
Rhubarb

services

Roger Barton Fish suppliers
Royal Albert Hall
Samia Khan
Sarah Nicolson
Sarah Sillah
Selfridges
Shoot Agency
Shure Microphones
S.I.R
SJM Concerts
Skinny Dip
Smashbox Studios
Splice TV
Stanley's Post
Staffordshire University
Steve Hatt Fishmonger
St Martins Lane Hotel
Stockyard Props/Backgrounds
Street Studios
Taylors of Harrogate
Trident Sound Studios
Themetraders
The Little Lantern Theatre
The Lowry Hotel
ThemeTraders
The Morrison Hotel
The New Rose
The Nursery Inn
The Old Queen's Head
The Sanctum Hotel
The Worx Studios
Twinkle
Union Models
Vauxhall City Farm
Videoheads
Virgin Atlantic
WeAreRare
Wild at Heart
Xtraprint

artists

Alex Kapranos
Biffy Clyro
Brandon Flowers
Brett Anderson
Brian May
British Sea Power
BT
Bullet For My Valentine
Buzzcocks
Sir Cliff Richard
Coco Sumner
Detroit Social Club
Dexter Holland
Diagram Of The Heart
Divine Comedy
Hadouken!
Eliza Dolittle
Ellie Goulding
Empire of the Sun
Erik Hassle
Example
Fairport Convention
Feeder
Flood
Francis Rossi OBE
Gabriella Cilmi
General Fiasco
Goldie Lookin' Chain
Howling Bells
Huey Morgan
Kids In Glass Houses
James Walsh
Johnny Borrell
Jo Wood
Juliette Lewis
Kasabian
Kate Nash
Katie Melua
Kelly Jones
Liam Fray
Lissie
Madness
Mani
Marina & The Diamonds
Melanie Blatt
Mick Hucknall

Mystery Jets
Newton Faulkner
Paloma Faith
Papa Roach
Paul Oakenfold
Paul Weller
Professor Green
Richard Hawley
Rob Zombie
Roger Daltrey CBE
Rolf Harris
Siouxsie Sioux
Sophie Ellis-Bextor
Sparks
Speech Debelle
Sugababes
The Feeling
The Kooks
Tiffany Page
Tinie Tempah
Tony Christie
Tony Hadley
Ty Bulmer
We Are Scientists
White Belt Yellow Tag
White Lies

IT ALL STARTED with a passion for photography, food and a Muse gig. Sitting in the bar after the show and chatting to Muse frontman Matt Bellamy, I discovered that Matt, living in Italy at the time, makes his own pasta. Having just seen the band amidst twenty thousand screaming fans this seemed a little incongruous, but even rock stars have to eat. So why not find out what rocks their foodie boats and, as a food photographer who loves music, put these two things together, combining two huge passions in a collection of images?

Shortly afterwards I happened to get some last minute tickets for Kasabian at the Royal Albert Hall in aid of Teenage Cancer Trust. This was the first time I'd heard of the charity and amidst that impressive setting we watched the film which explains what they do. It was incredibly emotive and I realised then that we should do it for this fantastic music-based charity whose dedication to young people with cancer has inspired artists to collaborate, perform and give generously in many ways.

LOVE MUSIC LOVE FOOD: THE STORY BEHIND THE PROJECT

So, I approached the charity with a tiny booklet made up of a few shots from my band shooting days spliced together with images of mushrooms, spaghetti and crab claws. I met the lovely Heather Burns-Mace and she greeted the project with such enthusiasm I walked out of the Newman street offices slightly daunted; there was no turning back now and I couldn't let her down or the teenagers I'd pledged to help.

The rest of the project started to evolve slowly with the odd pinch of serendipity and large tablespoons of encouragement from Heather. Andrew Harrison our wordsmith gave in to persuasion from his wife Lili and myself over dinner one night and agreed to spend a considerable amount of the next year talking to artists about their food fetishes. Sarah Muir, tour caterer to the stars, then agreed to create recipes out of all sorts of musical food fancies as she regaled tales from backstage kitchens in booming Yorkshire tones, making the clientele in Fortnum's tearooms blush.

What followed has been a testament to the power of immense determination, truckloads of emails and hard work and planet-sized dimensions of goodwill from individuals and companies. For all those who have believed in this project and given generously in time and services, from 200 bags of free wine gums or guitar-case-sized amounts of tea bags, to assisting, lighting and providing studios and post production, I hope we have created a piece of work you can be proud of.

To all the management and PRs who helped get their charges into studios and locations and selflessly did all the legwork that goes with that, our sincere thanks. To the artists who donated their time and got involved/covered in noodles/naked with haggis/strewn with pasta, thank you so much. We are in your debt. Now that I know a little more about the music industry, I understand that an artist has three states of being, either recording, touring or somewhere remote recovering from the first two, so if your favourite rock star is missing from this collection, it's because of one of the above. But all artists do whatever they can, when they can, for Teenage Cancer Trust or other charities.

Most importantly, this project belongs to those young people with cancer that the team at *Love Music Love Food* have sought to support. By purchasing this book you have helped contribute towards those efforts. I hope you feast on its contents and enjoy this celebration of life, which aims to raise funds and awareness for teenagers who just want the chance to go on into adult life and fulfil the potential that lives in all of us.

Patrice de Villiers

Teenage Cancer Trust is a registered charity: 1062559 (England & Wales), SC039757 (Scotland)

Love Music Love Food is a project which aims to raise money for Teenage Cancer Trust by combining passions for music, food and photography.

Teenage Cancer Trust is a charity devoted to improving the lives of young people with cancer. Every day in the UK, six teenagers are told they have cancer. This is a rising figure and there are already more teenagers than children with the disease. Teenage Cancer Trust believes teenagers shouldn't stop being teenagers because they have cancer. Usually placed on a children's ward or with elderly patients, young people often feel isolated when facing a cancer diagnosis. That's why Teenage Cancer Trust funds and builds specialist units in NHS hospitals where young people with cancer are treated with others their own age, in an environment suited to their needs. As well as state-of-the-art facilities to keep young patients occupied during long stays in hospital, the units provide a place where young people can meet others in a similar situation, as well as providing the best possible care and support. Teenage Cancer Trust gets no government funding.

TEENAGE CANCER TRUST : *about* THE CHARITY

For the last ten years, longstanding patron Roger Daltrey CBE of The Who has worked tirelessly to secure stellar line-ups for concerts for Teenage Cancer Trust at the Royal Albert Hall, held in March each year. Acts to have performed in the past include The Who, Coldplay, Muse, Eric Clapton, The Cure, Paul Weller, Stereophonics, Keane, Razorlight, Jools Holland, Noel Gallagher, Kasabian and Kaiser Chiefs. It was these shows that led award-winning photographer Patrice de Villiers to the charity and to one of our best-known members of the fundraising team, Heather Burns-Mace. Sadly in January 2010 Heather lost her own battle with cancer, but this project wouldn't have happened without her. Heather would have been immensely proud to see it in its completion.

Teenage Cancer Trust is lucky enough to have the support of many great artists, making the relationship with *Love Music Love Food* a perfect fit. The galaxy of music stars who signed up to be part of this unique collection of portraits pays testament to this. Some are longstanding supporters of Teenage Cancer Trust, others completely new to the charity. We cannot thank them enough for giving up their precious time to be part of what we can only describe as a feast for your eyes.

'*Love Music Love Food* really captures the fun essence of Teenage Cancer Trust,' says Simon Davies, Teenage Cancer Trust CEO. 'Music is a huge part of many young people's lives, no matter what they're going through and there is a strong bond between music, young people and Teenage Cancer Trust. We've never seen our passion for music combined with a passion for food quite like this before, though! We hope people love this book as much as we do.'

'Seeing Muse, The Who and Madness at the TCT shows at the Albert Hall literally rocked me. It opened up a whole new realm of music.'—***Prince***

With specialist Teenage Cancer Trust units in hospitals all over the country, it's no surprise that there are up and coming musicians among those involved in TCT. Prince Aidoo makes hip hop, r 'n' b and soul (think Usher meets 50 Cent). He was diagnosed with leukaemia at the age of 14 and was treated in a regular children's ward, but when he relapsed at 18 he was admitted to a specialist TCT unit.

'The difference between the treatment was just amazing,' says the voluble Londoner. 'It's just a world apart. That I could talk to and share experiences with people of the same age really helped. Much as having cancer was a painful experience, it was a real eye-opener. I learned a lot about myself. I've never kept a diary, so music was a way for me to escape and deal with what I was going through.'

Prince had a bone marrow transplant when he was 19 and it's been looking good since. He's living in South London, studying business and working on his music – which TCT helped with too. 'When I was growing up, my musical influences were just the things my parents used to play: the Bob Marleys and whatnot,' he says. 'But as I've grown up I'm inspired by loads more things now. Going to the TCT shows at the Albert Hall and seeing people like Muse, The Who and Madness literally rocked me. It blew me away and opened up a whole new realm of music-making for me.'

Alice Watts is a London-based singer-songwriter whose 2008 album *Your World* showcased a talent for unique melodies and a beguiling singing voice (think KT Tunstall or Joni Mitchell in a sudden good mood). She was invited to Bloc Party's TCT show at the Albert Hall 2006, and the show instantly energised her. 'I'd had cancer the year before so an invitation like that meant a lot to me,' she says. 'You know when you see something and you immediately think "That's what I want to do?" That was what happened to me.' Alice bombarded the TCT with job requests and is now the charity's Fundraising Exec for London, working with all non-corporate donors and helpers. And she's also developing her music, with new material out in 2011. 'I'm starting to make a living off it,' she says, not entirely joking.

TCT BENEFICIARIES — PRINCE & ALICE *love* FOREST FRUITS & JUNK FOOD

Prince and Alice chose deliberately contrasting foods for their *Love Music Love Food* picture. For Alice it's forest fruits. 'They always put you in a good mood, don't they?' she says. 'Whenever I feel under par, berries and strawberries make me feel good. And they make a good picture.'

And Prince Aidoo opts for burgers. Alice had all these healthy products so he thought he'd go for the opposite – pure indulgence alongside wellbeing and nutrition. 'You've got to have your yin and yang, haven't you?' he says.

Burgers & Fries

serves 4

450g lean steak, minced
1 small onion, peeled and grated
1 tbsp Worcestershire sauce
1 tbsp barbecue seasoning
6 large white potatoes
vegetable oil, for deep-frying
1 tbsp olive oil
good pinch of sea salt
4 bread buns, split in half

Put the meat, onion, Worcestershire sauce and seasoning in a large bowl and mix well, using your hands. Divide the mixture into 4 portions, roll each into a ball and flatten into a burger. Place the burgers on a plate, cover with cling film and place in the fridge.

Peel the potatoes and cut into chips, about 2cm thick. You will need to cook them in batches to avoid overcrowding the pan; they will fry quicker if they have more room. Heat the vegetable oil in a deep-fat fryer or heavy-based saucepan until very hot. Carefully drop a chip into the hot oil to test the temperature; if it gently fries the oil is hot enough. Lower the first batch of chips into the oil and fry until crisp and golden.

Remove the fries from the pan with a slotted spoon and place in a bowl lined with a couple of sheets of kitchen paper to drain. Keep warm while you cook the rest. Toss the fries with sea salt and remove the kitchen paper, which will have soaked up excess oil.

Cook the burgers at the same time as the fries. Heat the olive oil in a large frying pan, place the burgers in the pan and fry gently until the juice runs clear and the burgers are crispy brown, about 10–12 minutes. Serve immediately, in buns with the fries on the side.

N.B. These burgers can be topped with anything: slices of cheese, tomatoes, onion or any variety of relish.

artists' biographies

Brett Anderson

Louche, androgynous, bum-spanking frontman with Suede, the glam-punk outragers of public decency whose hits ***Animal Nitrate*** and ***Metal Mickey*** fired the starting gun for Britpop.
TOP MOMENT: Suede's 2010 reunion for Teenage Cancer Trust is acclaimed as one of the most astonishing shows ever seen at the Royal Albert Hall.

Biffy Clyro

Hairy, tattooed, red-meat Ayrshire hard-rockers and multiple ***NME*** and ***Kerrang!*** Awards winners. Peculiar name is attributed to a Cliff Richard pen once owned by a band member: the 'Cliffy biro'.
*TOP MOMENT: Biffy Clyro were bewildered when X Factor winner Matt Cardle 'chose' their song **Many Of Horror** for his first single.*

Mel Blatt

Co-founder of All Saints who mixed girl band looks with quality songwriting and street cred, bringing combat pants to the masses.
*TOP MOMENT: Shares the key verses in All Saints' 1997 number one **Never Ever** with Shaznay Lewis, creating the great love-gone-wrong song of the 90s.*

Johnny Borrell

Motormouth leader of North London garage-punk band Razorlight, contemporary of Pete Doherty and Carl Barât of The Libertines, and mate of cricketer Andrew Flintoff.
TOP MOMENT: Supported Queen and Paul Rodgers in front of 60,000 people at Hyde Park.

VV Brown

Statuesque, flat-topped r 'n' b pop queen with a sideline as a model for Marks & Spencer. A secret comic book fan, who has had a graphic novel, ***City Of Abacus***, published.
*TOP MOMENT: Single **Shark In The Water** took off in the US making her one of few British singers to break the US since Amy Winehouse.*

BT

The groundbreaking trance producer and DJ Brian Transeau has worked with artists as diverse as Tori Amos to Peter Gabriel and Britney Spears.
*TOP MOMENT: Composed the soundtrack for the movie **Monster**, the story of serial killer Aileen Wuornos.*

Bullet For My Valentine

Welsh metal band who took the long and winding road from skatecore and thrash back to pure, fundamental, it-ain't-broke-so-don't-fix-it heavy metal.
*TOP MOMENT: Named Best British Band three times by **Kerrang!** magazine and twice by **Metal Hammer**.*

***Tabita Bulmer** of New Young Pony Club*

Anglo-Trinidadian lead singer with punk-funk electro band NYPC and the beneficiary of an unusual childhood. With no schooling at all between the ages of 8 and 13, she's a self-educated prodigy.
*TOP MOMENT: Breakthrough single **Ice Cream** became a worldwide club hit.*

Buzzcocks

Much-loved Mancunians who took punk rock to the next level by daring to write about love on classics like ***Promises*** and ***What Do I Get?*** Also first with the reunion idea, they've been back together since 1989.
TOP MOMENT: Reunited band was invited to tour with Nirvana by hopeless fan Kurt Cobain. It turned out to be Nirvana's final tour...

Tony Christie

Sheffield's answer to Tom Jones, if the question is, 'Who's got a voice that could raise the dead and make a statue cry?'
*TOP MOMENT: Resurrected by **(Is This The Way To) Amarillo** in 2005 but his Northern soul-influenced 2011 album **Now's The Time!** is the real miracle.*

Gabriella Cilmi

Bellissima Australian pop-electro-soul chanteuse with a voice that's punchy and soulful beyond her years. Loves her food – that'll be her Italian blood.
*TOP MOMENT: Was first spotted when singing **Jumpin' Jack Flash** at an Italian festival at the tender age of 13.*

Roger Daltrey CBE

Godfather of Teenage Cancer Trust, self-taught master of trout husbandry, thespian portrayer of John McVicar, Franz Liszt, Rodney Marsh, the immortal Hugh Fitzcairn from ***Highlander***... and he's in The Who too.
*TOP MOMENT: Too many to count... but the epic mod concept album **Quadrophenia** will do.*

***Marina Diamandis** of Marina & The Diamonds*

Power-lunged one-woman pop army, sounding somewhat like a futuristic Kate Bush or a sci-fi Tori Amos.
TOP MOMENT: Winning over America as support on Katy Perry's national tour.

Sophie Ellis-Bextor

Soignée queen of British disco pop with a famous mum, ***Blue Peter*** presenter Janet Ellis. Married to fellow ***Love Music Love Food*** participant Richard Jones of band The Feeling.
*TOP MOMENT: **Groovejet (If This Ain't Love)** with Italian DJ Spiller is considered a timeless dancefloor classic.*

Empire of The Sun

Intergalactic Australian electro duo, resembling a poster for ***Labyrinth*** or ***The Empire Strikes Back*** come to life.
TOP MOMENT: Videos and lavish tour summoned up the madness of 80s sci-fi.

Example

Quick-witted West London MC and associate of Lily Allen, The Streets and Professor Green.
TOP MOMENT: Gave chicken chain Nando's so many shout-outs that they produced a special Black Card specifically for him.

Fairport Convention

The Folk Beatles, basically. The biggest band in British traditional song since 1967, inventors of electric folk and since 1979 the hosts of music, food and fine ale celebration the Cropredy Festival.
*TOP MOMENT: Their **Liege & Lief** album from 1969 remains the holy text for the rural raver.*

Paloma Faith

Anyone with red hair gets called 'fiery' but it's true of this passionate London singer, who's an actress (***St Trinian's***, ***The Imaginarium Of Dr Parnassus***) and former burlesque performer and magician's assistant.
TOP MOMENT: Belting duet on ***Forget You*** *with Cee-Lo at the 2011 Brit Awards.*

Newton Faulkner

Dreadlocked troubadour who's reinvented the singer-songwriter model by using his guitar as a percussion instrument. Though his middle name is Battenburg, he did not choose the cake of the same name for ***Love Music Love Food***.
TOP MOMENT: Plays stripped-down guitar-only versions of ornate songs like ***Bohemian Rhapsody*** *and Massive Attack's* ***Teardrop***.

The Feeling

The band that saved soft rock, with gorgeous radio-friendly hits like ***Never Be Lonely*** and ***I Thought It Was Over***.
TOP MOMENT: Played the Glastonbury Pyramid Stage in 2008 and did their take on The Buggles' ***Video Killed The Radio Star***.

Flood

Much sought-after record producer to elite clients including U2, Depeche Mode, Smashing Pumpkins, Sigur Rós, PJ Harvey and many more.
TOP MOMENT: Earning his nickname because of the constant flow of tea he brought to the studio when a junior engineer.

Brandon Flowers

The Killers frontman and multiple Sexiest/Best Dressed/Most Stylish Man award-winner was raised as a Mormon and then moved to Las Vegas – so he's seen salvation and sin close up.
TOP MOMENT: Acclaimed tour for solo album ***Flamingo*** *showed he's a powerful performer in his own right.*

Noel Gallagher

Leader of Oasis who piloted the combative Mancunians through 15 years as Britain's biggest rock band.
TOP MOMENT: First two albums ***Definitely Maybe*** *and* ***(What's The Story) Morning Glory*** *changed the course of rock music in the 90s.*

Tony Hadley

Mighty-voiced Spandau Ballet frontman who lent the New Romantic funk band a soulful edge. Reunited with his estranged bandmates in 2009.
TOP MOMENT: 'GOLD! Always believe in your soul!'

Rolf Harris

Wobbleboard inventor, kangaroo tier-downer, Stylophone spokesman, didgeridoo phenomenon, beloved painter and entertainer... can you tell who it is yet?
TOP MOMENT: Triumphant performances at Glastonbury since the 90s cemented Rolf's status as international treasure.

Erik Hassle

Rising soul-pop star from Stockholm, like a Swedish Robbie Williams.
TOP MOMENT: Won over Mika's audience when he supported the Beirut-born pop sensation on tour.

Richard Hawley

The Yorkshire Roy Orbison, blessed with a beautiful, understated voice and unaffected, honestly emotional songs.
TOP MOMENT: When Arctic Monkeys won the 2006 Mercury Music Prize, Alex Turner told the crowd 'Someone call 999, Richard Hawley's been robbed.'

Dexter Holland *of The Offspring*

Who says punks are lazy? The frontman for the LA garage band is a qualified pilot, has a Master's Degree in molecular biology, has written working software for the BlackBerry and now manufactures his own hot sauce.
TOP MOMENT: Their biggest UK hits ***Pretty Fly (For A White Guy)*** *and* ***Why Don't You Get A Job?***

Peter Hook

Infamous bass player with Joy Division and New Order, once described as 'dressing like a U-Boat captain.'
TOP MOMENT: Invented the bass guitar as lead instrument – see his famous riff on New Order's colossal hit ***Blue Monday***.

Howling Bells

Restless-minded Australian indie band who travel between Sydney, London and Los Angeles to create a unique mix of cosmic country and introspective rock.
TOP MOMENT: Debut album ***Howling Bells*** *named among the albums of the year 2006 by* ***NME*** *and* ***The Guardian***.

Mick Hucknall

Legendary epicurean frontman of Simply Red, bountiful with his favours to the extent that he once issued an apology to the estimated 3,000 women he'd slept with.
TOP MOMENT: Simply Red's 1991 album ***Stars*** *is the sixth best-selling album of all time in Britain, certified twelve-times platinum with sales of 3.6 million.*

Kelly Jones *of Stereophonics*

Stadium-packing, gravel-voiced Welsh rocker and heart-melter with a love of Leeds United FC, leather jackets and wine gums.
TOP MOMENT: Played to 200,000 people at their own two-day festival 'A Day At The Races' in 2001.

Alex Kapranos *of Franz Ferdinand*

Gastronomy-friendly frontman of the erudite Scots new-wave band, who gave British rock its groove back in the mid-2000s.
TOP MOMENT: Wrote a weekly column for ***The Guardian*** *detailing what he ate on tour with Franz.*

Kasabian & Noel Fielding

Heirs to Oasis's massive audience, the Leicester hooligan-dance crew appear in ***Love Music Love Food*** with their good friend, surrealist ***Mighty Boosh*** comedian Noel Fielding.
TOP MOMENT: Collaborated on the ***Vlad The Impaler*** *video – Noel still appears onstage with Kasabian in the guise of a bloodthirsty killer.*

The Kooks

The Kinks, the Beatles, the Police, Squeeze and the Stones all go into this Brighton indie band's pot.
TOP MOMENT: Debut album ***Inside In/Inside Out*** *went quadruple platinum in the UK.*

Juliette Lewis

The star of ***Natural Born Killers*** and ***From Dusk Til Dawn*** alternates her movie career with life in her own touring rock band.
TOP MOMENT: When she covered two PJ Harvey songs in the movie ***Strange Days*** *it ignited her musical career.*

Madness

The Crown Jewels of British pop, the Nutty Boys' run of hits from 1979–82 – ***My Girl, Baggy Trousers, Embarrassment*** – is unequalled for sheer fun.
TOP MOMENT: Reunited for Finsbury Park ***Madstock*** *show in 1992 causing an outbreak of dancing that officially registered as an earthquake.*

Mani *of the Stone Roses & Primal Scream*

The bass player who gave the baggy generation permission to dance, now doing the same for insurgent rock band Primal Scream.
TOP MOMENT: The fantastic bass-driven reprise of the Roses' ***I Am The Resurrection*** *is Mani's superstar showcase.*

***Francis Rossi** OBE*

Status Quo's lead singer and guitarist gave up his fabled ponytail in 2009 but in every other respect his commitment to both rock and roll remains intact.
*TOP MOMENT: The band appeared on **Coronation Street** in 2005, where they played at the disastrous wedding of layabout and Quo fan Les Battersby.*

Siouxsie Sioux

The former Susan Ballion was one of the original punks and over a 30-plus year career she's influenced artists as diverse as Tricky, Garbage, Morrissey and Jeff Buckley.
*TOP MOMENT: Her first solo album **MantaRay** in 2007 was just as musically exciting as the early Siouxsie And The Banshees releases.*

Sparks

Brothers from another planet Ron and Russell Mael have ploughed a unique furrow in a 40-year career, embracing glam rock, disco, electro-pop and grandiose orchestral music.
*TOP MOMENT: Created an entirely new form of symphonic pop on the 2002 album **Lil' Beethoven.***

Speech Debelle

British rap talent mixing original hip hop flavours with a fresh London feel.
TOP MOMENT: Won the 2009 Mercury Music Prize against stiff competition from Florence And The Machine and Bat For Lashes.

Sugababes

The most modular girl band in British pop, who are constantly being refreshed with new members.
TOP MOMENT: Most successful female band of the 21st century with six number ones and 18 top ten hits.

Coco Sumner

Daughter of one Gordon Sumner AKA Sting, now making smart electro-pop under the name I Blame Coco.
TOP MOMENT: Played pretty much every festival in the land in summer 2010.

Tinie Tempah

Britain's best hope yet for a worldwide rap superstar, Tinie Tempah combines UK grime with rave and electro and a burning sense of mission. He could be the next P. Diddy.
TOP MOMENT: Conquered the 2011 Brit Awards with two gongs and four nominations.

***James Walsh** of Starsailor*

Tim Buckley-inspired cosmic songwriter and Liverpool FC fan. Will star in the movie ***Powder***, a cautionary tale about how bands can sabotage their own success.
TOP MOMENT: Recorded a benefit single for victims of the Hillsborough Disaster with Liverpool legend Kenny Dalglish.

Paul Weller

The Modfather, an inspiration to generations of British musicians and still the sharpest-dressed man onstage.
*TOP MOMENT: His 2008 double album **22 Dreams** stunned everyone with thrilling new styles and musical invention, even though it was Weller's 21st album.*

White Lies

Dark and atmospheric indie band from West London, whose music still contains enough splashes of colour to summon up The Teardrop Explodes as well as Joy Division.
*TOP MOMENT: Named Best New Band at 2009 **Q** Awards.*

Rob Zombie

Gore-soaked star of industrial metal with the band White Zombie turned director of splattercore horror movies. But it's all in fun.
*TOP MOMENT: Directed the reboot of the **Halloween** series in 2007.*

Brian May

Queen guitarist, badger-defender and qualified astrophysicist with an asteroid named after him – 52665 Brianmay.
TOP MOMENT: Performing a full-on rock version of the National Anthem atop Buckingham Palace on his trusty homemade Red Special guitar, for the Queen's Golden Jubilee.

Katie Melua

She's from Georgia – the real Georgia, not the one REM are from – and hence she's torn between cosmopolitan sushi and the hearty dairy products of her home country in the Caucasus.
TOP MOMENT: Played the deepest underwater gig ever, 303 metres under the North Sea, at the Norwegian Troll A platform in 2006.

***Huey Morgan** of Fun Lovin' Criminals*

The garrulous New Yorker has a second career as a much-loved DJ on Radio 2 and BBC 6Music. Huey knows his food: he used to own a pizza joint and has written a magazine wine column.
TOP MOMENT: Won over a new audience when filling in during Lauren Laverne's maternity leave on 6Music.

Paul Oakenfold

Ibiza veteran, producer-remixer to Happy Mondays, Massive Attack, U2 and more, superclub resident and still the world's best-known club DJ.
TOP MOMENT: Became the first-ever DJ to play the Hollywood Bowl in 2005.

Papa Roach

Indestructible alternative rock band from Vacaville, California, who have gravitated from their rap-metal beginnings to a pure metal incarnation.
*TOP MOMENT: Played with Guns N' Roses on the notorious **Chinese Democracy** tour.*

Sir Cliff Richard

From lip-curling rock and roll rebel to disco-pop hitmaker to stalwart of devotional music, the artist formerly known as Harry Webb is the only singer to have a number one in six consecutive decades.
TOP MOMENT: Has played the Royal Albert Hall more times than any other artist, with 80 shows and a total audience of more than 450,000.

*Kasabian & Noel Fielding consult an early mock-up of **Love Music Love Food**.*

Muse...

First published in 2011 by
Quadrille Publishing Limited
Alhambra House
27–31 Charing Cross Road
London WC2H 0LS

www.quadrille.co.uk

Editor Janet Illsley
Editorial Assistant Louise McKeever
Book Art Direction Jason Kedgley / Tomato
Design Steph Gillies
Production Vincent Smith, James Finan

Concept © 2011 Patrice de Villiers
Interview text © 2011 Andrew Harrison
Recipe text © 2011 Sarah Muir
Photography © 2011 Patrice de Villiers except pages 19, 113, 165, 169, 187, 224, 226, 227, 229, 231, 239.

Picture acknowledgements
Page 19 © Adam Corbett, Page 113 © Dan Kendall, Page 165 © Emilie Bailey, Page 169 © Adam Corbett, Page 187 © Phil Dunlop, Page 224 © Paul King, Page 226 (left) © Marie Absolom, Page 226 (centre) © Adam Corbett, Page 227 © Emilie Bailey, Page 229 (centre) © Pablo Antoli, Page 229 (right) © Gideon Marshall, Page 231 © Dean Chalkley, Page 239 © Kevin Lake. Rolling Stones 'Beggars Banquet' image shown within photograph on page 179 © Michael Joseph.

The rights of the contributors have been asserted.

All rights reserved. No part of this book may be reproduced, stored in a retrieval system or transmitted in any form or by any means, electronic, electrostatic, magnetic tape, mechanical, photocopying, recording or otherwise, without the prior permission in writing of the publisher.

Cataloguing in Publication Data: a catalogue record for this book is available from the British Library.

ISBN 978 184400 994 7

Printed in China.